CRIMINAL CONSPIRACIES

ORGANIZED CRIME IN CANADA

Margaret E. Beare
York University

Nelson Canada

I(T)P An International Thomson Publishing Company

Toronto • Albany • Bonn • Boston • Cincinnati • Detroit • London • Madrid • Melbourne
Mexico City • New York • Pacific Grove • Paris • San Francisco • Singapore • Tokyo • Washington

I⟨T⟩P ™
International Thomson Publishing
The ITP logo is a trademark under licence

© Nelson Canada,
A division of Thomson Canada Limited, 1996

Published in 1996 by
Nelson Canada,
A division of Thomson Canada Limited
1120 Birchmount Road
Scarborough, Ontario M1K 5G4

Canadian Cataloguing in Publication Data

Beare, Margaret E.
  Criminal conspiracies

ISBN 0-17-604838-3

1. Organized crime—Canada. I. Title.

HV6807.B4 1995   364. 1 '06' 0971   C95–932262-0

Team Leader and Publisher	Michael Young
Acquisitions Editor	Charlotte Forbes
Projects Coordinator	Heather Martin
Production Editor	Tracy Bordian
Production Coordinator	Brad Horning
Art Director	Liz Harasymczuk
Cover Design	Julie Fletcher
Cover Art	Michael Herman
Senior Composition Analyst	Alicja Jamorski
Input Operator	Elaine Andrews

Printed and bound in Canada

1 2 3 4 WC   99 98 97 96

Contents

iii

Foreword

For several decades, the topic of organized crime has held sway over the public imagination. Countless movies, television dramas, and popular books have detailed the misdeeds of real and fictional organized crime figures, and in so doing have often obscured the line that needs to be drawn between myth and reality. Moreover, it seems that too often social scientists have done little to clarify matters. Much of the research and theorizing in the area of organized crime have lacked a critical viewpoint, and as a result they have legitimated rather than challenged popular stereotypes. When compared to other types of crime problems, organized crime has tended to escape rigorous and innovative analysis—particularly in the Canadian context.

Criminal Conspiracies by Professor Margaret Beare provides readers with the first systematic and comprehensive examination of organized crime in Canada. By drawing heavily on the available criminological literature and on the insights she developed as a member of the federal policy community, Professor Beare is able to illuminate effectively the complex social, political, and economic relationships that link the phenomenon of organized crime to the wider society.

For Professor Beare, organized crime is best conceptualized as a process or method of committing crime rather than as a distinct type or crime. This emphasis on process encourages movement beyond the narrow view that associates organized crime with a restricted range of criminal activities or with particular ethnic groups. By attending to both the content and the dynamic character of organized crime, Professor Beare is able to ask and answer meaningful questions about the characteristics of those who get involved in organized crime, about how the changing nature of international economies facilitates such crime, and about how adequately law enforcement has responded or can be expected to respond.

Readers of this book will discover that much of what passes for public knowledge about organized crime in Canada is simplistic and misleading. As in other areas of criminological investigation, however, the book also illustrates that the realities revealed by careful scholarly analysis prove far more intriguing.

Leslie W. Kennedy, University of Alberta
Vincent F. Sacco, Queen's University
Series Editors

Introduction

Organized crime has always brought with it a mystique. This book attempts to blend the accurate aspects of organized crime's image with the equally interesting reality of what is involved in attempting to control crime among the organized, powerful, wealthy, and potentially violent criminal segments of society. The links with the larger society are what characterizes organized crime today and make it an important area of study. Our present understanding of organized crime is defined by politics, the media, and the organizational interests of such key stakeholders as the police, governments, international pressure groups, and academics. All of these groups can and do use organized crime to gain headlines, wider mandates, and greater resources.

The topic of organized crime is fraught with discord: from those who see organized crime everywhere, to those who see it nowhere; and from those who argue that there is no more evidence of its existence than there is for the existence of God or (more recently) the Devil,[1] to those who have sat through the testimony, transcripts, and wiretaps of some of the deadliest of mobsters or found themselves tracing the paper trail of money launderers through a labyrinth of real and false corporations, offshore accounts, and underground banking systems.

This book is not specifically about crime families. There have been several well-written journalistic accounts of the stories and histories of Frank Cotroni, Rocco Perri, Paul Volpe, the Kung Lok Triad, and others.[2] Instead, while the book uses individuals and families to illustrate specific criminal processes, money laundering schemes, and enforcement problems, its primary goal is to study the *concept* of organized crime, and to present a picture of organized crime in Canada alongside a discussion of enforcement issues, legislation, governmental policies, and (where relevant) international comparisons. To the extent that the book has an integrative theme, it is to challenge the reader to question received wisdom about the nature of organized crime, organized crime policies, and organized crime enforcement.

Organized criminals are not all "mobsters" of the "Little Caesar"/Edward G. Robinson variety. Rather they are businesspersons, lawyers, politicians, financiers, and law enforcement officials. While some look like hoods, talk like hoods, and dress badly, others do not![3] When the Atlantic City casino managers were asked at Senate investigation hearings into casino credit practices why they tolerated, and in fact encouraged, the attendance of known organized criminals in their establishments, the straightforward answer seemed to be that these people were not only big spenders but were fun, interesting, and often charming people to have around (New Jersey 1983).

One is struck by the ordinariness of many of the people who either orchestrate criminal activities or agree to participate in crimes. The awe-inspiring aspects of the organized crime label vanish as otherwise law-abiding citizens support criminal organizations by buying smuggled cigarettes, hiring prostitutes, or selling their houses or valued goods for suspicious amounts of cash. In these ways the public knowingly facilitates the activities of criminals. This is not to diminish the destructiveness of the criminal activity, but merely to indicate the difficulty of discerning those among us who have decided to put greed and power ahead of law-abiding behaviour.

Law enforcement, both in Canada and internationally, has changed vastly in recent years. There are increasing demands for new skills and expertise, new resource requirements (at a time of fiscal restraint), and new political arrangements. Crime today is no longer local or even national, and law enforcement agencies are slowly attempting to address the international characteristics of a significant percentage of criminal activity.

Policing is a profession full of fascinating contradictions. On the one hand, police work is extremely political, high profile, and visible. On the other hand, it remains the domain of internal managers, undercover operations, and street-level practitioners. It is only recently that the traditional isolationism of the police-work environment has given way to a gradual recognition of the need to make use of expertise that extends beyond the confines of the police organization. Organized crime enforcement demands a commitment to longer-term strategic intelligence and to the specially trained civilian analysts who may be required; an incorporation of forensic skills into police recruitment, training, or contracting budgets; and an ongoing and supportive interaction with prosecutors and other professionals.

Financial investigations and, more specifically, investigations that make use of the proceeds of crime legislation require sophisticated and often resource intensive police work. A knowledge of business, bank procedures, accounting, and new computer technology is a prerequisite for identifying and following a financial paper trail, and, if required, documenting an association between the criminal proceeds and the criminal activity. As removed as these methods may appear to be from traditional policing styles, they are linked to wider forms of police work and serve to confirm the themes that run through all policing. Without a disgruntled or bleeding victim, without community intolerance of certain criminal acts, without the willingness of the public to participate (as witness or informant), the task of police work is made difficult or impossible.

The criticisms of policing expressed in this book are matched by an equally critical discussion of key court decisions, which at times appear to counter any advance made by law enforcement. Cross-border technologies and agreements can similarly threaten traditional policing methods, and government policies are at times seemingly designed to create organized crime markets. Criticism must also extend into the academic community. In Canada, we lack an academic literature that has attempted to advance knowledge or policy-making related to organized crime. Criminologists and others who study the police and policing tend to ignore the international, cross-jurisdictional, and criminal enterprise aspects of crime control. These "targeting-upwards" and "outwards" enforcement efforts are often less visible than other street-level police operations. Within the academic community there has arisen an interesting split between those who study policing without reference to organized crime and those who study organized crime without reference to policing.

This book attempts to capture the thinking behind policy decisions that culminated in legislative shifts in Canada. It also tries to convey the frustrations of law enforcement officers as they attempt to develop successful organized crime cases. While the Canadian and, more broadly, the North American experience constitutes the primary focus of the book, much of the discussion of Canadian legislation, police and prosecutional training, and law enforcement strategies as they relate to organized crime will be of interest to international jurisdictions as well.

In summary, I have attempted to illustrate the environment in which a serious study of organized crime occurs. Today's is not the environment of even five years ago. My intent is not to attempt to persuade the reader that the situation has become "worse." We do not know for sure. Estimates of the size, amount, and threat caused by organized crime are misleading. As was stated in *Tracing of Illicit Funds: Money Laundering in Canada* (Beare and Schneider 1990, xi), there is no verifiable method for determining the size of the illicit economy. Estimated figures, however carefully calculated, are only guesses. Once stated, however, they take on a reality they do not deserve.

The documented facts: a large underground economy related to organized crime exists; millions of dollars of illicit proceeds are laundered each year; lives are lost due to the operation of these illicit markets in Canada and abroad; law enforcement responses are changing and must change more.

The present organized crime environment makes it clear that organized crime today is far from an "alien" conspiracy operating outside the confines of legitimate society. As we look around the globe at the forces that determine the nature and scope of organized crime, we see criminal activity derived from political regimes, dictated by government policy, and defined by custom, tradition, and demand.

To study organized crime is to study the underside of legitimate society—activity that uses the same business/economic motivations; seeks political advantage and protection; and is often judged socially by the same measurements. The "difference" is the illicit nature of the commodity and the processes used to succeed.

METHODOLOGY

This book combines a number of methodologies. Eleven years of working at the Federal Department of the Solicitor General in Canada afforded me a valuable opportunity of working closely with the police at all levels of jurisdiction and rank. During those years, Canadian officials studied the attempts south of the border to fully implement and use the Racketeer Influenced and Corrupt Organizations (RICO) Statute. We then analyzed the substance of this legislation and its impact through the 1980s and early 1990s. Meetings were held with the drafter of the U.S. statute, Robert Blakey, and with U.S. spokespersons for organizations with the most to win (or lose) from this type of legislation. This exercise served as an important backdrop to the eventual passing of the Canadian legislation that allows for the seizure and forfeiture of illicit proceeds.

As a research officer for the government, I was initially charged with the task of studying legalized gaming outside of Canada, and then across Canada. Other projects included work on the creation of Canada's Drug Strategy and an extensive study on money laundering in Canada.[4] This environment allowed me a unique access to information relevant to organized crime.

Working within government gives one direct experience of the policy-making process. Compromise is an integral part of this process of getting a research idea accepted as policy and finally passed into legislation. Understanding these compromises is important to the sociologist because they represent pockets of power, ongoing exchange relations, and a negotiated sense of justice and order. This book combines the research and experiences accumulated throughout those years with a wide range of methodological techniques: interviews with law enforcement officers, government policy officials, and academic colleagues; analysis of police case files, documentary research, and literature reviews and an examination of the regulatory mechanisms present in the business and financial communities. Ongoing policing and policy experiences across a variety of issues are also incorporated into the text.

ACKNOWLEDGMENTS

Many individuals and organizations assisted in the writing of this book. I would like to thank Queen's University for allowing me to spend two years teaching and writing, and the Department of the Solicitor General for allowing me to take a two-year leave of absence from the Federal Government. Vince Sacco (Queen's University) facilitated my entry into the Queen's sociology department, and provided support and valuable debate throughout this project. This time, and the motivation and inspiration I derived from academic colleagues and friends, made the task of writing possible. Frank Pearce was particularly generous in reading and commenting on the manuscript. I was fortunate that John Tait (Privy Council Office, Ottawa) was spending a year at Queen's as the Skelton-Clark Fellow 1994–95. John had previously been both Deputy Solicitor General and Deputy Minister of Justice, and I benefited greatly from our discussions. Likewise, my Wolfe Island landlady offered constant support and reassurance that, without naming names, less lethal forms of organized crime are still thriving in that island community! In addition, a number of academics provided anonymous but extremely useful comments on both the proposal and the manuscript of this text, including Doug Skoog (University of Winnipeg) and David MacAlister (Kwantlen College), and others from Lakehead University and the University of Toronto.

Three individuals are particularly critical to my interest in the issues relating to organized crime. A key figure has been and remains Frederick Martens. Freddie introduced me to the world of criminal intelligence during the 1970s when he was head of the Intelligence Bureau for the New Jersey State Police, and we have remained friends ever since—throughout his tenure with the Pennsylvania Organized Crime Commission and after its politically induced demise. Peter Manning (Michigan State) has provided me with decades of advice and guidance. Tonita Murray (OIC Strategic

Planning and Corporate Policy RCMP) shared much wisdom gathered from her provincial experiences at the B.C. Coordinated Law Enforcement Unit (CLEU), her expertise gained at Solicitor General Canada, and most recently within the RCMP.

There would be no book without the assistance from the police and ex-police. Ten years of vigorous "discussion" with Rod Stamler (ex-assistant commissioner RCMP) provided the basis for some of the arguments presented in this text. His contributions nationally and internationally to organized crime issues over the years were part of the motivation for writing this book. Wayne Blackburn (RCMP) read not only this version of the text but one that was twice as long! He provided comments, factual information, and the encouragement that perhaps there might be a need for such a book. I got used to and appreciated the "for your dumb book!" faxes that would arrive on my desk. A number of RCMP members provided backup to Wayne, including, among many others, Brian Abrams, Chris Mathers (ex-RCMP), Gabe Marion, and John Neily.

RCMP members from across Canada as well as headquarters provided me with virtually any information that I "really" needed (there were some additional pieces of information that I occasionally thought that I wanted!). I fear attempting to list individual police officers because I will miss critical names. Having said that, Don Svendson (ex-RCMP Manitoba) provided ongoing encouragement and forced me to be aware that all organized crime does not restrict itself to Toronto, Vancouver, and Montreal. Tim Killam assisted with policy questions (RCMP Hdq). Michael Pelletier (RCMP Hdq) was always there to point me in the right direction regarding who in the force or in the U.S. DEA could provide me with the answers to my many queries. John Coleman and John Counihan provided some of that DEA material.

Likewise OPP, QPF, and municipal policing members shared with me their experiences in specific cases and their responses to particular legislation and relevant policing issues. Officers such as Bill Burke (ex-OPP) not only provided information directly to me, but also identified which other officers could best answer my questions. These officers include Wayne Frechette (OPP) and the Cornwall Regional Task Force members, including Mike Atkinson (RCMP), Jean Bourassa (RCMP), Paul McIsaac (OPP), and Chris Lewis (OPP). Moe Pilon (OPP) and Barry Hill (Metropolitan Toronto) provided valuable information during their periods as directors of Criminal Intelligences Services Canada and Criminal Intelligence Service Ontario, respectively. I have benefited greatly from my association with the Canadian Association of Chiefs of Police and with the individual committees on which I have been allowed to participate. This is not a complete acknowledgment of the contribution made by police officers. I apologize to those whom I have omitted.

Department of Solicitor General and Department of Justice officials including Fred Bobiasz, Kim Prost, Helen Banulescu, Scott Burbidge, and Joe Price attempted to keep me current and accurate on governmental developments and legislative changes important to organized crime. Jim McCollum (Finance) provided updates to me on financial legislation. Patricia Donald, Crown counsel in British Columbia, provided me with essential information relating to her experiences with conducting international organized crime cases and with the Mutual Legal Assistant treaties. Peter Engstad and Stan Shillington (CLEU) assisted me with intelligence from British Columbia and kept a constant supply of organized crime clippings coming into my mail box. Chris Nuttall (Home Office London) always responded quickly to my questions by supplying facts and contact people in the U.K. Finally, I wish to acknowledge the work that Stephan Schneider did on our 1990 Tracing of Illicit Funds report, and to thank again the hundreds of people in the financial and business community who supplied us with information during that previous money laundering research. Michael Ballard (Canadian Bankers Association) is just one of the people who has been consistently supportive during all of our research.

Nelson Canada has been a great introduction for me into the world of book publishing. I want to thank particularly Charlotte Forbes and Heather Martin for their interest in acquiring an organized crime book for the Crime in Canada series, and Tracy Bordian, the Senior Production Editor, for working with me to create this volume.

Margaret Beare, York University

NOTES

1. See Hawkins (1969); Morris and Hawkins (1970); and Albini (1993).
2. See, for example, Edwards and Nicaso (1993); Dubro (1985, 1992); and Possamai (1992).
3. RCMP agent Douglas Jaworski reports that unlike the Hollywood villains who wore superbly cut Armani suits to commit their crimes, in the real world of organized crime (Colombia cartels) even multimillionaires seldom wore anything but designer jeans, polo shirts, and leather jackets. Rolex watches were popular ... And while cartel barons might wear belts and loafers with the Gucci label, they were often the cheaper rip-off items, made in Venezuela. Not everybody loses their sense of what's

reasonable to pay for clothes. I never saw anybody in a suit..." (quoted in Edwards 1991, 53).

4. These research documents, produced as User Reports by the Ministry of the Solicitor General of Canada, are titled *The RICO Statute: An Overview of U.S. Federal and State RICO Legislation,* No. 1984-12; *Legalized Gambling: An Overview,* No. 1984-13; *Legalized Gaming in Canada,* No. 1988-12; *Tracing of Illicit Funds: Money Laundering in Canada,* No. 1990-05.

Overview

PART I UNDERSTANDING ORGANIZED CRIME IN THEORY AND PRACTICE

Chapter 1 presents competing definitions of organized crime, and outlines the theoretical, operational, and legal ways in which the term is used in Canada. Researching organized crime is uniquely difficult. These research and methodological issues are discussed. The chapter concludes with an examination of why the study of organized crime is particularly important now. Included in this discussion are such issues as globalization of trade and the move toward international enforcement regimes (and Canada's strategic position within these agreements).

Chapter 2 examines the criminological theories that attempt to account for organized crime and the involvement of individuals in specific types of organized crime activity. A typology of organized crime groups is presented. The relationship between theory, public policy, and the role of politics is also discussed. The chapter illustrates the gaps that can occur as public policy-makers strive to meet the needs of diverse masters.

PART II ORGANIZED CRIME ACTIVITY IN CANADA

Chapter 3 begins with an examination of the global social, economic, and political changes that are having a direct impact on organized crime in Canada. This chapter provides a historical overview of organized crime groups and activities in Canada, and then discusses the groups outlined in the typology discussed in Chapter 2. This chapter also addresses the extent to which different crimes and criminal groups overlap. Included in this discussion is the confusion between criminal and legitimate practices in the business world.

Chapter 4 examines national and international money laundering. Money laundering is a criminal activity of critical importance to organized crime. It is also an activity that is coming under increasing scrutiny by the police.

PART III   OFFICIAL RESPONSES TO ORGANIZED CRIME

Chapters 5, 6, and 7 provide an in-depth analysis of official responses to organized crime in Canada: policy, legislation, and policing. Canadian legislation and enforcement difficulties are discussed along with new enforcement tools and current restrictions on traditional policing methods. The chapters also examine global crimes and cross-jurisdictional enforcement strategies that require international agreements.

Chapter 8 concludes the book with an overview of future trends in organized crime and organized crime control. Underlying the chapter is a consideration of the most serious gaps in our understanding of organized crime and law enforcement initiatives against it.

Understanding Organized Crime in Theory and Practice

INTRODUCTION

Social science-related phenomena are "understood" via an interlocking grid of definitions, research, and theoretical frameworks. Each of these three components are problematic in relation to organized crime.

Every book or article on organized crime begins with a prolonged attempt at a definition. The problem, to quote Gertrude Stein, is that "there is no there, there." There is no one crime to focus on; there is no one type of group committing the crimes; there is no single jurisdiction to target. The action of defining organized crime tends to replace writing about organized crime! Attempts at definitions that have been satisfactory to law enforcement, policy-makers, or academics seldom are satisfactory to all groups.

Sources of data available to the researcher are extremely problematic. Critics are quick to indicate the weakness and potential biases in most research on organized crime, no matter which sources of information or intelligence are used. Traditionally, there has been a sense in the criminological literature that whoever is supplying the information will have something to gain from the specific interpretation and use of the information. These problems with definitions and research are compounded by the fact that there is no well-developed theoretical framework for organized crime.

Even the merit of the concept of "organized crime" has been challenged. A reviewer of the proposal for this book suggested that one had to question whether the concept of organized crime was a useful analytical tool in understanding a class of events that fall within the term. I have attempted to take this query very seriously.

The creation of concepts is not a neutral process. Robert Merton warns us that the acts of identifying and defining concepts have direct consequences. The created concept provides us with the definitions that make up our theory, guides our collection of data, and determines the comparability of data. Determining whether or not there is merit in identifying a category of crime as "organized crime," and then deciding how we will delineate that category, is critical to our understanding of the issues. As Merton observes, "Our conceptual language tends to fix our perspectives and derivatively, our thoughts and behaviour" (1967, 145).

If there is any gain from conceiving of an organized crime category, it is because of a *distinctive harm* that organized criminals can deliver. This distinctive harm stems from the process by which the crimes—often consensual crimes—are committed. The crimes committed for profit are often less serious than the fear stemming from the group's reputation, the violence committed to eliminate competition or detection, the corruption of officials, and the infiltration of legitimate businesses (Pennsylvania Crime Commission 1991, 3). Hence it is not the specific crimes that are key to understanding organized crime, but rather criminal activity that is carried out via a particular process, which is defined as an organized crime process. The task then becomes to determine which groups "qualify" for labelling as organized criminals based on their manner of operation.

When you do this, you discover that not only the crimes themselves but also the groups involved in them are very diverse in terms of motivation, sophistication, longevity, and commitment to the criminal behaviour. In contrast, if you begin with a fixed idea of the supposed organized crime groups, the task becomes self-fulfilling. You will be restricted to finding that which you look for, and enforcement efforts will therefore be targeted mainly at the predetermined organized crime "threats."

Defining the Concept of Organized Crime

ACADEMIC DEFINITIONS

To the extent that the term "organized crime" is useful,[1] its essential characteristic is that it indicates a *process* or *method* of committing crimes, not a distinct type of crime in itself, nor even a distinct type of criminal. Alan Block and Peter Lupsha take a similar position. Block emphasizes that it is the process itself, "the endless weaving of criminal conspiracies," that is at the heart of organized crime (Block 1990, 9). Lupsha similarly contends that "organized crime is a process—an activity possessing certain attributes and characteristics" (1986, 33).[2]

> Organized crime is a process or method of committing crimes, not a distinct type of crime in itself.

A good definition of organized crime must capture the essential aspects of the "process" that certain criminals use in carrying out criminal activity, increasingly within an international arena. As globalization of markets, financial institutions, and the electronic transfer of data increases, our understanding of organized criminal processes must continually evolve.

Maltz (1990) lists the following as characteristics of organized crime: corruption, violence, sophistication, continuity, structure, discipline, multiple enterprises, an involvement in legitimate enterprises, and ritual bonding. These characteristics, he concludes after an examination of actual organized crime examples, are not all necessarily present in each and every organized criminal activity. Reuter (1983) emphasizes three main characteristics that ought to be used when identifying organized crime organizations: durability, hierarchy, and involvement in a multiplicity of criminal activities (175). A definition that is too all-inclusive, that does not delineate what is unique about organized crime from an operational, enforcement, or economic perspective, fails to be useful. Whatever differences may exist between organized crime activities, the operations should have in common:

- a structure that allows individual criminals to be removed and substituted without jeopardizing the viability of the criminal activity;

- criminal activity committed via continuing criminal conspiracies (i.e., ongoing, repetitive criminal activity rather than one or two criminal acts committed for profit);

- the capacity to operate through political corruption and/or the potential of violence.

Organized crime is *ongoing* activity, involving a *continuing criminal conspiracy,* with a *structure greater than any single member,* with the potential for *corruption and/or violence* to facilitate the criminal process.

The same configuration will not exist in all organized criminal operations. History, economics unique to specific commodities, and political agreements have all played a role in the creation of distinct criminal organizations. For example, you may note that these "requirements" do not include a formal hierarchical structure as depicted on the charts of the mob "families." Although there usually is a structure, members may be associated fairly loosely or more formally positioned; organized crime groups appear increasingly to be structured horizontally rather than hierarchically.

Some writers have attempted to draw a continuum based on the notion that "Mafia"[3] organized crime activity is somehow closest to an "ideal type" organized crime group, with other groups perceived to be "looser" and therefore further removed from this pure form.[4]

While it is valid to acknowledge the durability, hierarchy, and multiplicity of the "traditional" Mafia, to use this form of organized crime as the polar end of a continuum is to distort the picture presented of other organized crime groups. There is a danger that historically we have focused disproportionately on the Italian Mafia, and have assigned it a particular status on the basis of habit, ease, and political/historical circumstance, rather than any unique organized crime characteristics. This becomes particularly problematic when one considers that even widely held assumptions about the structure of the Mafia may be flawed. Recent organized crime studies reveal structures and operations very different from those commonly associated with the Mafia.

Once the researcher moves beyond the more traditional models of organized crime, the degree and nature of the "structure" varies more than was originally assumed. In some criminal organizations, a seemingly loose structure is given substance by the presence of a "tithing" system whereby a percentage of the criminal proceeds is given over to the organization. In some organizations, this may involve a percentage of all criminal proceeds regardless of the nature of the activity or how individualistic the deed; in others it may mean only a percentage where the organization has been directly involved.

To understand organized crime, one must also understand the globalization of financial markets as well as the globalization of certain criminal activities. Organized criminals look for new opportunities, which are being offered by the growing body of facilitating laws and procedures that encourage legitimate cross-jurisdictional financial and business operations. While formerly a valid distinction was made between white-collar crimes, corporate crimes and organized crimes, increasingly white-collar and corporate crimes, are becoming global crimes and are being carried out in an organized crime manner. Similarly, with respect to the recent police and prosecutorial targeting of criminal proceeds, the extent to which white-collar and corporate crimes are being intertwined with organized crime is becoming more apparent. Often this is done in order to move, hide, and increase via legitimate businesses the criminal proceeds. A study by Edelhertz and Overcast (1993) confirmed the "central importance of investigating and prosecuting white collar crime violations in proceeding against organized crime groups. ... The body of embezzlement, fraud, breach of trust, and tax cases was truly impressive" (167–168).[5]

Even after concluding that it is the process that makes the organized crime activity, and after determining what characteristics of the process will qualify, we must still contend with the fact that organized crime groups differ in terms of the types (and degree) of threats they pose to society.

Once a group meets the required characteristics of an organized crime group, it must then be studied as its own entity. From a policy and enforcement perspective, one must acknowledge at least four differences among organized crime groups (and possibly within one organized crime group studied over time).

Four Variations across Organized Crime Groups with Policy/ Enforcement Consequences

Groups may:

* change over time;
* operate domestically and/or internationally;
* have a purpose separate from the criminal activity;
* be integrated into the social, political, and economic order.

First, groups can change over time and become, or cease to be, organized crime groups. There may be groups in the process of forming, or newly created criminal groups that fall into a grey area where there is disagreement as to whether they are a continuing criminal enterprise or merely individuals involved in criminal ventures.

Police intelligence must be such that these groups can be identified and action taken *before* sophisticated criminal operations are set in place. Similarly, if they cease to be a significant threat, law enforcement must reallocate any resources spent targeting them onto more relevant groups. Law enforcement officials must also remain aware of the fact that their actions may have very significant and unanticipated consequences. We know for example that law enforcement targeting of some criminal activities may result in the small or vulnerable groups being eliminated in favour of more sophisticated operations capable of securing a monopolistic market.

Second, organized crime groups can be either domestic or global in their emphasis. The groups that operate internationally may require different "policing" than their domestic counterparts. Reliance on cross-jurisdictional enforcement regimes, the need for complex accounting and financial investigations, and the likelihood that the international organized crime group is sophisticated in its operations, all add to the enforcement difficulties. In some cases, it is the international evidence of the organized crime operation that reveals the extent to which the group is "continuing," "conspiratorial," and "structured." Most organized crime is international in that the organization will look to capitalize on all sources of advantage, the greatest being its ability to operate across borders. The sophistication of international organized crime groups, their economic base (which enables them to buy police and engage in political corruption), as well as their potential for violence bespeaks the need for an innovative, collaborative government response.

Third, the focus on Mafia-type operations has diverted attention from the reasons the criminal group exists in the first place. From a law enforcement and policy perspective, it may be important to determine whether the group exists primarily to commit crimes or whether the criminal activity is secondary to the structure of the group. One can hypothesize a situation where a group's membership is changed, or even the committing of criminal activities is terminated, and the group continues to exist. Groups can thus be seen to fall along a continuum, which is discussed further in Chapter 2. This book takes the position that, while the groups involved in organized criminal behaviour may or may not have a purpose beyond the criminal activity, all policy and enforcement decisions must take into account this variation across organized crime groups. Any control strategy will benefit from an understanding of what motivates participation in the organized crime group. The criminal activity may turn out to be more peripheral than was formerly assumed.

Finally, organized crime groups are not all equally integrated into the larger society. Duration of the criminal operation, sophistication of the processes, and the cultural and ethnic similarities between the criminal operations and the social/political order all help to determine the extent to which the organized crime is invisibly interwoven through the legitimate system. The unanticipated consequences of some law enforcement strategies may inadvertently serve to deepen the entrenchment of the criminal activity by facilitating the development of powerful, well-integrated, organized crime operations instead of smaller independent non-monopolistic criminal activity.

The four variations across organized crime groups outlined above become most important when we attempt (as we do in Chapter 2) to apply causation theories to organized crime behaviour. To understand such behavior we must take into account and explain the "methods" of doing business adopted by some of these criminals, the complex money laundering schemes, the business empires (both onshore and offshore), the interactions across criminal groups, and the willingness to commit acts of violence.

LEGAL DEFINITIONS

In addition to academic accounts of organized crime, the criminal justice systems of countries engaged in law enforcement against the phenomenon that we term "organized crime" offer us legal definitions.

While the term "organized crime" does not appear in the current English version of the Canadian Criminal Code (CC), the

---

S. 462.3 (Criminal Code)

"Enterprise crime offence" means an offence against any of the following provisions:

- bribery of judicial officers
- bribery of officials
- frauds upon the government
- breach of trust by public officer
- corrupting morals
- keeping gaming or betting
- house, betting, pool-selling
- bookmaking
- keeping common bawdy-house
- procuring
- murder
- theft, robbery
- extortion, forgery
- uttering forged documents
- fraud, fraudulent manipulation of stock exchange transactions
- secret commissions
- arson
- making counterfeit money
- possession of counterfeit money
- uttering counterfeit money
- laundering proceeds of crime
- possession of property obtained by crime
- designated drug offence
- conspiracy or an attempt to commit the above
- an act or omission anywhere that, if it had occurred in Canada, would have constituted an offence listed above.

1989 Proceeds of Crime legislation makes reference to the term "enterprise crime."[6] The French version of the *Criminal Code* uses the phrase *infraction de criminalité organisée*. The *Criminal Code* reference to enterprise crime/*infraction de criminalité organisée* includes a list of 24 offences that are deemed to be enterprise/ organized crimes and designated drug offences to which the Proceeds of Crime legislation applies.

Clearly, any list of enterprise crime offences is bound to be arbitrary. There is ongoing debate about which offences should be covered by the Proceeds of Crime legislation. In 1992, the Canadian Association of Chiefs of Police (CACP) Organized Crime Committee recommended that the list of enterprise crime offences be expanded to include all profit-motivated crimes, not just the high-profile offences. The committee's list includes mail fraud (s. 381),[7] illegal arms trafficking (ss. 95, 96, 97), perjury (s. 131), break and enter (s. 348), smuggling,[8] and tax evasion.[9] As a result of new legislation, the proceeds of crime provisions under the Criminal Code now apply to tobacco smuggling. Bill C-102 amends the Excise Act and the Customs Act by making it an offence to be in possession of the proceeds of cigarette smuggling activities; it also makes the Criminal Code's proceeds of crime provisions applicable to the Excise Act and the Customs Act. Similarly, legislation creating an asset management and sharing regime will capture the proceeds of tobacco smuggling that have been forfeited under the new Act.

Given what have become extremely wide interpretations of the U.S. statutes, Canadian policy-makers must determine the intent of the proceeds legislation. The rhetoric that accompanied the new law enforcement approach spoke clearly of the need for enforcement tools designed specifically to target organized crime with a particular emphasis on drug trafficking.

RESEARCHING ORGANIZED CRIME

It is common to scoff at the idea of "organized crime" with the assertion that such a conception is based upon fantastic notions of a vast underworld organization with workers, lieutenants, captains and at the top a master mind, an organization which has no being except in melodrama. But "organized crime" does exist although it is not so nicely integrated as in the crime world of fiction (Moley 1926).

Daniel Bell, Dwight Smith, and others ... are properly sceptical of the existence of a tightly organized, singular conspiratorial group called the "Mafia." Yet it is equally foolish to be so closed-minded as to fail to recognize that loose interactions, and associational and goal commonalities do exist among organized criminals and organized criminal groups (Lupsha 1981).

This section examines the difficulties of researching organized crime. Controversial issues associated with the academic approach to organized crime are identified and discussed.

What other area of research could have rooms piled with files of sworn testimony, dozens of informants, hundreds of infamous figures behind prison bars, and still be the subject of aggressive debate as to whether or not the phenomenon exists! In their extensive study of organized crime business-type activities, Edelhertz and Overcast (1993) confront the "existence" issue as follows: "We avoided involvement in the definitional morass ... preferring to accept as 'organized crime' those cases that were selected for attention by dedicated organized crime law enforcement agencies" (vi). All critics might not agree.

METHODOLOGICAL ISSUES

There are a limited number of ways to gain knowledge about the operations of organized criminals—from the criminals themselves; from law enforcement; from membership or direct participation in the organizations; from analysis of newspapers, wiretaps, or court hearings; and from government documents and commissions. While access to one or more of these sources is essential to the researcher, each source has its pitfalls. In this section, we will discuss the problems associated with organized crime research.

Few social phenomena have the power that organized crime does to attract the press, to bolster law enforcement resources, and to animate public support for various legislative or enforcement crackdowns. This milieu encourages distortions, which are facilitated by the invisible nature of demand-driven organized crime. Most of the criminal offences associated with organized crime are consensual in that the illicit commodity is willingly sought and purchased by the public. This would be true for drugs, gambling, prostitution, pornography, and smuggling. However, it would not be true for extortion, arson, murder, and frauds. In these latter situations, a high level of fear, intimidation, and powerlessness replaces the consensual condition of the "sale."

What makes organized crime the "perfect" societal threat is that it can be presented to the public to be as large or as small a problem as the media, politicians, and law enforcement want it to be. The consensual (and hence invisible) nature of many organized crime offences allows this type of activity to be manipulated for an array of diverse gains by members of those industries that exist to control, report on, or study it.

LAYERS OF SECRECY

Secrecy plays a major role in making the research task difficult. While all research tasks require gumption and intelligence when it comes to locating the data, organized crime research involves convincing others to give you entry into their highly protected working environments, where they hold a near-monopoly on the flow of information. Organized criminals have traditionally had nothing to gain from divulging information to researchers. Of course, their intent has been to keep information about their operations hidden not just from researchers, but from all outsiders.

The Quebec Police Commission (1977) report recognized the importance of secrecy to organized crime groups in its discussion of what it viewed as an important consequence of the Quebec Inquiry into Organized Crime:

> One of the Commission's goals was to throw a wrench into the activities of criminal gangs, by exposing them, for secrecy and stealth are the main strength of criminal organizations. There is sufficient evidence that crooks feared these public appearances. Some lay low, some left the province, and some chose self-imposed exile in the United States, or even Central America, to avoid testifying before the Commission. ... In the final analysis, depriving criminal organizations of their secrecy undermines and weakens them (309 and 312).

Organized crime commissions are relatively infrequent in Canada. They have tended to be created in response to a short-term political desire to "look into" a particular organized crime operation and then disband. In Australia, existing on-going crime commissions have been created largely to bring order to corrupt law enforcement agencies.[10]

In Canada, a more traditional source of exposure of the criminal organization has been via the police, who face considerable difficulties as they attempt to penetrate organized crime groups. The structure and membership of these organizations are designed to reduce the potential for infiltration by undercover officers or agents. The importance of ethnicity in organized crime operations has much to do with the formation of a group where loyalty and secrecy can be assured on the basis of family ties coupled with intimidation. Outsiders can be readily spotted and excluded. Undercover officers and agents, except as buyers or sellers of the illicit commodities, thus seldom become part of organized crime organizations. Although various "stings" or "reverse stings"[11] may help the police to build cases against the organizations, they do not usually provide indepth knowledge about the functioning and membership of the larger organization.[12]

Secrecy provides both protection from exposure to law enforcement and the ability to create a distance between the illicit commodity being sold to the public and the realities of the organized crime operations. There is some indication that the public continues to buy the illicit commodities at least in part from a lack of awareness of the violence and exploitation that is involved in the criminal operations. As the Quebec (1970b) study of organized crime maintained, "The illusion must be maintained for the public that gambling, lending, or prostitution are simply services generously and harmlessly offered to the public" (99). On occasion, however, the organized crime group must weigh the benefits to be gained from certain acts of violence, even at the cost of publicity. For example, the Quebec study cited above acknowledged that, in order to "serve" the public with "regularity, volume, immunity, and profit," organized criminals will seek to establish and maintain a monopoly over a specific commodity (100).

The quest for a monopoly is, of course, not unique to criminal operations. However, while organized criminals may use acts of violence—including murder—to eliminate competition, most legitimate businesses avoid such strategies. In between are the supposedly lawful businesses and corporate entities whose practices, aimed at securing a large percentage (or a monopoly) of the market, have been found guilty of putting individuals or communities at risk of disease or death. Given the nature of some recent cases, one must question at what point corporate entities are, in fact, organized crime operations. Increasingly, the lines between white-collar, corporate, and organized crimes are blurring. Each type of crime is used to facilitate the others. White-collar crimes are used to hide the illicit proceeds from organized crime; corporate crimes are committed by organized criminals through the illicit operation of legitimate businesses; types of corporate crimes are, in fact, synonymous with white-collar crimes.

The secrecy so valued by the organized criminals is, unfortunately, also characteristic of the entire organized crime environment. The difficulty of the researcher's task is compounded by the fact that the other "players," who have some direct involvement in organized crime, work within a similarly confidential environment. Breaking through the barriers that surround organized criminals may seem simple compared to obtaining valuable information from law enforcement. Confidentiality and the integrity of police investigations is always at stake. The task of gaining access to data will prove impossible unless the researcher is successful in having his or her project sanctioned by top management, and even then the individual and the project must "make sense" to the police officers throughout the ranks.

Law enforcement agencies often have an overly heightened sensitivity to sharing knowledge with the outsider. This "knowledge" extends far beyond sensitive police intelligence to include almost any information held by the police. Like organized criminals, organized crime law enforcement officers have little or nothing to gain from providing researchers with their information—unless it is evident that doing so may in some way assist police officers. Unfortunately, in Canada there is no tradition of academic research being directly sought out with the express purpose of policy or operational usefulness in the area of organized crime enforcement. The fault here lies with both arenas—a law enforcement community generally closed to academic advice, and an academic community generally ignorant of, and condescending toward, applied police-oriented research.

Secrecy extends beyond the criminal and law enforcement to include government officials who habitually overclassify the most mundane of information. In my life as a public servant, I have received hand-delivered, double-bagged, top-secret classified documents informing me (or, conceivably, the surreptitious reader) of nothing but the time and place for a meeting to discuss general topics related to organized crime. The practice of overclassification forces the researcher who has been exposed to government information to hunt down public sources in order to reference what is known from confidential documents.

Investigative journalists with the right contacts can be very useful in terms of uncovering information. Moreover, they have the freedom (subject, of course, to the potential for libel charges) to print what they discover. There is at least one ex-RCMP officer who quotes extensively in his writings from newspaper and magazine articles on organized crime. When one traces the source of the media information, one finds that it originated with the officer himself—demonstrating that it is permissable to "say" certain things based on experience while on the job, but not to "know" things based on previous confidential experience.

EVALUATING THE SOURCES OF INFORMATION

Obtaining access to the information is only the first step. The researcher works very much within a social environment that in this case comprises such players as law enforcement officials, politicians, journalists, civilians, and, of course, the criminals themselves. It is necessary for the researcher to recognize the inherent biases in each of these potential sources. This task involves more than simply determining the truth or falsity of the data received. It involves the more complex process of understanding the information received from the perspective of the donor. To do this the researcher must first understand the organization that has provided the information. This *verstehen* research activity is essential in helping the researcher assign the appropriate meaning to the information and to the observable activity.

Data Sources

- Organized criminals
- Law enforcement
- Government-generated documents
- Media/journalists and forensic investigators
- Social science research

ORGANIZED CRIMINALS

Researchers and law enforcement officials who engage in close interaction with organized criminals are often accused of having been co-opted or duped. For example, while Ianni's (1972) study of the Lupollo family is considered an important insider's look at a crime family, critics have charged that the family kept from Ianni information about its more serious illegal activities. It is implausible, they argue, that the family was not involved in heroin distribution or in the use of violence. The nondisclosure of these aspects of the family's operation to Ianni casts doubt on his argument that the family was driven by a desire to move out of criminal activity into legitimate operations (Reuter 1987). In addition to deliberate deception, there is a growing sense that criminals themselves are being deluded by television and law enforcement accounts of their lives into thinking their operations are more extensive, organized, and professional than they actually are.

In the last few years a large number of autobiographies by organized crime figures and family members have been written. As well, organized crime informants have come forward in person to tell their stories in exchange for protection and/or immunity. Whatever the merits of each individual account as a potential research source, it would be unreasonable to dismiss out of hand the entire discourse from known organized criminals. Firestone (1993, 216) provides us with a list of what he considers to be the most important of the mob memoirs.[13] There are some valuable things to learn from each of these accounts: why their subjects chose to become involved in criminal activity; contradictory information regarding the structure of the criminal organizations; changes in the organized crime operations over time; and explanations of the changes in legislation that made it feasible for the informants to come forward to tell their stories.

The existence of the accounts themselves is revealing of the attitudes of organized criminals to their own lifestyles. In comparing white-collar and organized crime attitudes, Katz (1988) writes:

> With white-collar crime, we have a special problem in locating facts to demonstrate the lived experience of deviance. Despite their presumably superior capacity to write books and the healthy market that await their publication efforts, we have virtually no "how-I-did-it-and-how-it-feels-doing-it" autobiographies by corrupt politicians, convicted tax frauds ... Stick-up men, safecrackers, fences, and drug dealers often wear the criminal label with pride, apparently relishing the opportunity to tell their criminal histories in colourful, intimate detail (319).

Interestingly, organized crime memoirs reveal a maze of white-collar crimes woven through the organized crime activities. However, evidence of white-collar crime becomes available only when it is revealed as being an aspect of the organized crime "way of doing business" or, more specifically, the way of attempting to disguise how successful they have been at their criminal endeavours.

That the subjects of these memoirs have been members of the Mafia rather than organized criminals in general may partially be explained by the fact that certain organized crime operations may be more vulnerable to exposure by informants due to their structural features. For example, evidence supporting the notion of distinct "cells" of responsibility in the Colombian cartels suggests that individual informants from those particular criminal organizations will be able to provide only incomplete accounts.

Why have so many mobsters in the United States come forward and broken *omerta*, the Mafia code of silence? Firestone (1993) proposes two explanations. The first has to do with changes in law enforcement strategies. Firestone identifies as the main influence the U.S. Racketeer Influenced and Corrupt Organizations (RICO) statute provisions that allow prosecutors to link separate offences and make it easier for the state to build successful organized crime cases and then impose triple damages and severe prison terms upon conviction. He also cites the existence of an effective witness-protection program that creates a new identity and relocates the informant with less risk (211). (The U.S. RICO statute, the Canadian Proceeds of Crime legislation, and witness-protection programs are discussed in depth in Part 3.)

The second explanation has to do with the erosion of mob values. Memoirs written by both sons and their fathers seem to indicate that the older generation accepted the oath of obedience and loyalty over individual safety or preference. Firestone uses the differences between Angelo Bruno and Nicky Scarfo to illustrate the two positions. Bruno would have expected loyalty from crime family members, and would have taken care of the dependents of those in jail. In contrast, Scarfo would expect the arrested crime family member to turn state's evidence (hence an attempt would be made to have him killed prior to arrest or trial). In Canada, the "new Mafia" of the Commissos has been contrasted with the older operations of figures like Paul Volpe. Dubro maintains that Volpe had standards and granted to human life a value that the Commisso brothers never did (Dubro 1985, 185).

There may be no contradiction between Firestone's two explanations. Increased enforcement powers coupled with the potential for "life after informing" may well combine with a different value system. As loyalty for the sake of loyalty weakens, it is replaced with fear of the sentences accruing to those found guilty of maximum RICO charges. Prosecutors in the United States claim that since the late 1980s over 300 top and middle-echelon leaders in the seven New York/New Jersey crime families have been convicted or are awaiting trial, and that this targeting by law enforcement has had a significant impact on how the Mafia has chosen to operate. Social clubs once openly frequented by the mobsters have closed; code names and hand signals are used instead of the real names of mob leaders; and members are resisting gaining any type of profile that will make them likely targets for law enforcement. It has been suggested that the Genovese family alone has been able to retain its power, due to its ruthlessness and the secrecy imposed by Vincent Gigante. According to top Mafia informant Anthony Accetturo, former head of the Lucchese family, "If anybody survives it will be the Genovese. The Genovese gang was probably the only family in the region that had not been weakened by a new generation of leaders whose lust for money and power had created dissension and betrayals" (*New York Times* 1994, 1). While the Canadian Proceeds of Crime legislation may be argued to have similar powers to the U.S. RICO statute, several provinces still hesitate to use this relatively new legislation— primarily due to the undertaking that the attorneys general must sign to accept liability.

It is not only in North America that informants are turning on their former criminal organizations. Ties between the Cosa Nostra and politicians in Rome and Sicily have been described by six former members of the Mafia who testified against Giulio Andreotti, seven times Italy's prime minister and one of the country's longest serving politicians. The key informant was Tommaso Buscetta, who was largely responsible for the convictions won against 360 crime family members during Italy's 1987 anti-Mafia trials (*Economist*, May 28, 1994, p.49). The testimony of Italian informants (*pentiti*, meaning repentants) allowed the police to arrest Salvatore ("Toto") Riina, the alleged head of the Sicilian Mafia. The increasing willingness of crime members in Italy to turn state's evidence has been attributed to a new series of anti-Mafia laws, a special anti-Mafia national police force, a program for protecting the *pentiti*, and improvements in traditional policing techniques such as wiretaps.

The making of deals with informants is a controversial police activity, since in organized crime cases informants tend to have strong criminal backgrounds themselves. Aside from the questionable ethics of trading evidence against one criminal for the freedom of another, there are problems associated with the discretionary nature of these deals as well as with the task of keeping the informant alive before and after the court appearance. In response to accusations that the evidence may have been put to political uses (and also because of the vast number of *pentiti* requiring protection), Italian justice officials are now reviewing their laws regulating the use of Mafia *pentiti*.

Perhaps the most well-known U.S. informant was Joe Valachi, who came forward (before RICO existed) after having killed a fellow inmate while in a federal penitentiary. Two American criminologists, Joseph Albini and Dwight Smith, have made much of the apparent contradictions in Valachi's testimony during the 1963 McClellan hearings. The testimony of an informant, however, may be valuable even with inconsistencies. Where you sit in any organization—at the top or near the bottom—will determine what you see and how clearly you understand the functioning of the larger operation. No one claimed that Valachi was at the top of the organized crime hierarchy and it would be expected that he in fact could be wrong in some of his testimony. As Reuter (1983) argues, secrecy is a precious asset to a criminal enterprise, and only a select few have a comprehensive knowledge of how the entire operation works.[14] With respect to the Valachi testimony, the contradictions are less important than the general descriptions that have been substantiated by numerous sworn testimonies and wiretap transcripts.

Although informants are a critical link in building organized crime cases, they are usually individuals who have been identified by the police (possibly through undercover work) and are central to an ongoing police investigation. Douglas Jaworski, who approached the RCMP with an offer to be an informant against the Colombian cartel, is an exception. In his case, the motivation was fear of U.S. and Canadian law enforcement, an impending IRS investigation, and a realization that the cartel members could have him killed for idiosyncratic reasons or on orders from their leader, Escobar.

Cecil Kirby is perhaps the best known of the Canadian informants, due in part to the controversy surrounding the immunity granted to him for past acts of violence, including murder. In exchange, the government received what was argued to be extremely valuable information against the Commissos. Dubro documents criminal defence lawyer Eddie Greenspan's outrage at the "deal" given to Kirby. What Greenspan neglected to mention was that he had served for over 10 years as the lawyer for Cosimo and Remo Commisso, the main targets of the Kirby investigation (Dubro 1985, 216).

In Canada, the issue of undercover work and the use of informants recently came under review, partly as a result of the 1989/90 publicity surrounding dubious law enforcement activities undertaken in the Cogger case.[15] Criticism of the RCMP resulted in a public inquiry.

LAW ENFORCEMENT

The reliability of law enforcement information is a subject that has generated much controversy in the academic community. Law enforcement sources are seen to be critical by some researchers, and critically flawed by others. Some organized crime researchers argue that law enforcement agencies over the years have developed a particular view of organized crime, one that excludes all other views. They claim that the preferred law enforcement view is one that accomplishes three things that are directly advantageous to law enforcement. The police interpretation creates

- a public image of organized crime that will result in increased police resources to fight the "threat";

- a justification for the fact that police actions are not having the impact that the public might expect from the resources consumed due to the size, scope, and imperviousness of the perceived organized crime threat;

- an "alien" conspiracy notion of organized crime that separates this activity from "normal" society and shifts the focus away from police corruption and/or collusion in organized crime activity.

Even when police information is backed up by recorded wire-tapped information direct from the criminals, critics point out that this information is suspect because it is transcribed, summarized, and interpreted by law enforcement officers or prosecutors.[16] What we end up with is a conspiratorial view held by some academics of a conspiratorial view of organized crime held by law enforcement. This kind of scepticism can lead the researcher to neglect valuable law enforcement-generated "by-products" such as public records of indictments, court records, and appellate briefs.[17]

Unlike some of his colleagues, Robert Kelly (1991) does not believe that law enforcement has engaged in a conspiratorial manipulation of data. He argues instead that while police case-building and intelligence gathering become shaped by beliefs that are congenial to law enforcement, the processes involved in identifying and defining "threats" are more complex, more interesting, and far more relevant than mere conspiracy.

Following on Merton's discussion of the Thomas theorem ("If men define situations as real, they are real in their consequences"), the danger is the creation of a self-fulfilling prophecy (Merton 1968, 475). Particularly during the 1960s and 1970s the police, believing in a national Mafia criminal conspiracy, focused their attention on these groups and individuals, with the result that the majority of the police cases were Mafia-related. The police experience, as reflected in police case data, therefore confirmed the initial assumption.

In addition to any bias in the law enforcement perspective on organized crime, some researchers and government officials have acknowledged the problems caused by misinformation deliberately provided by the police in order to create impressions that they hope will assist law enforcement operational objectives. This misinformation is provided to the media for public consumption and then used by unsuspecting researchers.

Overall, it is difficult to gauge how informed the police and law enforcement are regarding organized crime. A researcher must be able to distinguish between those situations where police information is withheld, actually absent, distorted, or purposefully wrong and those situations where the information is available, correct, and valuable. It is important to acknowledge that the quality of police intelligence varies over time depending on the personalities and abilities of those in charge, the resources available, and current law enforcement priorities. An example of improved police intelligence can be seen in the police penetration of New York City's Chinese gangs and tongs. Kelly et al. (1993) found that law enforcement authorities possess a more valid and reliable picture of the activity and structure of these gangs than in the past. The successful prosecution of several Chinese gangs and drug-trafficking groups stemmed from the assistance of a gang member-turned-informant. Likewise, in Canada and the United States, there has been a steady increase in the knowledge of the police regarding Russian organized crime operations in North America.

There are serious difficulties in attempting to empirically determine how effective the police and related law enforcement agencies are, and likewise how efficiently the resources are being utilized. The Canadian Drug Strategy 1992 renewal included $33 million for the funding of three special anti-drug profiteering units to be located in Vancouver, Toronto, and Montreal. What was somewhat unusual was the specification that there be an ongoing evaluation process carried out by the Solicitor General Secretariat officials or external researchers on contract. The objective of the government was to learn what the units were able to do and where the difficulties were. In addition to providing the public with some notion of impact from resources spent, this project was to be a learning experience for the police forces involved in the three sites, and possibly have an effect on policing techniques and strategies across Canada.

The law enforcement information that we possess on the nature and extent of organized crime in Canada comes primarily from the following sources:

- *Criminal Intelligence Service Canada (CISC)*. The primary internal intelligence coordinating national mechanism has a mandate to collect and analyze intelligence related to organized crime. CISC has nine provincial bureaus across Canada that are operated by police officers on loan (secondment) from the RCMP and from provincial and municipal police forces. Two main factors—restricted resources and a failure to secure the commitment of police forces across Canada—continue to compromise the effectiveness of this organization.

- *Canadian Association of Chiefs of Police (CACP)*. The CACP Organized Crime Committee worked with the CISC to compile an annual report on organized crime. The *Organized Crime Committee Report* served as the only nationally distributed report on organized crime. The CACP Organized Crime Committee met twice a year to discuss the changing organized crime environment and to make recommendations to governments or to the CACP. During Spring 1995 the committee decided that their function was a replication of CISC responsibilities, and the committee was disbanded. The commissioner of the OPP has been appointed to serve as a liaison between CACP and CISC.

- *Royal Canadian Mounted Police (RCMP).* As of April 1995, the main directorates within the RCMP that have a role in detecting and reporting on organized crime are Criminal Intelligence and Federal Services. Economic crime, the anti-profiteers units, and drugs fall under Federal Services. RCMP officers are spread across Canada, and work with municipal and provincial police forces in joint-force, multi-force, and permanent structures—such as the British Columbia Coordinated Law Enforcement Unit (CLEU)—and in the regional CISC bureaus. In the Northwest Territories and in all provinces except Ontario and Quebec, the RCMP works on contract as the provincial and (in some jurisdictions) the municipal police. In those "contracting" jurisdictions the RCMP takes even greater responsibility for organized crime enforcement.

- *Provincial and Municipal Police.* Organized crime activities in Canada present a serious crime problem for all major urban police forces. Organized crime intelligence is generated by such specialized units as drugs, criminal investigation, anti-rackets, and homicide, in addition to the ongoing street development of police cases. Joint-force operations are a way of pooling the resources and intelligence of individual police forces.

- *The Coordinated Law Enforcement Unit (CLEU).* Combining federal, provincial, and municipal police and civilian resources, CLEU has a mandate to identify, prevent, and suppress organized criminal activity in British Columbia. The organization has two components, the Joint Force Operations Section and the Policy Analysis Section. Organized crime intelligence is collected and analyzed for both enforcement and policy purposes.

- *CSIS.* Although the Canadian Security Intelligence Service has to date not been directly involved in organized crime intelligence work, information of interest to the RCMP does come to CSIS in the course of its mandated activities.

- *Other Government Enforcement Agencies.* Other government departments having some involvement in organized crime control include: Immigration (VISA Intelligence, handled by

RCMP); Customs Canada, Enforcement Directorate, Intelligence Services; External Affairs International Drug Policy Section; Coast Guard; DND and the Communications Security Establishment; Attorneys General and Solicitors General departments (provincial and national).

GOVERNMENT-GENERATED DOCUMENTS, ROYAL COMMISSIONS, INQUIRIES, AND TASK FORCES

Canada lacks a tradition of frequent and extensive national organized crime commissions, although there have been a number of provincial organized crime commission reports and a major federal/provincial study (Justice 1983). As a source of organized crime information, royal commissions, task forces, and inquiries may, like their counterparts in law enforcement, have a preferred view of organized crime—one that may have more to do with politics than fact-finding. Having said that, valuable information can still be derived from the various reports.

The creation and operation of commissions or inquiries is a study in itself. The researcher must always consider the conditions that prompt the inquiry; the process by which the chairperson is selected; and the timeframe within which the group is expected to produce its findings. In policing and law enforcement inquiries, there often exists a tension between the lawyers, police practitioners, and researchers who are assigned to work together. In Canada, it is most common for a prestigious lawyer or judge to be appointed Chair. By habit and training, these chairpersons are more comfortable with both the thinking and the timeframes within which their lawyer colleagues work. The perceived merit of including the "rhetoric" of a research component to these inquiries may be greater than the perceived merit of the research itself!

In addition to possible bias, the researchers and other officials on these working teams are usually not given sufficient time to generate new data or even to develop new, solidly based interpretations. Research activities that may produce results in ten months' time are sometimes recognized politically and may, therefore, be included in the working group, but the thinking, commitments, and report writing (including the recommendations) often move along quite independently of this slower, "esoteric" aspect.[18] The result may be pseudo-research that is manipulated into a politically acceptable response aimed at relieving a politically defined, media-generated crisis.

MEDIA AND FORENSIC INVESTIGATORS

The domestic and international media are important sources of information on organized crime. Ironically, researchers, policy analysts, and intelligence analysts often use media reports for information on organized crime issues. The advantages of this information source are that it is international in scope and focuses on timely issues; as well, journalists are often better investigators than academic researchers, willingly present their information to the public, and often have better and/or more diverse sources than police. On the negative side, media reports are often highly reactive, sensational, or speculative. Nevertheless, this body of data should not be ignored. Canada's limited canon of organized crime studies is dominated by the writing of journalists and ex-journalists whose books hold much information of interest and value to the public and to the researcher.

In ways similar to the media, professional forensic investigators can play a significant role in organized crime investigations. In domestic situations, they are hired either by private corporations to untangle complicated organized frauds and scams or by law enforcement to complete the lengthy and complex financial investigations needed to build money laundering and international organized crime cases.

As a source of knowledge for researchers, a limitation of forensic investigators may be the range and depth of investigations that the paying client requires. Instead of a longitudinal focus, there is likely to be a "solution" obtained in exchange for the fee. This may consist of a mundane accounting task or something more unique. In more esoteric circumstances, private forensic investigators are hired by governments to trace stolen funds absconded by previous regimes or to complete the international investigations needed to enable businesses to operate in foreign countries without the fear that they are dealing with organized crime figures.

In addition to these paper-trail auditing tasks, there is an area of "policing" that can no longer be adequately addressed by the public police. Commercial crimes, international frauds, and a wide array of technologically facilitated crimes relating to the use of computers, credit cards, stock market manipulations, and insurance scams are too resource-intensive for many Canadian public police forces whose priorities are often driven by a political need to "keep the streets safe" and to maintain a highly "visible" presence.

Access to organized crime information from forensic investigators is limited by the investigators' requirement to protect the paying customer's confidentiality. Like the criminals themselves, these investigators are in a pay-for-results business—a business they will not jeopardize to satisfy the informational needs of researchers. In some instances, the customers will have gone to the forensic investigator rather than to the public police specifically in order that the criminal activity—organized or otherwise—never becomes a matter of public knowledge. The only factor that works to the researcher's advantage is that forensic investigators must bring in business to their umbrella companies. One way to do this is to remain in the public eye as an expert on certain types of ongoing criminal activity, and to serve as the media's source on certain high-profile issues.

In addition to the investigatory skills that forensic investigators may have themselves, they are often ex-public police officers and as such benefit "informally" from the formal data sources maintained by public police systems and from their continuing friendships with police-force members. Likewise the "exchange" of information may on occasion go in the opposite direction. For example, private police, who are less affected by the procedural requirements that restrain public police, can pass along valuable information to focus (or refocus) a public investigation. This give-and-take between private and public police will increasingly be an issue as the private industry continues to grow. At present, private policing is estimated to be over three times the size of the public police. Issues of concern include the training, regulation, and accountability of private police.

SOCIAL SCIENCE RESEARCH

> The field of organized crime research, to say it modestly, suffers from "intellectual atrophy." Little is written that deserves our attention, and that which is written often does not reflect reality. All in all, research into the mechanics of organized crime is in need of an infusion of new thinking. Particularly when it comes to addressing public policy issues with respect to organized crime control, the field could use a healthy dose of "real world" experiences (Martens 1993, 27).

Research on organized crime has tended to be somewhat limited and shallow in its focus. The most fruitful areas are those that emphasize the diversity of organized crime activity, and the consequences that this diversity has for law enforcement and policy. Case studies have been the preferential approach, due mainly to the impossibility of attempting a broad empirical study across diverse organized crime groups. While many of the traditional social science research methodologies are of dubious value when it comes to gathering empirical information on organized crime, it must be acknowledged that all methods have been used with some success by some researchers. The following list is not exhaustive and merely serves to indicate the range of research strategies.

- *Case studies involving in-depth participant observation.* Includes the work of Bill Chambliss (1978) in Seattle; Gary Potter (1994) in "Morrisburg," Francis Ianni (1972) in New York City. In some studies, a particular organized crime family was chosen; in others a particular illegal market was analyzed.

- *Analysis of police files, seized documents, and interviews with informants.* Includes the work of Peter Reuter (1983) in New York City, Donald Cressey (largely) in New York, Joseph Albini (1971) in Detroit, Margaret Beare and Stephen Schneider (1990) on Canadian money laundering, and Mark Haller (1991) on the Bruno family in Philadelphia.

- *Analysis of the by-products of law enforcement and court activities.* Includes public-accessible indictments, court records, appellate briefs: Herbert Edelhertz and Thomas Overcast (1993) in the United States, and Diego Gambetta (1993) in Italy.

- *Interviews with government and law enforcement officials, historical records, and media analysis.* Includes the Canadian work of James Dubro on the mob (1985) and the Asian underworld (1992), Mario Possamai on money laundering; and Peter Edwards (1991) on an RCMP Colombian cartel sting.

- *Economic oriented market-analysis studies of illicit commodities plus estimations of demand and supply size.* Includes the work of Peter Reuter and the Rand Foundation, Herbert Edelhertz and Thomas Overcast, and Mark Moore (1987; 1992).

NOTES

1. See Kelly (1986).
2. This focus sets aside for the moment the question of who or what constitutes the organized crime activity. While these debates serve to elucidate the dominant form of organized crime at any one period in history, they bring to our understanding of the general concept only dissension and distortions.
3. This book uses the term "Mafia" when referring to traditional Italian organized crime.
4. See Hagan (1982) and Albini (1971).
5. Edelhertz and Overcast (1993) emphasize the need for police and prosecutors to use in their white-collar investigations forensic ac-

counting skills that will detect irregularities such as "the maintenance of false records, the submission of false claims, collusion
between customers and suppliers, commercial bribery, kickbacks, ver-
tical and horizontal monopolies and ... omnipresent tax violations"
(168).

6. The phrase "part of a pattern of criminal activity planned and orga-
    nized by a number of persons acting in concert" appears in Section 183
    of the *Criminal Code* pertaining to authorizations for interception of
    private communications. *Martin's Criminal Code* (1975) added to this
    definition the phrase "and that such pattern is part of the activities of
    organized crime" (s. 178.1, 101).

7. Interestingly, it is the mail and wire fraud predicate offenses under
    RICO that have caused the most controversy. As Justice Marshall
    stated in his dissenting opinion in *Sedima*, "The single most signifi-
    cant reason for the expansive use of civil RICO has been the presence
    in the statute, as predicate acts, of mail and wire fraud." Nonna and
    Corrado (1990) argue that virtually any commercial action can be
    brought under RICO, since most operations require use of the U.S.
    mails.

8. Customs Tariff Act, R.S.C. 1985 c. 54 s. 37.

9. Income Tax Act, S.C. 1970-71-72, c. 63, ss. 238, 239.

10. A study of crime commissions would be interesting, particularly fol-
    lowing the controversial 1994 demise of the Pennsylvania Crime
    Commission following its investigation into the conduct of Pennsylva-
    nia Attorney General Ernest D. Preate (Pennsylvania Crime Commis-
    sions, April 1994). See Rogovin and Martens (1993) for a discussion of
    the typologies and mandate of diverse crime commissions.

11. In a typical sting operation, a police officer working undercover, or a
    paid agent working for the police, will attempt to buy drugs from a
    suspect. Reverse sting operations are more controversial and poten-
    tially open to court challenge. In these operations, the police sell drugs
    to the suspect or launder money for traffickers in order to make their
    cases against users/distributors or criminals whose illicit proceeds
    are great enough to warrant a "professional" money launderer. These
    operations are discussed in greater detail in Chapters 4 and 7.

12. There are, however, cases in which considerable information has been
    gained. Pilot Douglas Jaworski had worked with the Colombian cartel
    almost as a member before becoming an agent. Jaworski's ability to
    fly planes to Colombia placed him in an advantageous position. Simi-
    larly, reverse stings in which police set up a storefront operation to
    launder illicit proceeds provide considerable intelligence.

13. Appearing within parentheses is the name of the mob figure who ei-
    ther wrote the book and/or was the subject of the book. *Quitting the
    Mob: How the "Yuppie Don" Left the Mafia and Lived to Tell His Story*
    (Michael Franzese), 1992; *Contract Killer: The Explosive Story of the
    Mafia's Notorious Hit Man* (Tony Frankos), 1992; *Blood and Honour:
    Inside The Scarfo Mob: The Mafia's Most Violent Family* (Nick Cara-
    mandi), 1990; *Body Mike: An Unsearing Exposé by the Mafia Insider
    Who Turned on the Mob* (Joe Cantalupo), 1990; *Mafia Enforcer: A True*

Story of Life and Death in the Mob (Cecil Kirby), 1987; *Donnie Brasco: My Undercover Life in the Mafia* (Joe Pistone), 1987; *Wiseguy: Life in a Mafia Family* (Henry Hill), 1985; *A Man of Honor* (Joe Bonnano), 1983; *The Last Mafioso* (Jimmy Fratianno), 1981; *Honor Thy Father* (Bill Bonnano), 1971; *The Valachi Papers* (Joe Valachi), 1968; *My Life in the Mafia* (Vincent Teresa), 1973; *Killer: Autobiography of a Hit Man for the Mafia,* ("Joey"), 1973 .

14. See also Southerland and Potter (1993).

15. See Palango (1994) for an account of former assistant commissioner Rod Stamler's police cases, including the Cogger case. See also the Marin Inquiry (Marin 1991).

16. However, practices vary between jurisdictions. Unlike their U.S. counterparts, Canadian courts usually require verbatim transcriptions.

17. These documents provide much valuable information in Edelhertz and Overcast's *Business of Organized Crime* (1993).

18. Examples of current policing inquiries that exhibit this tension include the Judge Oppal Policing Inquiry in British Columbia (1994); the Sheehy Inquiry in the United Kingdom (1993); and numerous inquiries in Metropolitan Toronto, including Lewis (1989) and Bellemare Report in Quebec (1988).

C   H   A   P   T   E   R   **2**

The Theory Behind Organized Crime

This chapter attempts to provide a theoretical framework to explain organized crime. The first two parts in this section attempt to explain why organized crime exists, and why certain criminal associations take on the characteristics of organized crime groups. The third part offers a typology of organized crime groups, while the fourth attempts to explain why particular individuals participate in organized crime activity.

EXPLAINING THE EXISTENCE OF ORGANIZED CRIME

> We must not make a scarecrow of the law,
> Setting it up to fear the birds of prey,
> And let it keep one shape, till custom make it
> Their perch and not their terror.
>
> (William Shakespeare, Measure for Measure, 11.i.1–4)

Explaining why organized crime exists may be the easiest of the tasks. In all societies there are goods and services that are kept illegal but remain as desired commodities. As long as there continues to be a market for these illicit items and services, someone will offer to fill the void and violate the formal laws of the society in order to supply the market in exchange for considerable profit. Profit from illicit commodities remains the raison d'être of organized crime operations. The factors discussed in the following sections help to explain variations in organized crime activity across jurisdictions and time. Awareness of the functions fulfilled by organized crime in no way justifies or excuses the criminal behaviour, but it does serve to facilitate the development of policing strategies and policies that may more effectively control the activity.

Our purpose here is to illustrate the subtle interactions among control agencies, officials, and organized crime. "More" enforcement does not necessarily translate into "less" organized crime. What is required, as Merton (1967) and Martens (1978) suggest, is an understanding of the latent functions being served by organized crime. Only then can clear and deliberate "goal-oriented" enforcement resources be brought to bear on the exploitive activities.

MACRO-LEVEL VARIABLES

While organized criminals are motivated by a micro-level desire to make a profit, there seem as well to be certain macro-level variables that facilitate organized crime. For example, Lupsha (1988) notes the important role that natural ports and harbours played in the era before air travel and instant communication. He points out, in support of the "out-group" explanation of criminal behaviour, that it was the rough port environment that provided a niche for the new immigrant and other excluded individuals as well as a facility that enabled extortion, corruption, and distribution of illicit goods.

LAWS AND REGULATIONS

Organized crime involves supplying a desired commodity or service that for some reason has been classified as illegal or illegitimate. Laws and regulations are responsible for shifting the supply and demand out of the legitimate economy and into the realm of crime and the underground economy. As H.L. Packer observes,

> Regardless of what we think we are trying to do, when we make it illegal to traffic in commodities for which there is an inelastic demand, the effect is to secure a kind of monopoly profit to the entrepreneur who is willing to break the law. In effect, we say to him: "We will set up a barrier to entry into this line of commerce by making it illegal and, therefore, risky, if you are willing to take the risk, you will be sheltered from the competition of those unwilling to do so" (quoted in Edelhertz and Overcast 1993, 163).

Saying that the illegal enterprises would not become the domain of organized crime without the regulation of these activities by law and by the police is not the same as saying that without the specific laws organized crime would not exist. Organized crime has proven itself to be infinitely flexible in identifying profit-making illegal commodities. Unless the society is prepared to legalize all such activities/ commodities, the illicit markets will merely shift. Having said that, there are some commodities (such as illicit drugs) that are particularly lucrative, and legalization has become part of the rhetoric surrounding the issue of crime control.

MARKET ECONOMICS

Most of the business rules that apply to legitimate enterprises also apply to criminal operations. Such factors as degree of risk and the nature of supply and demand all help to determine a commodity's price and hence the profit garnered by the criminals. By applying economic theory, it is possible to identify the economic incentives and limitations within a particular environment. When the commodity is a service rather than a product, organized crime, like legitimate business, attempts to gain the maximum control possible by managing the "choke points" of an industry. With respect to the concrete industry, for example, once organized crime gained control of this time-sensitive activity, the rest of the construction industry was at its mercy (Edelhertz and Overcast 1993).

CORRUPTION

There is no consensus on how essential it is for organized crime to be able to corrupt officials (i.e., political officials, law enforcement officers, and those in business and finance). Some prosecutors and investigators see corruption as a critical factor, while other observers see it as less relevant (Edelhertz and Overcast 1993, 128). Whether or not corruption is essential, Reuter (1987) is correct in arguing that a corrupt political authority at the local level can be a "uniquely powerful instrument for organized crime" (1987, 181). There may be blatant corruption in exchange for kickbacks or the power at the disposal of the criminal group may allow its members to gain control over a public process and in that way corrupt the system:

> The capacity to corrupt public processes provides significant regulatory advantages in terms of protecting an organized crime enterprise or operation as it moves into a new sphere of illegal activities, and to a large extent also can be used to protect existing markets from non-organized crime competitors (Edelhertz and Overcast 1993, 129).

> **Chicago:** The Department of Streets and Sewers has been a ready source of employment for organized crime members and associates. In one case, an associate had a job with Streets and Sewers that consisted of inspecting street signs in one section of the city. His only responsibility was to submit a monthly report noting the location of street signs that needed repair or replacement. To perform these duties, he was provided a city-owned vehicle. In addition to performing his duties for the city, he also was a collector for a bookmaking operation, making his daily pickup rounds in the city vehicle at the same time he was inspecting street signs (Edelhertz and Overcast 1993, 143).

More serious than the corruptibility of individual political officials is the threat of political systems colluding with organized crime in order to stay in power, eliminate opposition, or raise funds through involvement in illegal commodities such as drugs.

THE INTERPLAY BETWEEN VIOLENCE AND CORRUPTION

The amount of monopolistic control by organized criminals over one jurisdiction or one market is in various ways related to the likely degree of violence and corruption. Both of these factors can be adversely manipulated as a result of the unanticipated consequences of law enforcement activities. Violence within an organized crime market may mean that there is no monopoly and therefore separate groups are fighting among themselves for control. An absence of violence may mean that the monopoly has been established or that the market is such that competition is not seen as threatening. However, once you introduce aggressive enforcement, these two variables may, in fact, exist in opposition to each other. Violence within organized crime operations may be indicative of less corruption given that one function of corruption is to allow for monopolistic control over the illicit market. Aggressive enforcement may result in the elimination of small operations and the creation of a monopoly, or may eliminate "select" operations and may reflect the corrupt relationship between the control agencies and the remaining illicit operation (Geis 1966; New Jersey 1978; Dintino and Martens 1980).

Explaining the Movement of Gangs or Criminal Enterprises into Organized Crime

From the organized criminal's point of view, there are certain advantages associated with organized crime membership that are absent from individualistic criminality. While these benefits vary depending upon the type of organized crime activity, some of the main ones are outlined below.

INTIMIDATION

For some criminal enterprises, the main benefit is the ability to intimidate. In those criminal operations that require the "organizing" of hundreds of employers (as in the case of criminal-controlled corrupt unions), effective control is maintained through the ability to make "credible threats of continuing violence" against competitors or resisters (Reuter 1987, 182). To some extent this is a "reputational" capacity. However, there must be the potential capacity (tested in reality or rumour) to inflict violence or economic destruction upon an individual opponent. According to Edelhertz and Overcast (1993),

> An over-riding objective of such groups is control, to some extent an even more important objective than organizational or personal enrichment—it is important to control other criminals and to be in control of their activities, and to ensure that they have respect for the authority that is exercised over them (121).

Gambetta (1993, 3) emphasizes the link between the state decreeing a particular transaction or a commodity illegal and the creation of a private protection market operated by organized crime. As Gambetta states:

> The definition of what constitutes an illegal commodity is subject to change as legislation varies from country to country. There is one feature, however, that all illicit markets have in common: they are both unprotected and subject to legal action (1993, 226).

STABILITY AND STRUCTURE

Another feature of organized crime operations that may not be present in looser gang or individual operations is stability. The "tithing" system, whereby a percentage of the proceeds is paid into an existing structure, provides a sense of longevity, assistance against encroachment from outsiders, continuing links into the political structure, "lobbying" strength on occasion, and, in some jurisdictions, economic support for imprisoned members' families. In addition, the extensive organized crime network facilitates access to those with specialized skills. The Colombian cartel groups, for example, require for their international operations the expertise of money launderers, lawyers, and accountants.

PAYMENTS, JOBS, AND SUPPORT

A thorough investigation into the "services" granted to organized crime members, conducted by Edelhertz and Overcast (1993), concluded that rewards/payments varied across cities. Listed below are some of the cities and advantages of membership:

- Kansas City: cash, legal services, real (legitimate) employment, support for families of imprisoned members.

- Cleveland: share of the illicit proceeds, support for imprisoned members' families, support for members' families with economic/health problems.

- Philadelphia: legitimate jobs—associates are required to make their own living and contribute a percentage into the organization.

- Chicago: a modest "salary" (there is little evidence of support for the families of arrested members). Most associates hold legitimate jobs, often with the city.

- New York: legitimate and, in some cases, "no-show" jobs.

Gambetta's (1993) research in Sicily emphasized that capital was one of the services that the Mafia supplied to high-risk or illegal enterpreneurs. He describes a process whereby the Mafia would allow the entrepreneurs to operate independently until the Mafia's investments seemed at risk:

> The financial exposure of the Mafia has crucial consequences, for it is no longer just money which is at stake but the credibility of the guarantor as well ... when it becomes problematic, Mafiosi responded by internalizing key smugglers ... According to Tommaso Buscella "it became necessary for the Cosa Nostra to turn the major smugglers into men of honour—in order to make them more amenable to its will (1993, 231).

STATUS, PRESTIGE, BELONGING

In addition to profit, prestige and status may be attached to membership in specific organized crime operations. Edelhertz and Overcast (1993) emphasize that organized crime provides members with a sense of belonging and identity—the perfect combination for creating loyal "company men." This loyalty, as we have discussed, is increasingly being tested by the legislative incentives to turn informant.

A Typology of Organized Crime Groups: A Two-Dimensional Model

In Chapter 1 we argued that once you focus on organized crime as a "process," you see great diversity across a wider range of organized crime groups. In this section we attempt to create a typology within which the distinct organized crime groups can be plotted. A two-dimensional model is proposed.

The evolutionary model of organized crime, originally advanced by Stier and Richards (1987) and expanded by Lupsha (1988), postulates that organized crime groups go through an evolutionary process. The model categorizes organized crime groups on the basis of their interconnectedness to the state in terms of use of corruption, scope of activity, and power and exchange relationships. However, the relationship between the organized crime group and the society is only part of the picture. It does not determine what forces propel the group into the next stage of evolution. In addition to the Stier-Richards-Lupsha continuum, organized crime groups can be seen to fall along a second continuum ranging between legitimate groups that engage in organized crime as a secondary activity and organized crime groups that exist for no other reason than to commit crimes.

THE EVOLUTIONARY MODEL

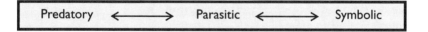

The first phase or stage, termed the *predatory stage*, tends to be characterized by violence and has little connection to the political system. As Lupsha (1988) states, the organized crime group "may be used by that system but is subordinate to it" (3). Predatory organized crime tends to "control" via the use of physical violence aimed at problematic clients or competition. As groups evolve toward other stages, the violence becomes more economic in nature, and may be carried out by the withdrawal of a vital service such as hazardous waste-disposal, concrete delivery, and control of labour.

In the second stage, known as the *parasitical stage*, the interaction between the criminal system and the political system is stronger. Risks of doing business are minimized by corruption and contributions to government parties. The criminal activity is still, however, bottom-up in that it is initiated by the organized criminals and introduced into the society. In the final stage, termed the *symbiotic stage*, the reverse occurs. The political system seeks to minimize risks by using organized crime as its extra-government force. Lupsha suggests that organized crime groups operating in Mexico, Italy, and Colombia are closest to the symbiotic stage. Scandals have exposed the fact that "legitimate" government officials acknowledge their presence and consult with them on economic and state matters.

Conceptualizing organized crime in this manner allows one to compare organized crime groups in terms of their link into the political system, and also to identify the catalysts that served to relocate the groups in relation to positions of power. The policies and political climate that gave rise to the Prohibition era can be seen as catalysts for the development of a predatory group that was to evolve into a parasitic one. As Stier and Richards (1987) state;

> In its most advanced form organized crime is so thoroughly integrated into the economic, political, and social institutions of legitimate society that it may no longer be recognizable as a criminal enterprise. Such integration represents the most serious potential for social harm that can be caused by racketeers. However, the criminal justice system is least effective in dealing with organized crime when it reaches this level of maturity (65).

The biggest threat posed in the final stage of the evolutionary model is not the illicit commodities themselves, but rather the dependence of legitimate businesses or political regimes on the services provided by the organized crime group.

LEGITIMATE AND ILLEGITIMATE GROUPS

Table 2.1 provides an outline of organized crime groups in Canada that reflects their varying degrees of dependence on organized crime activity. This continuum attempts to capture the differences between the groups in terms of their commitment to crime. Between the two polar extremes are two intermediate positions that although arguably distinct also serve to indicate the shading that occurs between the two extremes.[1]

There may also be movement across the model over time. For example, legitimate groups that "stumble" onto highly lucrative

TABLE 2.1

The Commitment of Legitimate and Illegitimate Groups to Crime

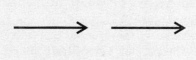

Existence of group is independent of, and therefore separate from, OC activity		Existence of group is dependent on, and therefore explained by, OC activity	
Characteristics	**Characteristics**	**Characteristics**	**Characteristics**
Criminal activity is secondary to the ongoing purpose of the existing group structure.

Existing structure or circumstantial advantages may facilitate the OC activity, but OC is not the reason the group exists. Group is seen to be legitimate in spite of OC activity. Group activities are much broader. | Structure is in place for political/ideological or task-oriented reason. OC may be used to provide the funds to reach the goals.

OC activity is accepted as a necessary part of the operation of these groups. However, without the OC activity, the groups would change but continue to exist. | The sense of tradition/ethnic cohesion is provided within the continuation of a historical structure that may have been created originally around a political ideology.

The group's main reason now for existing is to carry out OC. | Groups are created strictly for the purpose of efficiently carrying out OC crimes. If OC was no longer a group activity, the group would have no reason to exist.

This category tends to include the newer OC groups that are still in a state of flux. |
| **Examples** | **Examples** | **Examples** | **Examples** |
| Aboriginal groups that engage in OC criminal activity. | Terrorist groups involved in OC to generate funds

Outlaw motorcycle gangs | Asian triads/ Mafia | Russian, Jamaican, and Nigerian OC groups

Colombian cartels |

(illicit) activities may actively seek other illicit opportunities when the initial money-making opportunities change, or they may break away from the original legitimate group structure and engage exclusively in organized crime activity. Similarly, groups may move out of organized crime activities in response to increased legitimate opportunities or increased risk. Other groups come into being specifically to commit organized crimes, and change only as is necessary to maintain an effective and efficient criminal operation. Figure 2.1 illustrates the four "ideal type"[2] categories of organized crime groups. In reality, of course, all of organized crime groups fall somewhere along the predatory–symbiotic/legitimate–illegitimate continuum. It is highly unlikely, for example, that there exists in Canada an organized crime group that operates at the pure symbiotic level, with the government relying on its criminal members for services and support. However, there are groups that fall somewhere between the parasitic and the symbiotic levels. Similarly, even the categories of legitimate and illegitimate groups are blurred since some organized crime groups may still retain an aura of legitimacy from a bygone era or enjoy that status within some circles but not in others. Further, the international nature of organized crime raises the problem that groups seen as legitimate in some countries may be seen as criminal in others, and vice versa.

The typology of organized crime groups is important in terms both of explaining why the crimes are committed and of attempting to devise anti-organized crime governmental policies and diverse law enforcement control strategies. The implications of the typology for law enforcement are discussed in Chapter 7.

EXPLAINING INDIVIDUAL PARTICIPATION IN ORGANIZED CRIME

Having defined organized crime as criminal activity that is carried out according to a particular process, we must now ask what it is that compels certain individuals to engage in organized crime activity. The answer to this question lies in the dynamic relationship between the criminal participants, their organization, and the larger society. The profit motive alone does not explain engagement in criminal conduct: why one individual or one group chooses crime while others strive to obtain legitimate profit; why one specific illicit activity is chosen over other illicit options.

A number of theories have been offered to explain why individuals engage in organized crime operations. Because definitions

Typology of Organized Crime Groups

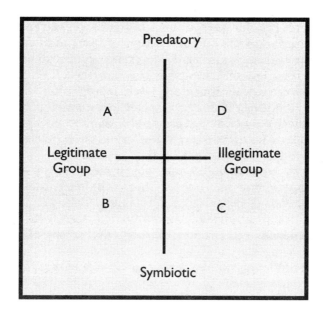

A
- predatory in relation to the larger society
- has some claim to being seen as a legitimate group
- members may use the pre-existing (legitimate) structure to facilitate their crimes

B
- has a symbiotic relationship to the larger society
- may be hard to identify as being an organized crime operation given its "legitimate" nature
- members may be the most pernicious criminals because of the degree to which they are integrated into the society

C
- exists specifically to carry out organized crime activities
- has a symbiotic relationship with the state
- may still bear the remnants of a former legitimacy

D
- may be the easiest group to detect, and perhaps also to target
- has no legitimate status
- operates at a predatory level without the benefits of political or enforcement corruption

of organized crime have tended to focus on the criminal activity as a distinct type of "crime," it has been assumed that one or two theories can be uniformly applied across all of the groups involved in these particular crimes. However, when one starts from the perspective that organized crime is a process, it becomes clear that there can be very different groups with very different "commitments" to the criminal activity. Attempts to apply one or two theories across all organized crime groups are inadequate because they fail to distinguish between the different types of organized crime operations and even between the same groups studied over time. This is not to deny the validity of applying *specific* theories of crime to *specific* groups.

Whatever category of organized crime we are discussing, it is imperative that the discourse of the organized crime participants themselves be introduced into our discussions of motivation. Although evidence has refuted those who once questioned the very existence of organized criminals and their activities, there persists in the academic community a lingering hesitation to grant credence to the words of the criminal actors. The lifestyles and ambitions of some organized criminals are so far removed from the lifestyles of bureaucrats and academics that a deliberate attempt must be made to understand the criminal behaviour from the criminal's perspective. What is being proposed is not a naive acceptance of the criminal's justification, but rather a *Verstehen* appreciation of the criminal environment.

Two lessons of postmodernism can be meaningfully applied to our task. The first is to listen to the discourses of the participants for explanations of their criminality, and to assign particular significance to the role of language and symbolism (Katz 1988; Gambetta 1993; Schwartz and Friedrichs 1994). The second post-modernist lesson is to develop a willingness to look beyond the artificial constraints imposed by theories that sociologists and criminologists have offered over the years. At times, theorists have been more concerned with out-theorizing their predecessors than with bringing a fresh perspective to bear on issues that have been bandied about over the past six decades. Schwartz and Friedrichs (1994) call for an energizing of criminological work by way of two postmodernist incentives:

- an appreciation of the ephemeral, fragmentary, and chaotic emergent tendencies in contemporary society; and

- the exposure of some of the pretences of both mainstream and critical forms of criminological analysis (238).

This text will emphasize the complexity of factors and the challenging interplay of variables that influence individual behaviour. It will also focus attention on the participants themselves.

In the same way that it would be convenient if all organized crime groups came into existence and were motivated to act criminally for exactly the same reasons, it would also be convenient if one general, all-encompassing theory of crime could be found to be adequate to explaining this phenomenon. Unfortunately, neither of these convenient situations is a reality.

There is little of value in general theories of crime that are dismissive of criminal skills and pride of criminal abilities, that reject the validity of different nonsocially prescribed priorities, and that ignore the need to ground even the vaguest of theories in empirical fact. Theories that claim no need to know what is actually happening at the level of the criminal or the organization will fail to advance our understanding of crime or criminal organizations.

Gottfredson and Hirschi's *A General Theory of Crime* (1990) espouses a "general" approach to organized crime that fails to consider the realities of the subject. Their book brings to mind Robert Merton's discussion of the "principle of cerebral hygiene" Auguste Comte sought to achieve while writing *The Course of Positive Philosophy*. Comte's objective was to maintain the originality of his peculiar meditations by "washing his mind clean of everything but his own ideas by the simple tactic of not reading anything even remotely germane to his subject" (Merton 1967, 33). The problem, as Merton observes, is that originality may be achieved through an "emancipation" from valuable antecedent ideas and pertinent facts. Gottfredson and Hirschi's discussion of organized crime reflects this condition. Their general theory does to social control theories what Hirschi (1987) accused the integrative theory of Elliott et al. (1985) of doing:

> Once the theory was at least adventurous and fully [sic] of ideas, now it is exceedingly cautious, concerned more with living than with living well. It may be able to save itself for a time with an operation here and a transplant there, but the end would seem to be inevitable and not faraway" (200).

The Gottfredson and Hirschi model ignores the realities surrounding the globalization of crime today. There is no disputing the fact that money laundering schemes demand of those who engage in them an ability to defer gratification as well as a sophisticated knowledge of computers, finances, and international trade. The disengagement of Gottfredson and Hirschi (1990) from such contemporary realities of organized crime is evident in discussions like the following:

> There is nothing in crime that requires the transmission of values or the support of other people. There is nothing in crime that requires the transmission of skills, or techniques,

or knowledge from other people. On the contrary, *it is in the nature of crime that it can be invented instantly* [italics added], on the spot, by almost anyone (151).

One of the most questionable features of the Gottfredson and Hirschi theory is its focus on the mundane aspects of lawbreaking and denial of the skills, experience, and selective abilities that are conducive to facilitating criminal behaviour. As Edelhertz and Overcast's (1993, 125) study found, while some organized crime activities involve the use of brute force, others require more than the sort of knowledge that is gained "on the spot". Accumulated knowledge, expertise plus practised skills, and social ease (if not actual charisma) must often combine to enable criminals to carry off some of the more sophisticated crimes. The level of sophistication is having an impact on enforcement strategies as police discover that undercover "sting" operations aimed at these criminals require a high level of business expertise. Police training, dress, and manner have all had to change.

Perhaps the greatest weakness of Gottfredson and Hirschi's theory is the tautological nature of their definitions—or, as Reed and Yeager (1991) state, "theory by definition" (16). Once you define crime as "acts of force or fraud undertaken in pursuit of self-interest" (Gottfredson and Hirschi 1990, 15), and then set up a model whereby criminal acts are juxtaposed against self-control, the one becomes by definition the opposite of the other. Or, as Akers states, "Propensity toward crime and low self-control appear to be one and the same. The hypothesis is true by definition: low self-control causes low self-control" (1994, 123). Having equated crime with lack of social control, Gottfredson and Hirschi can then reject Cressey's (1967, 1969) notion of organized crime (as a highly structured, disciplined, all-controlling criminal monopoly) because it is incompatible with their ideas of crime and self-control. They thus succeed in looping one tautological thesis through a tautological verification of it! For the time being, we must be satisfied with lower-level (possibly middle-range) theorizing, which is grounded more in knowledge of the specific crime category.[3]

CATEGORY "A" ORGANIZED CRIMINALS

The "A" category of organized criminals consists of those groups that exploit an existing legitimate group structure in order to facilitate organized crime activity. The commission of the crimes may be entered into as a temporary measure in order to capitalize on a highly profitable situation. In most cases, the circumstances favourable to the criminal activity will not have been actively sought or deliberately created, but also will not have been rejected in favour of legitimate oportunities (to the extent that they exist).

Theories that best match the criminal behaviour in this first category are those that focus on the urban ecology of crime and delinquency. Theories of this kind are rooted in the assumption that such factors as social order, stability, and integration are conducive to conformity, while disorder and nonintegration are conducive to crime and deviance (Akers 1994). Building on Durkheim's concept of anomie, Robert Merton's anomie theory focuses on the socially constructed contradictions between promises of achievable prosperity and real-life opportunities (Pfohl 1994, 261). According to Merton, when access to legitimate societal goals is made differentially accessible within the population, one option for those segments of the society that are adversely affected is to use illegitimate methods to reach the same socially prescribed goals. In most societies today cash is an important or essential commodity. Individuals who cannot earn sufficient amounts through legitimate methods have the option of turning to illegitimate methods such as crime or delinquency. According to this theory, when a person's access to societal goals is blocked— whether by poverty, racism, geography and/or lack of educational opportunities—a "strain" or pressure is imposed on the person, who still shares the larger societal goals. The person may respond by accepting the status quo, withdrawing, or achieving those goals through illicit/illegal means.

Richard Cloward and Lloyd Ohlin (1960) add to Merton's theory by emphasizing that some groups or individuals have a much greater illegitimate access than legitimate access; for them, choosing illegitimate means, such as crime and deviance, makes infinite sense. Cloward and Ohlin reject the assumption that all

FIGURE 2.2

Merton's Theory

Limited socially approved access ╱ Societal goals ╲		Goals	Means
	conformity	+	+
	innovation	+	−
	ritualism	−	+
	retreatism	−	−
	rebellion	(∓)	(∓)

people denied legitimate access to shared goals would, in fact, have equal illegitimate means. A deviant "learning environment," they argue, must be present to provide the role models, justifications, and learned methods that facilitate access to illegitimate means. Therefore, shared societal goals and blocked legitimate but accessible illegitimate means, and a supportive criminal environment provides the most complete explanation of criminal participation in category "A" circumstances.

Cigarette smuggling and the organized crime activity that built up around this "opportunity" provides an illustration of category "A" organized crime activity. The location of the aboriginal reserves—straddling not only the Canada–U.S. border, but also borders between Ontario and Quebec—and their tax-free status were major facilitating factors behind the criminal activity. Added to this were the massive price differences between Canadian and U.S. cigarettes and the willingness of Canadian cigarette manufacturers to export excessive amounts into the United States. The excess, for which there was no U.S. market, then became the

F I G U R E   2 . 3

Cloward and Ohlin's Theory

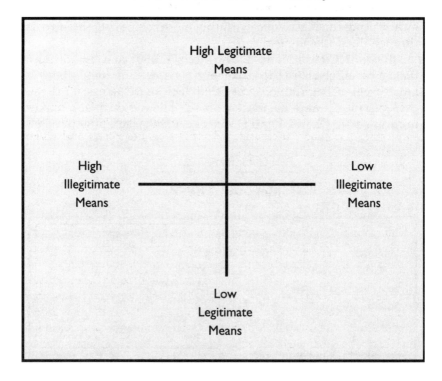

"supply" as it was smuggled back into Canada. Coupled with the severe lack of legitimate opportunity within the Mohawk communities is the realization on the part of its inhabitants that there is very little to lose by engaging in certain forms of behaviour—defined by some as organized crime, but for which there is at least the semblance of a justification based on arguments of self-government, tax-free "rights," and the illegitimacy of a disproportionate tax on nonexport cigarettes. (See Figure 2.4.)

David Matza (1992) speaks of neutralization processes that allow the actor to drift toward deviant or criminal behaviour. He identifies a "sense of injustice" as an important condition that, while it does not in itself lead to crime, "provides a simmering resentment—a setting of antagonism and antipathy—within which the variety of extenuating circumstances may abrogate the moral bind of law" (101). The perception of a long tradition of exploitation at the hands of various Canadian governments, the 1990 OKA crisis, and institutional discrimination that has resulted in high rates of unemployment and criminalization are all factors that, from the aboriginal perspective, feed into this sense of ongoing injustice. This reached into the international sphere when a Mohawk delegation visited Libya, in June 1992, to receive a "human rights award" honouring centuries of struggle against "imperialism."

It is important to emphasize that entire aboriginal communities are not involved in organized crime activity. Many community members chose continued poverty over crime, and there is evidence that some of those who look for and take advantage of opportunities to acquire low-risk wealth view their criminal involvement as a temporary aberration as opposed to a core group who will switch from one criminal opportunity to another. Spontaneous "opportunities" for category "A" criminal activity, however, may result in more permanent distribution networks and wider markets coming into existence.

CATEGORY "B" ORGANIZED CRIMINALS

While group "A" organized criminals are attracted to the same goals as those held by the larger society, group "B" criminals redefine the notion of success to fit their own priorities. Group "B" organized crime groups are involved in a lifestyle or in an activity that is much larger or more important than the organized crime activity. Organized crime groups that fall in this category would include terrorist groups, which use organized crime as a means of funding terrorist activity, and outlaw motorcycle gangs. Outlaw motorcycle gangs are able to recruit members for reasons that

FIGURE 2.4

Smuggling Routes

Two of the many smuggling routes into Canada through the Akwesasne reserve. [Before the taxes were reduced, police estimated] $1 million in illegal cigarettes [were] shipped daily.

1. Cigarettes are loaded onto boats from marina on U.S. side of reserve. This route bypasses Canadian Customs, which is housed on the island.

2. When the St. Lawrence is frozen, contraband is shipped across the river by truck and snowmobile to landings on the north side.

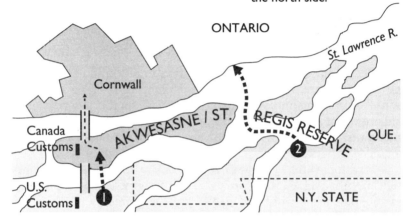

Reprinted with permission—The Toronto Star Syndicate.

combine legitimate biker membership incentives such as excitement and status with a willingness or desire to fulfil mandatory criminal membership obligations that can become increasingly violent and potentially profitable in nature. Outlaw motorcycle gangs, as described by Daniel Wolf (1991), are

> pre-adapted as vehicles of organized crime. Paramilitary organization lies at the core of their tight-knit secret society. It is a society capable of enforcing internal discipline, including an iron-clad code of silence which ensures that information about club operations never goes beyond the walls of the clubhouse (265).

Category "B" organized criminals hold a unique view on life that seems relevant to membership. In Katz's rejection of the Merton explanation of deviance and crime (for certain criminal activities), he states that for some criminal acts "the aims are specifically unconventional: to go beyond the established moral definition of the situation" (1988, 315).

Wolf's study of outlaw bikers is full of quotes that express the cultivated separateness of these individuals from the rest of society. In the book, one Rebel (Saint) member is quoted as saying, "The run is really what it's all about. That's where it all comes together." Wolf describes the run as

> rich with symbolism and charged with excitement and emotion. It provides meaning within a context of danger, power, and mystique. The run confirms a patch holder's claim to personal and social validity as an outlaw biker. Members are able to validate their identity as outlaw bikers by acting out their freedom ethic (1991, 225).

Outlaw motorcycle gangs thrive on their "outlaw" status and the excitement of club membership, in addition to the illicit profit derived from criminal activity. Interestingly, even the economic aspects of criminal involvement serve to reinforce a club's status as a community separate from, and independent of, mainstream society. Neither ethnicity nor social class determines the composition of these gangs (although there tends to be a right-wing, lower-middle-class, white bias). Gang membership relates more to a quest for a particular lifestyle, and to a willingness to violate the law and engage in physical violence in the pursuit of illicit profit. In a similar fashion, the ideological commitment to a "cause" justifies and overshadows involvement in organized crime activity for members of terrorist groups.

According to Matza (1992), outlaw club members take an "oppositional response to the pious legality of bourgeois existence" (34). Biker gang members know what the societal norms and values are—they just don't like them. In the words of Wolf (1991),

> Bikers often perceive straight society as a theatre of deception, a back-stabbing scenario that is hypocritically disguised by a thin veil of respectability; it is polite, but it is also superficial. Straight society is seen as lacking anything in the way of meaningful commitment or emotional depth (229).

The fact that many bikers hold legitimate jobs points to the inadequacy of "blocked access to legitimate means" (or other sources of strain) as an exclusive explanation of the delinquent or criminal behaviour.

CATEGORY "C" ORGANIZED CRIMINALS

Category "C" organized crime groups exist exlcusively to commit organized crimes. Of the four categories, category "C" groups have the structure most conducive to committing these types of crimes. The objective is not only profit but also the status associated with being a high-profile criminal or at least a member of a significant criminal organization.

Separating this group from category "D" is a sense of history or tradition that plays some role in the justifications provided by mobsters who have come forward to tell their stories. For example, testimony before the U.S. Senate Subcommittee Studying Asian Organized Crime revealed the existence of a "Triad subculture." Even those criminal groups that were not Triads themselves were influenced by a sense of such "Triad" traditions as the ritualism, obsessive secrecy, and loyalty. The mythology of the Mafia is similar to this sense of tradition.

Differentiation Association or Cultural Deviance Theory

In his analysis of mobster memoirs, Firestone (1993) concludes that differential association theory has the most to offer as an explanation of why individuals become involved in organized crime. In contrast with our category "A" criminals,

> None of the mobsters [covered by Firestone's study] claims to have chosen crime because he was denied the opportunity to pursue a legitimate career. In fact, quite to the contrary, most of the authors indicate that they could have had legitimate careers but simply preferred to be criminals (Firestone 1993, 203).

There is little indication of social alienation or weak social control with respect to these Mafia members. Most of them were very involved with their families and communities, held summer jobs, graduated from high schools, made and kept friends. Any separation between "family life" and "crime family life" reflected the complex mastering of social values rather than alienation from them. The "visible" mobster was the good community citizen who cultivated a solid church-going, charity-supporting image. Numerous accounts illustrate that the New York Mafia members took a special and generous interest in community members in trouble. To some community members these criminals were role models, even heroes.

At the 1992 U.S. Senate Subcommittee Studying Organized Crime, one member of the Hong Kong 14K Triad gang testified that, for him, triad membership served an integrative function in that it granted him introductions, assistance, and opportunities for involvement in criminal schemes. Comparisons were drawn between Triad membership and membership in exclusive men's clubs that provide the same functions for legitimate businessmen.

Ethnic Succession Debate

Various academics (Bell 1960; Ianni 1974; Haller 1971–72) discern in organized crime in North America an important ethnic succession feature whereby new immigrant groups use organized crime activity as a "queer ladder of social mobility." Certain ethnic groups in society, they argue, are excluded from the use of a legitimate passage into the middle and upper classes. As a result, they use illegitimate means as a temporary measure that enables them to ascend into the higher positions in society—at which point these ethnic groups strive to "go legitimate," or at least encourage their offspring to do so. This succession has been traced through Irish immigrants, Jews, Italians, blacks, Hispanics, Southeast Asians, Africans, and Russians.

The ethnic succession thesis builds on other theories that see a system of stratification as an important source of social strain. This stratification system, coupled with a culture that values achievements and possessions, encourages new immigrants to look for those openings that are relatively less closed to outsiders. Unique abilities and talents, as demonstrated in the arts and sports, are other examples of "ladders" that will allow entry. While there is some evidence that new immigrant groups must find a niche that is more open to their participation, there is less evidence that organized criminals see their lucrative crimes as mere stepping stones to lower-paying, less exciting, but legitimate jobs.

Lupsha (1981) rejects the ethnic succession thesis. His own research suggests that entrance into organized crime:

> [was a] self-choice based on individual skills and personal rationalization ... They did it because they—Luciano, Teresa, Lansky, and the others—saw in American values and culture an alternative easy, exciting, and romantic route to wealth. Namely "something for nothing, there's a sucker born every minute," lawlessness. Plus, they were good at crime and depersonalized violence, and received peer and material reinforcement from it (4, 13).

Timing was another important factor. The fact that some of the original Mafia were in North America and approaching adulthood at the beginning of Prohibition "provided opportunity, capital, and organization to routinize nationwide syndicated crime" (13). Becoming a gangster was seen as a legitimate, even desirable, career path.

This aura of "legitimacy" extends to the high status bestowed upon upper-echelon Mafia members by the media. One analysis of *New York Times* obituaries found that not only were Mafia members chosen for inclusion in what is in fact a fairly restrictive process, they were often lauded as well. Their good community deeds as well as their criminal affiliations were usually mentioned. Hence:

> Carlo Gambino was described as a "quiet godfather ... who kept muggers off the street." Vito Genovese led a "quiet life ... he was a good father who raised his children to be well-behaved, honest, and religious ..." And Joseph Zerrelli was "an intensely private man ... a good father ..." (Martens and Cunningham-Niederer 1985, 64).

The 1995 funeral of Ronnie ("The Colonel") Kray, in England, attracted such headlines as "Crowds line London streets as East End buries hero mobster" (*Toronto Star,* March 30, 1995, p. A3). The "dapper, chain-smoking sadist who razor-slashed and shot his victims," died of a heart attack. Kray's mobster twin brother, Reggie Kray, released from prison to attend the funeral, was photographed waving and winking to the thousands of people who lined the streets to watch the hearse as it went by—pulled by six jet-black horses.

As the reporter states:

> As East End "aristocracy," they consorted with movie stars such as Judy Garland and the odd politician. Leonard (Nipper) Read, the Scotland Yard superintendent who brought them to justice, once noted: "If someone had a drink with them, it was like having tea with Princess Margaret."

Category "C" organized criminals are the most integrated into and through society. While no organized crime group should be viewed as something foreign to and "outside" of the political and economic structure (capitalism or communism), this particular category enjoys greater integration than other (often newer) groups. For example, in March 1995, the former Italian prime minister Giulio Andreotti was finally ordered to stand trial on charges of having been a member of the Mafia. Magistrates had spent over two years gathering an estimated 90,000 pages of evidence against Mr. Andreotti. While the case continues, these types of examples illustrate most clearly the potential for political advancement being tied to certain organized crime activities and organized crime loyalties.

CATEGORY "D" ORGANIZED CRIMINALS

In addition to large amounts of money, power seems to be a critical motivating force for organized criminals. We see this perhaps most dramatically in category "D" criminals (about whom relatively little is known). In reference to the Colombian cartels, informant Douglas Jaworski was quoted as saying,

> I enjoyed working with Diego because he presented a view of life that I could never even imagine myself. I liked him because he was so interesting. They're the scumbags of the world and they're proud of it ... He used to describe the drug dealing as his hobby. He loved doing it. He loved the action and the pace and the power that he got from having thirty bodyguards. These guys would come out of the woodwork, young guys with .38s. ... You might ask why he didn't quit after he made his first $20 million. Go back to square one, pal. *It's his hobby. It's the power thing. He's like a little dictator. Those bodyguards don't move without asking him* [emphasis added] (56).

Bodyguards have come to symbolize the power that is held by these criminals. As one Russian mobster stated,

> The richer you are the more dangerous your life is. Some people are trying to get just enough money so that they remain inconspicuous. Others are ostentatious and pay for security. "Bodyguards are the name of the game" *(Evening Standard,* 1994).

Criminals who perform only one isolated task in a network of activities that add up to the organized crime activity may be able to justify their involvement due to their relative unimportance in the organization. The informant Jaworski, who did not come from a community that idolized mobsters, was able to appreciate not only the profit but also his own dispensability:

> Jaworski knew he was in the company of gangsters, but he didn't particularly care. The money was great, the company perversely unique, and Jaworski could rationalize his association with Caycedo by saying that he was only selling planes, and that if he didn't sell them to the cocaine cartel, someone else would (55).

Information coming out of Russia, Nigeria, and Colombia suggests that a combination of political and economic factors has given rise to a dominant culture that supports as normal such characteristics as being street wise, exploiting the trust of others, and treatings frauds and scams as clever business schemes. The political upheaval in Russia has exacted social costs. A sense of lawlessness and normlessness pervades the society. The slaying in March 1995 of a popular television star in Moscow was portrayed in the media as "a mafia ritual to show that they can do anything in this country" (*Globe and Mail,* March 3, 1995a, p. A12).

However, in addition to this state of social disorganization, in the case of Colombian organized criminals, their power can extend into direct political corruption. In August 1995, the Colombian defence minister resigned amid accusations that he used money from drug traffickers to help President Ernesto Samper win last year's election (*Globe and Mail*, August 3, 1995, p. A19). This is claimed to be the highest-reaching scandal linking organized crime and politics in Colombian history.

There has been much debate around the relative merits of differential association theory vs. control theory (the former argues that association with debate around people precedes deviant/criminal behaviour, while the latter argues the opposite). However, as Thornberry et al. (1994, 75) suggest, the value of these two approaches lies in the complex, reciprocal relationship between their variables. With respect to category "D" organized crime groups, the explanatory "cause" may borrow from several theories a range of variables, including risk-taking, opportunity, differential association, (also known as cultural deviance) and control.

NOTES

1. The Colombian cartels, for example, are hard to place. While lacking the historical "legitimate" period sometimes attributed to the Triads or the Mafia, the cartel's political ties to various Colombian regimes bestows this type of mythology upon them.

2. "Ideal type" in the Max Weber sense of being pure models that do not exist in the real world, but represent categories that allow one to differentiate across a population.

3. Merton advocated middle-range theories that allow one to link theory to empirical fact with a wide enough application to allow for meaningful generalization.

Organized Crime Activity in Canada

INTRODUCTION

Early forms of organized crime and linkages between old and new forms of criminal operations provide the foundation for current activities. A historic perspective serves to illustrate how illicit activity responds to new legislation, new technology, and new forms of competition. For example, as early as 1717 an organized counterfeiting "industry" was operating in response to a scarcity of paper notes in the United States. Today, law enforcement is attempting to control the highly sophisticated and international counterfeiting of plastic credit cards, with even greater risks looming as advances in technology allow for diverse methods of "symbolic" and immediate money transfers.

In December 1994, police in Toronto arrested 11 people alleged to be part of Asian organized crime. They were charged with running a $1,5-million fraud scheme in which stolen credit-card information was used to finance heroin trafficking. The conspirators used details from all of the credit-card purchases made at the CN Tower between January 1989 and May 1994. Approximately 28,000 credit-card purchases were made. Cooperating merchants accepted and processed the credit-card information in exchange for a share of the profits from the fraudulent transactions (*Globe and Mail*, December 15, 1994, p. A5).

Some illicit markets, reflective of the male- (and bachelor-) dominated public culture of the 18th and 19th centuries, persist today in similar forms of prostitution, pornography, and gambling (Johnson 1987), 5). A desire for alcohol, drugs, and nicotine has remained fairly constant, while government policies and economic conditions affecting these markets have fluctuated.

An *inaccurate* picture of organized crime will result unless the reader can envision a layering of criminal activity interwoven throughout the economic and political system. While from a limited perspective organized crime may seem to consist of relatively tidy hierarchies or families, a broader view reveals cooperative, economic-driven illicit enterprises that cut across different organized crime groups and jurisdictional boundaries. The objective of organized crime is profit. Commodities will be matched with markets to produce these illicit proceeds. This is the reality of organized crime in Canada and elsewhere today.

C H A P T E R **3**

Characteristics of Organized Crime in Canada

The organized crime forces at play during the 1990s make the earlier Mafia obsession of academics, the media, and crime commissions appear parochial by comparison. Today, organized crime activity is recognized to be diverse, collaborating, and ever changing. While the ongoing threat posed by established Mafia families cannot be dismissed, their "familiarity" must provide for law enforcement authorities a degree of comfort that is absent in their dealings with new organized crime forms and players. Traditionally, one of the greatest organized crime threats was seen to come from drug trafficking. But even this threat may pale in comparison to the possible involvement of organized crime in the smuggling and sale of nuclear weapons and materials.

With respect to the involvement of ethnic groups in organized crime activities, no ethnic group has shown itself to be immune from the lure of illicit profit. While some groups are at present of more concern than others, this fluctuates over time. As James Dubro states:

> Organized crime is not a racial construct, although it is a sad fact that many criminal organizations are restricted to criminals of the same ethnic background. ... just about every ethnic group has participated in a major way in organized crime over the years ... Essentially organized crime has always existed to make money by providing services and products that are illegal.[1]

This search for illicit markets is illustrated by the global penetration of the organized crime groups into foreign turf, and by the increasing cooperation among traditionally separate and distinct organized crime groups. It is instructive to read accounts of Italian officials' fear of the "yellow mafia" (as police in Rome speak of the invasion of the Mafia's kingdom by Asian gangsters); Eastern Europe's fear of the Italian Mafia moving into Bulgaria, Romania, Hungary, Czechoslovakia, and Russia; international fear of Colombian cartels working together with the Italian mafia; and, in North America, fear of organized crime activity from Russia and the Commonwealth of Independent States (CIS) moving across the ocean.[2]

In 1993, a Russian N.Y.-based mob collaborated with the Gambino organized crime family in what was claimed by law enforcement to be the largest fuel tax evasion scheme in U.S. history. As he unsealed a 101-count federal indictment against the 13 defendants, U.S. Attorney Michael Chertoff stated, "This was a marriage between traditional organized crime and emerging organized crime" (quoted in *CLEU Line,* May 1994, 58).

If there is a greater sense of "danger" from the current organized crime activities, it is due to the sophistication of the operations, the violence, the diversity, and the collaborative nature of many of the operations. Control agencies can no longer treat organized crime groups as separate and competitive ethnic-based operations. Not only are organized crime groups tolerating each other, but they are building the networks required for efficient business operations. While one may still challenge those analysts who make comparisons between the corporate organizational structure and the organized crime operational structure, the "thinking" of the organized crime operator has definitely become corporate. For example, Colombian cartels are actively changing both markets and commodities in order to reach a wider buying public. If there is more money to be made in heroin, they will grow opium. If the image or expense of a particular drug is too extreme, a different form and a "lower-price special" will be offered in a less-intimidating form. Thus, crack cocaine became the answer to enticing new cocaine users. Likewise cocaine was sold at a discount when it was first introduced into Russia. If the Eastern European/Russian markets are bigger than the North American market, organized crime groups will obligingly serve them.

Complete shifts between source country and demand country are being orchestrated by organized crime groups that, in some cases, are external to either jurisdiction.[3] To the extent that organized crime operations are "client based," the Canadian population—and thus the size of the market for illicit commodities—may not support the size of operations desired. Hence, Canada can serve as a source country (rather than as a market) for stolen cars, jewellery, and large-scale frauds and scams. Triads, Colombians, and Russian criminal groups will transfer these commodities to the huge markets of Eastern Europe,

Russia, and China. Similarly, organized crime analysts now speak of groups such as the Triads "contracting out" certain street-level crimes, while the dominant Big Circle Boys move back to China in order to capitalize on more profitable activities that involve the linking of Canadian commodities to the China market.

GLOBAL ORGANIZED CRIME AND ITS IMPACT ON CANADA

The world is in a state of rapid transition. Political realignments, economic shifts, and new crime patterns all affect Canadian society in the same way that other nations are being affected. Crime—particularly organized crime—is becoming increasingly global in nature. The law enforcement response to this activity is caught somewhere between the local, national, and the international borderless environment. This section provides an overview of the key political and economic shifts that are having a direct impact on organized crime activity in Canada. Three geographic areas in particular will be discussed: Hong Kong and South East Asia; Eastern Europe and the Commonwealth of Independent States (CIS); and Colombia and South America.

SOUTH EAST ASIA: HONG KONG AFTER THE BRITISH ADMINISTRATION

On July 1, 1997, the administration of the territory of Hong Kong will be transferred from the United Kingdom to the People's Republic of China (PRC). The consequences of this shift are being anticipated by law enforcement in Hong Kong and abroad. U.S. officials have identified Chinese organized crime as one of the most significant and prominent of all the emerging ethnic criminal organizations today.[4] Canadian officials have similarly identified organized crime groups of Asian descent as having gained a dominance in such criminal activities as importation and trafficking of cocaine and heroin, home invasions, extortion, alien smuggling, counterfeiting, fraud, forgery, gambling, prostitution, and murder.[5]

Despite the guarantee in the 1984 Sino-British accord that Hong Kong's change in political sovereignty will not affect its status as a capitalist economy for the next 50 years, uncertainty persists. The United States, Canada, and other nations fear that, as 1997 approaches, Hong Kong officials may cooperate less with Western officials in order to appease mainland China.[6] In addition, enforcement exchanges in intelligence, in place through

Britain, will cease, and all informal cooperative measures will have to be renegotiated.

EASTERN EUROPE AND THE COMMONWEALTH OF INDEPENDENT STATES (CIS): THE TEARING DOWN OF WALLS

The entire configuration of Europe has changed rapidly—through war in the case of Yugoslavia, and through political design or accident in other areas. The disintegration of the USSR and the changing of borders throughout Eastern Europe have facilitated drug-smuggling routes from Central Asia to Europe. The Balkan drug routes through Turkey, Yugoslavia, and Northern Italy are now shifting to Eastern Europe. The former Soviet Union contained Asian republics capable of producing heroin equal to that produced in the more traditional golden triangle countries.

While it is not possible to generalize about the organized crime activity in these diverse countries, there are general themes that Canadian officials are concerned about. For example, as Western nations argue the merits of one form of bank reporting/recording versus another, there are countries whose financial structures are too primitive to meet any of the current standards required to detect money laundering or financial frauds. Law enforcement and banking staff are often undertrained and underfunded, and legislation is often not in place to deal with organized crime and laundering activities.

Increasing problems of state corruption and organized crime in the successor states have had a major impact on law enforcement within those countries.[7] Corruption of government and law enforcement officials is a critical issue that has negatively affected the feasibility for sharing law enforcement intelligence between countries, the ability to engage in joint-force operations, and the confidence with which business interests can look to invest. President Boris Yeltsin, speaking at a Kremlin meeting in February 1993, identified organized crime as Russia's most urgent problem. He described a country where "everything is for sale," where corrupt police officials, ministries, and entrepreneurs are engaged in exploiting the collapse of communism and the now porous border. In the words of one observer,

> It is sad but probably fair to say that organized crime is about Russia's only growth industry. Official estimates of the number of organized crime groups rose from 2900 in 1989 through 3500 in 1990, to 5100 in 1991. ... The rise of these "mafias" is more than a social problem, a criminological curiosity, and a law enforcer's nightmare, though. It also has def-

inite implications for the national security of the post-Soviet states, and indeed, their neighbours near and far (Galeotti 1993).

COLOMBIA AND SOUTH AMERICA: ORGANIZED CRIME, TERRORISM, INSURGENCY, AND POLITICS

The third area in our overview of recent developments in global organized crime affords us insight into the diverse factors that impinge on official responses to such criminal activity.

Any objective discussion of organized crime in South America must at least acknowledge the culpability of the CIA and other U.S. government officials who advance foreign policies at the expense of drug enforcement.[8] According to Senator John Kerry, chairman of the Senate Foreign Relations Subcommittee on Terrorism, Narcotics and International Operations, the congressional hearings into the Contra drugs and arms scandal showed that "stopping drug trafficking to the United States has been a secondary U.S. foreign policy objective. It has been sacrificed repeatedly for other political goals" (quoted in Sharkey 1988, 33).

While Nadelmann (1988, 1) may rightly identify drug-related corruption among foreign governments as the major obstacle that confronts "the government of the United States in its global battle against international drug trafficking," we must also acknowledge the role that North American political exploitation plays in facilitating the growth and spread of drug trafficking, as well as the role that the North American demand for drugs plays in creating the market in the first place.

Latin America's drug trade is closely linked to violence, political corruption, insurgency, and terrorism. Just as we must distinguish between gangsterism and organized crime in Eastern Europe and the CIS, so too we must distinguish terrorism (ideological or criminal) and insurgency from organized crime in South America. Several factors make this difficult. Analyses vary depending on who is writing the intelligence reports. "Narcoterrorism" has been flagged as a top threat to the United States in the 1990s. The term itself serves to forge a link between drug trafficking and terrorism. As national security agencies seek to justify their existence in the post–Cold War era, the word "terrorism" is broadly invoked. Officials from M15 in the United Kingdom, the CIA in the United States, and CSIS in Canada begin to discuss drug trafficking in terms of the threat it poses to national security. They then invoke this "threat" to argue that enforcement activities should fall partially under the jurisdiction of their own organizations. Their position was strengthened when a U.N. crime conference in May 1995 adopted a controversial resolution acknowledging links between terrorism and organized crime *(South China Morning Post,* May 9, 1995, p. 15*)*.

VARIATIONS IN ORGANIZED CRIME ACROSS CANADA

As mentioned in Chapter 2, certain physical and geographical features of cities make them either more or less "agreeable" to organized crime. Ports or other entry points, adequate population/ markets, and a degree of heterogeneity add to the likelihood that the urban centre will attract and cultivate criminal conspiracies.

The proximity of western Canada—particularly Vancouver—to Asia, both in terms of immigration and travel, has resulted in patterns of criminal activity that differ from those in Toronto and Montreal. Ontario and Quebec have responded most directly to the desire of U.S. mobsters to expand their empires north. While one can easily appreciate that the geographical links between two countries can result in a sharing of organized crime activity, the role of political cultures is more nebulous. It has been argued that the political cultures that prevail in different cities are, to varying degrees, also responsible for the historical roots of some organized crime.

In attempting to explain why the Mafia initially gained a firmer foothold in Montreal than in Toronto, Mann (1968) refers to the fact that the Duplessis regime was so corrupt that it bred a tolerance in the public for bribery and corruption. The premier was alleged to have said to the Quebec Provincial Police that any policeman who could not earn his keep independent of the police force salary was not worth having on the force (Mann 1968, 143). According to Tepperman et al. (1976),

> the police and political figures in Canada are not equally incorruptible. Specifically, organized crime figures have had more success in bribing public officials in the province of Quebec, particularly in Montreal, than elsewhere. ...Quebec appears to provide a fruitful field for the expansion of organized criminal enterprises, since the prerequisites of public complicity and political corruption are available to mobsters (23).

In a five-part series in *Maclean's* magazine on "The Mafia in Canada," Phillips (1963–64)[9] credits gambling with providing the enormous sums with which criminals bribed the Montreal police. "In alliance with politicians," he writes, "the Montreal Mafia by 1960 had completely corrupted police in the province and city" (Part 5, 12).

In a controversial document, two priests, Gerald Dion and Louis O'Neill, denounced political corruption in the province of Quebec. Their pamphlet, first published in the bulletin *Ad Usum Sacerdatum*, was written expressly for the clergy. A copy, titled *Political Immorality in the Province of Quebec*, was leaked to *Le Devoir* on August 7, 1956. In it, the priests discuss vote buying and selling, corruption of political officials, and political interference by clergy:

> Such proceedings as vote buying, corruption of the electoral law, threats of reprisals against those who do not support the "right party," false oaths, substitution of persons, the corruption of election officers, also seem to be becoming normal elements in our social life at election time ... that which should cause us the greatest anxiety is the fact that so few people seem to be scandalized by it all (Dion and O'Neill 1956, 10–11).

According to Phillips (1963–64), Montreal in the 1940s carried the mystique of having a Paris-like underlife, complete with diverse entertainments and famous bordellos, but this foundation eventually gave way to violence and corruption—largely due to the city's links with the U.S.-based Mafia, which saw Montreal's potential to serve its operations in a number of ways.

One police officer referred to Montreal recently as being "a city on the dodge." Some of the largest near-systemic corruption scandals in Canada have involved Quebec. One example is a *Toronto Star* headline, from September 2, 1994, which announced, "Entire police force [Chambly] busted in drug raid: Crime corruption said well known in Quebec town." While there is some concern within Quebec and within the wider police community that perhaps the actions of the QPF were overly extreme in the Chambly case, five police officers were charged with offences that included trafficking in steroids, running an illegal gambling operation, possessing bootleg alcohol, and illegally distributing confidential police information (*Globe and Mail*, September 16, 1994, p. A4).

Police officers who have worked in small Quebec towns like Chambly report an attitude that encourages officers to become involved in profit-making operations, both legal and illegal. But it is not just the small, municipal forces that are vulnerable in Quebec. A particularly nasty corruption case culminated, in 1992, in the suicide of a RCMP Inspector who had been a former head of the Montreal drug squad. Six years earlier, a RCMP Montreal drug squad Staff-Sergeant had been sentenced to jail in another high-profile corruption case.

None of this is to suggest that the other major centres have not had their own corruption cases. British Columbia witnessed the first case in which a RCMP Anti-Drug Profiteering (ADP) member was arrested for stealing from the cash exhibits. The history of the Toronto police (municipal, provincial, and RCMP) is similarly dotted with examples of corruption. It was in part the 1961 discovery of police corruption in the anti-gambling squad of the OPP that led to the establishment of the Ontario Police Commission, and to the appointment of Justice W.D. Roach to head a royal commission into organized crime (Ontario 1964). No jurisdiction should assume immunity from corruption, although all may not historically be equally vulnerable to it.

It is hard to make empirical comparisons regarding the prevalence of corruption across jurisdictions since corruption only comes to the attention of the public when it is unsuccessful. Some argue that the smoother and more sophisticated elite networks of "corruptive influence" that may steer politics and policing in some other jurisdictions may go undetected (or, at least, not be interpreted as corruption), while the more visible and awkward forms of corruption become headline news.

THE DENIAL OF ORGANIZED CRIME IN EARLY INQUIRIES

Canada's reluctance to label criminal activity as organized crime is revealed in the reports produced by early commissions and inquiries in the 1960s and 1970s.

ONTARIO

The 1963 Roach Royal Commission (on Gambling), often cited as a significant denier of organized crime, concluded that with the exception of gambling there was little organized crime in Canada:

> My investigation did not disclose that there was organized crime in the Province to any alarming extent except in the field of organized gambling... (Roach 1963, 357)

Until the late 1970s the message remained the same. In 1973, the *Report of the Royal Commission on Certain Sectors of the Building Industry* (chaired by Judge Harry Waisberg) established a clear picture of bombings, violence, and organized corruption. However, the term "organized crime" was rigorously avoided. The numerous bombings, shootings, assaults, arson, burglaries, and cases of fraud were instead described as "symptoms of a disturbed industry":

A statement that the construction business is not a lily-white business neither explains nor excuses illegal activities ... To the extent that they are offences per se, they can be adequately dealt with by the law enforcement agencies. To the extent that they are symptoms of a disturbed industry, they must be examined to ascertain the cause (Ontario 1974, vol. 1, p. 3).

The recommendations that accompany the report indicate an approach that targets individual acts while ignoring the interconnections between the highly lucrative exploitation, threats, and frauds committed within the building industry—as evidenced by the union's response to entrenched union control and abuse:

- The shooting incidents involving the Acme premises and Bruno Zanini, together with the indiscriminate possession of arms as revealed in the investigation, suggests the necessity for *more rigid arms control* (Ontario 1974, vol. 1, p. 342).

- The bombing incidents, coupled with the casual possession of dynamite, suggests the necessity for *more rigid control of explosives* (Ontario 1974, vol. 1, p. 342–43).

- Evidence of deliberately falsified or nonexistent bookkeeping, and an absolute lack of accountability, was countered with the recommendation that *minimum standards be set for union books and records* (Ontario 1974, vol. 1, p. 343).

Although the two-volume report included a section on the introduction of organized crime into the industry—including the participation of Paul Volpe—organized crime was not treated as integral to the violence that was occurring throughout the building industry. The notions of "criminal conspiracies" and "linked" criminal schemes were not widely appreciated (nor was there adequate legislation with which to tackle organized crime groups). Nevertheless, the Ontario report did succeed in bringing attention to the deeply ingrained nature of violence within a particular industry.

QUEBEC

Quebec was a little more inclined than Ontario to label certain criminal activity as organized crime. The *Maclean's* magazine series of articles by Alan Phillips on "The Mafia in Canada" documented the movement of New York mobsters into Montreal during the 1950s, and the re-election of Jean Drapeau in 1960 and subsequent attempts to clean up corruption within both politics and law enforcement.

During the 1970s, a series of organized crime reports were produced by the Province of Quebec. Illegal gambling was identified as a major money-making activity for organized crime in Canada as well as the United States. The 1970 report entitled *Crime, Justice and Society* begins with a discussion of the U.S. organized crime initiatives, and quotes at length from the 1963 Roach Report, which was also tied closely to ongoing U.S. commissions on organized crime. The 1977 *Report of the Commission of Inquiry on Organized Crime* documented the levels of corruption and violence among key organized criminals, and exposed two key organized crime families operating in Montreal—the Dubois brothers and the Cotroni–Violi organization (Quebec 1977).

Vincent Cotroni

"He is soft-spoken, polished, decisive, a power in east-end politics. To Italian immigrants, Cotroni is the "padrone." They speak with awe of his sixty-thousand-dollar Rosemount duplex, his limousine and chauffeur, his summer house in Lavaltrie ... They accord him respect for the thousands of dollars he gives to church and charity. In the service of evil he has won moral stature" (Philips 1963, 15).

The commission report linked mobsters like William Obront with a vast network of ongoing criminal activity. It also found connections between a network of Canadian mobsters and the Cotroni crime family, including evidence that Obront laundered over $89 million for Vic Cotroni. Accused in the report of having an "almost brotherly relationship" with Willie Obront was Mitchell Bronfman, who maintained that he was a victim of loansharking at the hands of Obront (Newman 1978, 225).

Historical records and inquiries illustrate that criminal activities and individuals intersect across the borders between the provinces and between Canada and the United States. "Nests" of crimes are committed. Illegal gambling operators are involved in loansharking. Tax evasion links in with everything from which money could be made: illegal booze, illegal gambling, loansharking, extortion, securities fraud, prostitution, and union manipulation.

ORGANIZED CRIME ACTIVITIES

Organized crime in Canada involves a wide range of profit-making activities, including:

- narcotics

- extortion

- loan-sharking

- white-collar crimes, frauds, and scams

- smuggling of cigarettes, alcohol, guns and other weapons

- smuggling and other illicit schemes involving illegal aliens

- pornography and prostitution

- credit-card theft and frauds

- murder and contract killings

- gambling (both illegal operations and organized crime activities that take place within legal gaming facilities).

Canadian legislation recognizes the need for organized criminals to manipulate their proceeds in order to protect these illicit earnings from law enforcement and taxation. Under the 1989 Proceeds of Crime legislation, money laundering schemes are treated as organized crime activities. Criminal sanctions may involve the seizure of networks of assets invested by criminals in legitimate and illegitimate enterprises. In Chapter 4, we analyze various money laundering schemes and related law enforcement issues.

ORGANIZED CRIME GROUPS

The following categories of organized criminals in Canada (see Stamler 1992; CACP 1993; Sacco and Kennedy 1994) correspond to the typology of organized crime groups outlined in Chapter 2:[10]

- Category A: Aboriginal organized crime groups

- Category B: Outlaw motorcycle gangs

- Category C: Traditional Italian Mafia crime groups, ethnic groups such as Asian Triads, and Vietnamese gangs

- Category D: Colombian cartels and emerging crime groups from Russia and Nigeria

The word "traditional" is often used to describe the Italian groups—Mafia, La Cosa Nostra, and 'Ndrangheta[11]—while the word "ethnic" is usually used in reference to Asian organized crime (although, of course, there is an ethnic core running through most international criminal activity).

Given the diversity and integrated nature of Canadian organized crime, no credible analyst would suggest that organized crime is an "alien conspiracy" inflicted upon Canada by foreign, "ethnic" enclaves. To suggest that ethnic groups are involved in organized crime is not to imply that they exhibit any particular proclivity to criminal activity, but rather to indicate that there are very real advantages to be gained from creating a *closed and loyal* criminal operation that is unified and difficult to penetrate.

Outlaw motorcycle gangs achieve similar group unity through their club rules, initiation rights, willingness to retaliate, and lifestyle. Another way to achieve loyalty and cohesion is through ethnicity requirements. The goal is to

- make it difficult for the police to use undercover operators to penetrate the group.

- increase loyalty if actual families or community members are involved, possibly through the intimidation of a community or through actual loyalty.

- facilitate international organized crime by enabling the use of intimidation and extortion in both the country of origin and the new country. Relatives in the homeland can be held "hostage" to foreign-based criminals who can threaten violence as a consequence of disloyalty.

- facilitate the control of criminal activity, from the first stage of production through to the final stage of street selling. The two countries may serve as the "source" and "demand" countries, with one ethnic network controlling both ends of the criminal operation.

As we have seen, the make-up of ethnic organized crime groups is often determined by the specific criminal activity, the changing crime environment, and such factors as economics, political sensitivities, and the availability of the criminal skills needed to fulfil certain criminal tasks. It is essential to acknowledge that organized crime represents a marketplace in which *all ethnic and racial groups* (with varying visibility or exclusiveness) are involved. Analyses of recent large-scale police investigations reveal relatively stable networks of individuals who interact with one another in order to most efficiently accomplish the criminal tasks and make the largest amount of profit. In some instances, the groups consist of recent immigrants who share a distinct language and culture. Just as often the group comprises a network of criminals made up of Canadians of every background who work with other nationalities to carry out international offences, and who are bound together by little more than crime and profit.

ABORIGINAL ORGANIZED CRIME GROUPS

Only a small percentage of aboriginal community members are involved in criminal activities. Aboriginal organized crime, particularly with respect to the smuggling of cigarettes, illustrates the close relationship between government policy and the creation of organized crime. As discussed in Chapter 2, organized criminals within the aboriginal community make use of their legitimate group status (location of the Mohawk land, rights accruing to community members, jurisdictional disputes regarding policing of aboriginal communities) to facilitate such activities as the running of illegal gaming operations and the smuggling of cigarettes and alcohol. Of particular concern to law enforcement are the links that have been made between Asian criminals, traditional organized crime, and aboriginal criminal operations.

Although many people regard cigarette smuggling and illegal gambling as relatively trivial offences, both of these activities generate enormous profits that can then be used in ways that the public might consider more worthy of enforcement. For example, a recent investigation revealed evidence that cocaine traffickers within the Edmonton Vietnamese community were using smuggled cigarettes as the medium of exchange for cocaine. A "flashroll" of $200,000 worth of cigarettes was to be exchanged for 1.1 kilograms of cocaine (Linquist 1994, 34).

Aboriginal organized crime centres on "opportunistic" crimes. In the initial stages of operation, a significant profit-making opportunity is taken advantage of rather than sought out and developed. However, once the infrastructure of a distribution network is in place alternative commodities can and will be substituted. The smuggling of alcohol, drugs, guns, and illegal aliens is a matter of increasing concern for law enforcement. Weapons are of particular concern. What began as the smuggling of guns to support the military activities of a small number of Mohawk communities has become a profit-generating commodity. Nonaboriginal customers include a Jamaican street gang, the Montreal West End Gang, and motorcycle gangs.

OUTLAW MOTORCYCLE GANGS

Belonging to a motorcycle club is a legal pastime, and motorbikes appear to be one of the purchases that aging baby boomers are increasingly making. Unfortunately, in addition to motorbike clubs there are outlaw clubs that combine riding with committing serious organized crimes. Once classified as "predatory" (i.e., having no links into the political fabric of society) these organized crime groups have changed greatly in recent years. Not only have they begun to tap into the influence networks controlled by the Mafia organizations with which they affiliate, but they have been building their own relationships with the economic and social establishment. For example, police intelligence from Quebec indicates that members of the Hell's Angels are using their spouses and other close associates to infiltrate and gain information from legitimate businesses and government departments.

While initially biker gang members were used in secondary roles or as hit men for more sophisticated operations, they now have the sophistication to carry out their own complex organized crimes and to operate in a more equal partnership with other criminal groups. One case in Alberta indicates that outlaw motorcycle clubs have begun to hire underlings to perform the type of criminal acts that the Mafia used to hire bikers to carry out. In this instance, an outlaw club used a skinhead to collect a drug debt (CACP 1993, 10). Police believe that these connections are being made in jails. Motorcycle gangs tend to be racist (and sexist), which may continue to restrict membership and affiliations with non-Caucasian organized crime groups—unless the profit motive prevails.

Part of the strength of bike gangs derives from their worldwide contacts. For example, the reach of the Hell's Angels membership now extends to 30 chapters in the United States, five in Australia, 12 in England, various "bootleg" chapters in South America and South Africa, and additional chapters in Austria, France, Germany, the Netherlands, Switzerland, Sweden, Scandinavia, Norway, Finland, and Italy. Their criminal activities include drug trafficking and manufacturing of narcotics, extortion, prostitution, contract killing, frauds, fencing of stolen property, and money laundering. Surveys indicate that approximately 95 percent of Hell's Angels, out of an estimated 1 100 members worldwide, have criminal records or have been suspected of a criminal offence (*RCMP Gazette* 1994, 37).

Of the over 41 separate outlaw clubs across Canada, the two main clubs with national and international status are the Hell's Angels and the Outlaws. In some provinces, such as Quebec, the Hell's Angels control all of the exotic-dancer clubs, as well as many other bars, through extortion and intimidation. To date, the Hell's Angels are not established in Ontario, but police intelligence indicates that they may be preparing to move in.

Metropolitan Toronto has nine outlaw-biker clubs that usually, fairly peacefully, share the profits from illicit drugs, strippers, unlicensed drinking establishments, contraband gasoline, and stolen motorcycle parts (*Globe and Mail*, August 4 1995, p. A5). This peace was broken in August 1995 by the torching of a

FIGURE 3.1

Hell's Angels World Membership

Austria   Ireland
Denmark   Norway
France   Sweden
Germany   Switzerland
Holland   United Kingdom

Canada
USA
Brazil
South Africa
Australia
New Zealand

Source: RCMP, "Outlaw Motorcycle Gangs," *Gazette,* vol. 56, nos. 3 and 4 (1994). Reprinted with permission.

used-car business linked to the Loners motorcycle gang, a rocket from an antitank weapon through the armoured door of a Satan's Choice club house, the firebombing of a Loners' tattoo parlour, and, later, the firebombing of a Satan's Choice-affiliated restaurant. These attacks are either demonstrations of rivalry between Satan's Choice and the Loners or an attempt by Hell's Angels to stir up violence between these competing groups so that they can move into Ontario. The answer may be a combination of both of these explanations.

In the spring and summer of 1995, the Hell's Angels were involved in gang warfare with the Rock Machine biker gang in Quebec. It is estimated that as many as 40 people have been killed in the battle between these two clubs as they battle for control of the Quebec drug trade (*Toronto Star*, April 5, 1995, p. A9). An assassination (in broad daylight) of a Rock Machine member, coupled with the police discovery of two separate vans loaded with dynamite and nails, prompted the Montreal Urban Community Police to form an anti-gang squad. This squad was formed not out of concern that other outlaw biker members might get killed, but more specifically to protect the public from increasingly frequent bombings and shootings (*Globe and Mail*, March 3, 1995, p. A10). As feared, an eleven-year-old boy became an innocent victim of this rivalry. In September 1995, Richard (Crow) Émond was the first member (rather than an associate or hanger-on) of the Hell's Angels to be assassinated. Police anticipate retaliation. Outlaw bike gang members have powerful weapons and powerful lawyers at their disposal. In April 1995, the police arrested 13 Hell's Angels on charges that included murder, drug trafficking, and possession of illegal weapons. In the past, laying charges has proven easier than getting convictions.

In the early morning of September 14, 1994, the RCMP, OPP, Ottawa, Nepean, and Gloucester police terminated Project Flat Bed by raiding over a dozen Outlaws clubhouses scattered throughout Ottawa and the Valley and arresting 17 members on 55 charges relating to drug trafficking and firearms. This action gives rise to the legitimate fear that the Hell's Angels might see the weakened Outlaws gang as an opportunity to move into the territory.

Recalling stories of traditional mob leaders who "serve" their communities, the Hell's Angels are trying to clean up their image. In 1992, several thousand members of the public attended a Hell's Angels-hosted concert, which featured Willie Nelson, Waylon Jennings, and other well-known singers. The Boy Scouts collected tickets at the entrance, the Jaycees sold beer, and a percentage of the take went to the Sturgis (South Dakota) community. The hint of bike-club legitimacy, the romance of the Harleys, the "1 percenter" rhetoric, the imagined risks and excitement, the illicitly earned money and power—all combined to produce a public ambivalence and tolerance.

Policing outlaw motorcycle gangs is problematic for the same sorts of reasons that it is difficult to police ethnic gangs. First, police efforts to infiltrate these clubs is hampered by strict membership and initiation rites, and by expectations that members will commit certain criminal acts. Second, informants are rare due to the threat of retaliation. Finally, outlaw clubs have begun to use sophisticated counter-surveillance equipment and security on their premises. Outlaw motorcycle club members have evolved from scruffy, brawling bikers into businessmen with the education and specialized skills needed to execute financial frauds and complex money laundering schemes. The increasing use by clubs of legitimate businesses as a front for criminal activities makes it harder for the police to convict key outlaw club members and seize the club's illicit proceeds. In British Columbia, home to five Hell's Angel chapters, business deals tend to be conducted through the use of numbered companies and nominees. These techniques are used to disguise or conceal the true nature of the business and real owners of the operation.

The financial success of some outlaw clubs makes it increasingly necessary for them to develop money laundering operations. These are the types of "services" that the police can offer as undercover operators. In addition to undercover operations, the police have used Joint Force Operations (JFO) against outlaw gangs with considerable success when combined with a viable witness-protection program to keep potential informants alive (RCMP *Gazette*, 1994). In Canada, Criminal Intelligence Service Canada has been gathering intelligence on outlaw gangs since 1978. Project Focus maintains a data bank and shares information related to club membership, criminal activities, clubhouse security, financial status, power demonstrated in each area, acts of violence, intimidation, and major police actions and prosecutions. Internationally, Interpol operates a similar project called Project Rockers, which collates and shares with member countries information on criminal motorcycle gangs.

TRADITIONAL ITALIAN ORGANIZED CRIME

The so-called traditional Italian organized criminals comprise at least three separate groups: the Calabrian 'Ndrangheta, the Sicilian Mafia, and the Camorra from the Naples region.

All of the provinces with active Italian-based organized crime operations identify drugs as a major revenue-producing commodity. Also contributing to their criminal proceeds are such activities as illegal gaming, stock-market manipulation, fraud, loan-sharking, union racketeering, counterfeiting, extortion, money laundering, control of aspects of the construction and food-supply industries, and distribution of illicitly operated video poker machines.

Of concern to law enforcement, in addition to the actual criminal activity, is the extensive use of legitimate businesses in criminal operations. Edelhertz and Overcast (1993) point out the interconnections between criminal and legitimate operations. The resources available to criminal organizations give their "legitimate" operations an unfair advantage over any competition. Moreover, the legitimate business may provide "services" that further the interests of the criminal operations. These operations are used to invest criminal profit, serve in a money laundering capacity, and generally cover as a front for criminal activity.

In addition to the proceeds of crime and drug units, in Ontario two permanent joint-force operations carry out investigations specific to the activities of traditional organized crime groups. The Combined Forces Special Enforcement Unit (CFSEU) includes the RCMP, the OPP, and the Metropolitan Toronto, Peel, and York police departments. The second joint-force operation includes RCMP, OPP, and Hamilton–Wentworth Regional Police.

The willingness of so-called ethnic-based organized criminals to work with other criminals is perhaps most evident in the seemingly compatible working relationships that exist between the Italian-based Mafia operations and the outlaw motorcycle gangs. Their mutual involvement in drug trafficking forms the basis of this cooperative association. Mutually beneficial relations also appear to have been formed—across North America and internationally—between the Sicilian and Calabrian Mafia operations as well as between the Mafia and Colombian cartels.

At a symposium held in Toronto in November 1994 it was argued that Canadian immigration laws, banking regulations, and sentencing standards all serve to encourage international organized criminals such as the Mafia groups to operate throughout Canada. Lending credence to this argument, on November 8, 1994, Salvatore Ferraro, the reputed crime boss of a Sicilian Mafia family, was ordered deported from Toronto to Italy where he will face prosecution. According to Italian authorities, "Ferraro replaced Guiseppe Madonia as the head of the Sicilian crime family in 1992 after Madonia was arrested during a massive crackdown of mob activity across Italy." (*Toronto Star*, November 8, 1994, p. A5). Ferraro had been living peacefully in Toronto for the past three years.

ASIAN TRIADS AND VIETNAMESE GANGS

Although Asian organized crime is a nationwide phenomenon, its primary centres of activity seem to be British Columbia, Ontario, and Quebec. The crimes are similar to those perpetrated by the traditional Mafia organizations, but law enforcement is concerned about the violence and the automatic weapons often associated with Asian organized crime operations. There is some fear that

1997 may bring an influx of Asian criminals into Canada in response to the Chinese takeover of Hong Kong.

Organized crime groups like Triads have been successful at corrupting officials in order to facilitate their operations. In Hong Kong, the legal field abounds with Triad members. According to one 1986 estimate, 95 percent of law clerks in Hong Kong were Triad members (Clement and McAdam 1993). In the past, local Chinese were employed as interpreters for British barristers and solicitors working in Hong Kong—a position that has evolved into a more powerful and aggressive "profession."

Triad influence has also extended to the Hong Kong police. It has been estimated that 35 percent of all Chinese police officers were Triad members in the 1960s and 1970s. Systemic bribery was a reality. In 1976, the Independent Commission Against Corruption (ICAC) found that a number of high-ranking Triad members had fled to Canada or the United States. Approximately 30 wealthy ex-Hong Kong policemen invested heavily in Vancouver and Toronto real estate.

Triads
Triads originated in the mid-17th century in China. They comprised secretive societies working to overthrow the ruling Manchu or Ch'ing Dynasty through overt force and subversion. They derive their name, the Triads, from the groups' sacred picture—a triangle whose three sides represent heaven, earth and man, the three basic forces of nature for the Chinese (CACP 1993, 47).

More recently, joint force operations have targeted Asian organized crime across Canada. Full time Joint Force Asian Crime Investigative Units (JFASIA) operate in Toronto and Ottawa. In Toronto, the RCMP, the OPP, and the Metropolitan Toronto, Peel and York police departments are involved; the RCMP and Ottawa police force participate in the Ottawa operation. In British Columbia, the Coordinated Law Enforcement Unit (CLEU) receives assistance from the RCMP and Vancouver police, and works extensively with law enforcement authorities in the United States.

Of all the organized crime groups, the Triads are perhaps the most difficult to police. Asian communities only recently have begun to turn to the police for protection from the crime and extortion perpetrated upon them by Asian criminals. The police have identified a number of schemes that specifically target Asian people. For example, the Big Circle Boys created a shell corporation and advertised for employees in the Chinese daily newspaper. By this means, the gang gathered identification and personal information on over 100 potential victims and used this information to apply for credit and open bank accounts, and to facilitate the passing of forged cheques (CACP 1993, 52). Language and cultural differences, combined with a distrust toward public police on the part of Asian communities, has led to such trust-building measures as the recruitment of Asian police officers in urban Canadian police forces (in some cases, trained police are recruited from Hong Kong for this purpose).

The main Triad groups include the Kung Lok, 14K, Sun Yee On, United Bamboo, and Wo Hop To. Associated with these main operations are the Big Circle Boys or Dai Huen Jai gang. Police intelligence indicates that the higher-ranking Triad members and the Vietnamese gangs will use Big Circle Boys as enforcers, but the relationship between them is more complicated than that. The Big Circle Boys are not themselves a Triad, but many of the gang's members do belong to a Triad society, and most Triad groups include Big Circle gang members. Big Circle Boys are said to specialize in heroin smuggling, but are also involved in alien smuggling, credit-card scams, extortion, armed robberies, and home invasions.

On September 14, 1994, a series of simultaneous raids against members of the Big Circle Boys resulted in the arrest of 25 people in Toronto, Vancouver, and Montreal, and effectively terminated the Joint Drug Task Force Heroin Project, "Luen Hop" (*Toronto Star*, September 15, 1994, p. A3). The Combined Forces Asian Investigative Unit (CFAIU) worked with several other Canadian police agencies in concert with the Royal Thai Police and the Royal Hong Kong Police. What was particularly significant about this case was the nature of the heroin that was seized. Over the last couple of years, at least 112 deaths in Canada had been linked specifically to a lethal brand of Asian heroin. This high-purity China White (No. 4 variety) has been termed "The Killer Heroin." During this 18 month investigation two of the targeted individuals were killed in turf battles, indicating the level of violence that is involved within this particular criminal organization.

Unlike some of the organized crime cases where the police are noticing unique partnerships across organized crime groups, in this case the Big Circle Boys controlled the process from the poppy fields of Laos, Cambodia, and China to the streets in Canada—in this case, Toronto and Vancouver (*Toronto Star*, 1994, p. A3).

The presence of such high purity heroin is a reflection of the accessibility and low cost of heroin. One week after the September

14 raids, the police again raided the Chinese area of downtown Toronto and made 25 additional arrests. A member of the Metro Toronto Morality squad stated: "Last week it was the importers and today we took out a sophisticated distribution network" (*Toronto Star*, September 22, 1994, p. A7).

However successful the police may be in separate cases such as these, the drug is evidently entering Canada with little difficulty. The 80 percent to 90 percent pure heroin product indicates that the supply of heroin is in fact glutting the market so that the economics of this market does not encourage traffickers to cut/ dilute their illicit commodity. In July 1994, however, the purity level of the heroin in British Columbia dropped to 54 percent as publicity over the deaths and policing over heroin traffickers, increased.

In addition to the Chinese/Hong Kong gangs, Vietnamese gangs operate across Canada. Quebec law enforcement has recently identified a newer gang comprising members from Cambodia. Employing a combination of intimidation and force, these gangs commit a vast array of crimes, including extortion, illegal gambling and legalized gaming frauds, smuggling (aliens, alcohol, and cigarettes), trafficking in cocaine and heroin, prostitution, home invasions,[12] sophisticated frauds such as credit-card schemes, organized break and enters, and forgery. Triad membership, once restricted to Chinese born in China or Hong Kong, has recently expanded to include Vietnamese members, who contribute to the group both their money and their violent practices.

Another Asian presence is the Japanese *Boryokudan (Yakuza)* organizations. These Japanese organized criminals focus on tourist scams, narcotics smuggling, and the sextrade. In March 1993, Canadian newspapers reported that the Japanese crime boss Masaru Takumi had purchased a house in Vancouver. Takumi is claimed to be the "underboss" of the 26,000 member Yamaguchigumi group, considered the dominant group in the *Yakuza*. At the same time, records indicated that he was the president and a major shareholder of a B.C. company called T.M. Canada Investment Corp., and sole owner of a Vancouver tour company (*Vancouver Sun*, March 20, 1993). The media controversy deepened when it was learned that Takumi had for a time run a business out of an office in Canada Place. The Coordinated Law Enforcement Unit (CLEU) acknowledged the presence of 41 Japanese organized crime operations in British Columbia. CLEU'S director Peter Engstad stated that law enforcement did not yet know how great a threat the *Yakuza* could be to British Columbia or to the rest of Canada.

COLOMBIAN CARTELS[13]

It is estimated that Colombian cartels (Medellin and Cali) supply 70 to 75 percent of the cocaine consumed in Canada and the United States. The coca itself is not cultivated in Colombia but rather comes from places like Peru and Bolivia, and is flown to Colombia for processing and distribution. Some indigenous trafficking groups in these countries are actively engaged in altering the coca leaf into cocaine base before selling it to the Colombian cartels.

The Colombian cartels control the bulk of the cocaine distribution in South America, the Caribbean, and Europe (Stamler 1992). The cartels are expanding throughout all of the newly opened regions and have formed affiliations with the Mafia in Italy and with Russian criminals in order to effectively distribute their drugs to a growing market. In Canada, partnerships between Colombian cartel members and the Mafia have been formed to facilitate the distribution of cocaine across Canada as well as internationally.

Law enforcement officials are particularly concerned with an increase in the cultivation of opium and the conversion of the crop into heroin. Canadian police have detected only the beginnings of the distribution of Colombian heroin. Money laundering schemes—for both legitimate businesses and drug traffickers have been documented as a major law enforcement concern by the Drug Enforcement Agency (DEA). The Jaworski sting operation, discussed in Chapter 2, revealed to Canadian law enforcement officials the extent and the sophistication of the Colombian criminal presence in Canada.

One case that illustrates the extent of Colombian criminal involvement in Canada, entitled Project TOME, was initiated as a drug case by the Major Projects Unit of the Metropolitan Toronto Police in February 1991. In the fall of that year, a joint financial investigative unit comprising the RCMP, the OPP, and Metro Toronto Police was formed to carry out an intensive proceeds of crime investigation. The case was terminated in May 1993 (RCMP News Release, May 19, 1993). The drug and proceeds investigation had exposed an international network of cocaine traffickers originating in Colombia. The method of importation illustrated in Figure 3.2 was used to transport into Toronto $3.6 million in cash and 600 kilos of cocaine *per month*.

The police estimate that over 5 800 kilos of cocaine entered Canada before the arrests were made via the Colombian cartels, allegedly headed by Diego Serrano (Calabria), Rocco Morra (Mississauga), and Bernardo Arcila (Medellin Colombia). Some of the criminal proceeds were converted into U.S. cash at currency

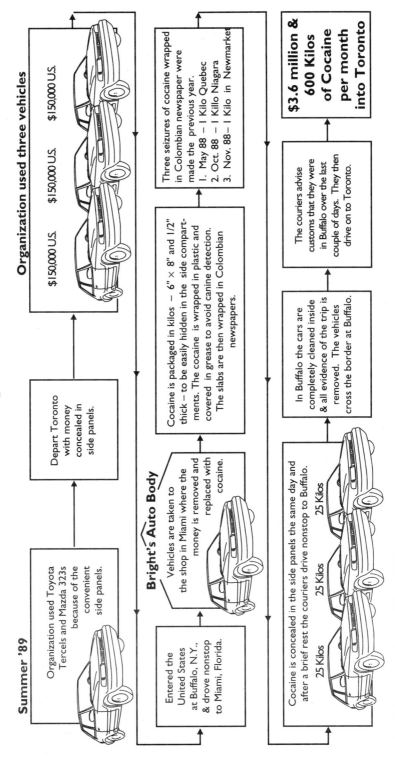

F I G U R E 3 . 2

Method of Importation—Cocaine

Summer '89

Organization used Toyota Tercels and Mazda 323s because of the convenient side panels.

Organization used three vehicles

$150,000 US. $150,000 US. $150,000 US.

Depart Toronto with money concealed in side panels.

Bright's Auto Body

Vehicles are taken to the shop in Miami where the money is removed and replaced with cocaine.

Cocaine is packaged in kilos — 6" × 8" and 1/2" thick – to be easily hidden in the side compartments. The cocaine is wrapped in plastic and covered in grease to avoid canine detection. The slabs are then wrapped in Colombian newspapers.

Three seizures of cocaine wrapped in Colombian newspaper were made the previous year.
1. May 88 – 1 Kilo Quebec
2. Oct. 88 – 1 Killo Niagara
3. Nov. 88 – 1 Kilo in Newmarket

Entered the United States at Buffalo, N.Y., & drove nonstop to Miami, Florida.

In Buffalo the cars are completely cleaned inside & all evidence of the trip is removed. The vehicles cross the border at Buffalo.

The couriers advise customs that they were in Buffalo over the last couple of days. They then drive on to Toronto.

$3.6 million & 600 Kilos of Cocaine per month into Toronto

Cocaine is concealed in the side panels the same day and after a brief rest the couriers drive nonstop to Buffalo.
25 Kilos 25 Kilos 25 Kilos 25 Kilos 25 Kilos 25 Kilos

Reprinted by permission of the RCMP.

exchange houses in Toronto. This cash was then returned to Florida and used to fund the next drug shipment as well as some property investments in that state. Most of the illicit profit, however, took another route (see Figure 3.3).

Police discovered that the cartels had over 200 properties in and around Toronto and in Florida. Two people worked full-time in Toronto to make monthly payments on the mortgages. A "laundering" scheme was developed whereby the criminals would write mortgage-payment cheques that would bounce, and then hire "runners" who would appear and offer to pay the amount owing in cash (usually to the relief of the bank or mortgage holder). This cash would not generate any paper trail, and the idea was that the criminals would eventually claim legitimate ownership of the land, houses, businesses, and recreational facilities.

The police alleged that illicit funds were used to buy Cayuga drag strip for $1.2 million, Treasure Valley Amusement Park in Oshawa for $1.4 million, and restaurants and apartments in Toronto (*Toronto Star*, May 20, 1993). Many of the mortgages were negotiated through one branch of the Canadian Imperial Bank of Commerce (a former bank branch manager was among those people arrested). Some of the most luxurious properties were purchased in Italy (*Toronto Star*, May 8, 1993). One of the principals in the criminal organization, Diego Serrano, owned a condominium in Calabria called the Taj Mahal, which was estimated to be worth $13 million. Italian police officials worked with Canadian police to seize this property and to arrest 18 people in Italy, including two police officers.

In November 1994, Diego Serrano was sentenced to 10 years in jail and fined $50,000 after pleading guilty to two counts of importing and trafficking in cocaine. His sentence, as a result of his guilty plea, was considerably milder than those received by three of his underlings—Joachin Sevillano, 20 years; Joseph DeFrancesca, 15 years; and Domenic Condello (who had served mainly as a courier), 14 years (*Globe and Mail*, November 2, 1994).

EMERGING ORGANIZED CRIME GROUPS

Although only Russian and Nigerian organized crime groups are discussed in this section, this is not to suggest that they are the only two emerging criminal groups in Canada. Additional organizations that could have been discussed include the Jamaican Posses. The Posses are often classified as an organized crime group, but their loose structure, near-random violence, and the lack of sophistication of their offenses (robberies, weapon trafficking, drug trafficking,

FIGURE 3.3

Organization Chart

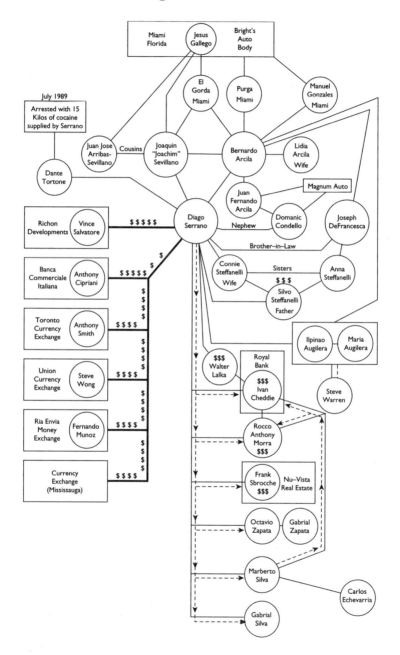

Reprinted by permission of the RCMP.

and murder) makes them similar to a violent street gang on their way to becoming an international organized crime threat.

Russian Organized Crime

Police investigations indicate a wide and, to some extent, unruly range of criminal activity committed by Russian organized criminals, who tend to engage in excessive violence, including seemingly haphazard retaliation and murder. Canadian and U.S. law enforcement agencies are still determining the nature of these Russian crime operations. While some of their participants appear to be operating in an organized crime manner, others are functioning more as independent street criminals in search of opportunities to commit fraud or steal. During June 1995, international law enforcement officials met at Meech Lake, Quebec, to discuss organized crime. Lt-Colonel Valerly Serebrikov, head of organized crime investigations for Russia's Interior Ministry, confirmed that Russian crime gangs were establishing themselves in Canada. Internationally, authorities are concerned that Russian organized criminals, in concert with criminals from such countries as Colombia and Spain, are engaged in the smuggling and sale of nuclear weapons-quality plutonium. Claire Sterling argues that an aspect of the nuclear smuggling scare that is particularly appalling is the role of secret agents around the world in obfuscating the situation, making it difficult or impossible to know the truth about nuclear leakage from Russia (1994a, 125).

Nigerian Tribal Organized Crime Operations

Some law enforcement officials fear that Nigeria is becoming a major drug-trafficking and transit point. Heroin and cocaine are the major commodities, although neither originates in Nigeria. Heroin is received in bulk from the Far East, often via Lebanon or Pakistan; cocaine comes from South America. It is estimated that as much as 80 percent of all heroin seized at John F. Kennedy airport in New York has gone through Lagos at some stage in its trip.

While the public is somewhat familiar with at least the mythology surrounding the "family" structure of the Italian Mafia and with the triad structure of Asian organized crime, the tribal-family-based operations of Nigerian organized crime are only now being recognized and addressed by law enforcement. The goal of these criminal groups is to make large amounts of money in Canada and then return to Nigeria. For reasons that include the intimidation of family members in the home country and a lack of desire on the part of these criminal to be "relocated" in witness-protection programs elsewhere in Canada, the police have found it hard to gain informants within this community.

F I G U R E   3 . 4

Flight Connections

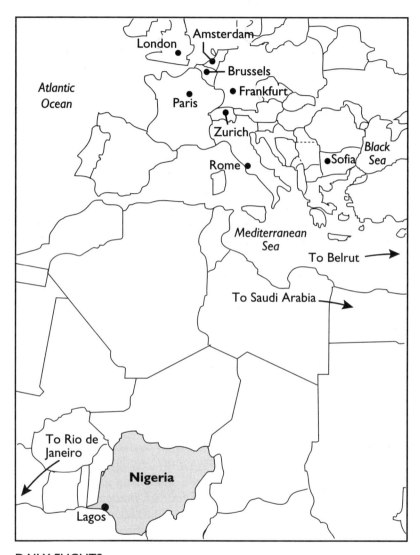

DAILY FLIGHTS

To Europe
London 6; Rome 5; Brussels 4; Frankfurt 4; Zurich 4; Paris 3; Amsterdam 3; Sofia 1

To African capitals 54

Other service
Saudi Arabia 2; Rio de Janeiro 1; Belrut 1

Lax security checks at airports and corruption of officials serve to reduce the risks associated with being a drug courier. According to police intelligence, the Nigerian crime syndicates promise to care for the families of those couriers who are caught. The couriers (women as well as men) sign a vow of secrecy, which if violated has severe consequences for their families. The sophistication of these operations is revealed in the high-quality of the forged documents and the training/coaching that the couriers receive prior to beginning work as drug smugglers. A preferred method of smuggling is to place the heroin in condoms and then swallow them. Airline personnel have been advised to watch for passengers who refuse to eat or drink on long flights.

Any country that has a direct flight from Nigeria is a target for the drugs pouring through what has been called "one of the world's leading drug conduits" (*L.A. Times* 1994). It is the sheer number of the couriers as well as their skills that is of major concern. Officials at London's Heathrow airport estimated that they arrested one Nigerian drug courier every day during 1993. In the same year, Nigerian organized criminals were estimated to be the second largest heroin importers into Canada. Because there are no direct flights between Nigeria and Canada or the United States, cities in Europe, Mexico, and the Caribbean are part of the courier's route to North America.

In addition to drug importation, Nigerian organized gangs have been involved in wordwide sophisticated scams and frauds. The RCMP's economic crime directorate estimates that $15 million has been taken from Canadians from one particular Nigerian sting operation that began in the early 1990s. Canadian business executives or professionals are sent "confidential" letters from someone posing as a Nigerian government official. In the hope of making 30 to 40 percent of a multimillion dollar fund, Candians agree to begin the transactions required to allow the Nigerian official to move his funds into a foreign bank account. Some victims have lost over $500,000: "One Calgary businessman who took $500,000 cash to Nigeria ... found a machine gun pointed at his temple ... The businessman was told to leave his money and get out of the country or die. He fled." (*Calgary Herald,* June 15, 1995, p. B10).

Nigerian police tend not to welcome assistance from foreign police, and Canada has no extradition treaty with Nigeria.

Collaboration among Organized Crime Groups

Figure 3.5 illustrates the interdependent relationships that characterize the major organized crime groups. On the periphery are those violent, "independent" operations (e.g., Russians groups) that have yet to fit into the evolving criminal landscape.

OPERATION CONTRAT/COMPOTE/ CREDITOR

On August 31, 1994, the RCMP out of Montreal announced the culmination of a four-year three-part undercover investigation called Operation Contrat/Compote/Creditor. Twenty-six persons with international connections were charged with conspiracy to traffic in cocaine and with engaging in Canada's biggest money laundering scheme to date: a $47-million money laundering ring. Of particular interest was the collaborative working arrangement that existed between the Colombian cartels, traditional Italian Mafia, and the Hell's Angels. The Mafia members went down to Colombia to obtain the cocaine from the Colombia cartel members, who then shipped the drugs by boat or plane back to Montreal. The Mafia in Montreal distributed the cocaine either on the street or to traffickers. Involved as partners in collecting the

FIGURE 3.5

The Interdependence of Organized Crime Groups

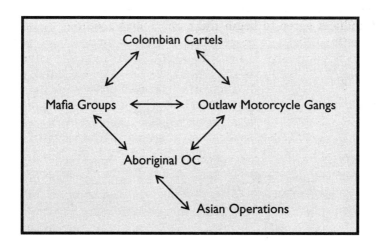

FIGURE 3.6

Contrat–Compote–Creditor

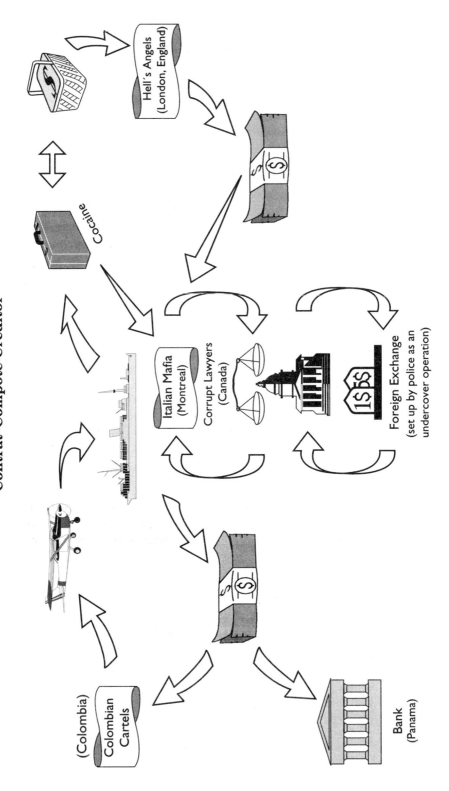

money and in distributing the drugs were the Hell's Angels in Montreal and the International Hell's Angels in London, England.

The RCMP had at the outset established a phony foreign exchange house to facilitate undercover money laundering sting operations. In addition to money laundering for the criminal organization, RCMP undercover operators were involved in transporting some of the drugs to England for distribution by the International Hell's Angels out of London. The law enforcement objective in this case was to identify the upper echelon criminals and to debilitate the organized crime operations by stripping them of their proceeds. As Sergeant Claude Lessard stated, "We seized their dope, we froze their houses, their bank accounts. They're just left with 25 cents for a phone call" (*Globe and Mail,* August 31, 1994, p. A1). Over 200 bank accounts in 29 banking institutions were frozen, including all of the records and bank accounts of 34 companies. Three lawyers were arrested and charged with laundering the proceeds of crime. Lawyer Joseph Lagana was sentenced to 13 years in prison. He was described in court as the brains behind the operation and the only man in direct contact with Vito Rizzuto—reputed Montreal Mafia chieftain (*Montreal Gazette,* June 30, 1995, p. A4). Reports on this case at the time of the bust revealed that these mobsters had provided funding to a Montreal restaurateur who obtained concession rights at Expo 92 in Spain.

In addition to the strictly illegal activity of all of the groups involved in organized crime, a network of legitimate involvements (with people and businesses) exists to facilitate the illicit activity. An analysis of organized crime must somehow capture the interconnections between the core criminals and the facilitators; the legitimate and the illegitimate activities; the criminal operations and the changing environment (government policies, economic conditions, and competing operations).

NOTES

1. The James Dubro quote is taken from *The Globe and Mail,* "Organized Crime," March 26, 1993, p. A16; Dubro was responding to an article on immigration and Triad members. He rejected the claim that organized crime in North America would increasingly develop "an Asian face." Dubro argues that, despite the U.S. hype, the face of organized crime is "white," with the powerful Italian Mafia still very much in control of unions, industries, and traditional crimes.

2. See *The Globe and Mail,* "Mafia Quick to Move When Money Begins Flowing," September 18, 1993, p. A15.

3. Conversation with Superintendent Wayne Blackburn, RCMP, Anti-Drug Profiteering Section, Toronto, Ontario, April 22, 1994.

4. See U.S. Department of Justice, Immigration and Naturalization Service, Investigations Division, "Chinese Organized Crime," March 1989.

5. See Canadian Association of Chiefs of Police, *Organized Crime Committee Report,* produced by the Canadian Intelligence Service Canada, 1993.

6. See *The New International Criminal and Asian Organized Crime,* a report by the Permanent Subcommittee on Investigations of the Committee on Governmental Affairs, United States Senate, December 1992.

7. See Shelley (1994).

8. Initially, only a few left-wing accounts accused the U.S. government of having facilitated the drug-trafficking industry for political ends. Now the literature is too vast and well-documented—including public hearings into the Iran Contra scandal—to be ignored or rejected. See, for example, Scott and Marshall (1991) and Mills (1986).

9. Following the publication of this series, Alan Phillips faced one trial and 10 libel suits that were eventually dropped. See also Mann and Hanley (1968).

10. This order does not relate to any perceived ranking of increasing dangerousness but rather to the "boxes" resulting from the dimensional model created by differentiating organized crime groups based on their predatory vs. symbiotic characteristic and the degree to which the organized crime group is strictly created and serves to facilitate organized crime. See Chapter 2.

11. While all three terms are used quite loosely to refer to "organized crime," the term "Mafia" was originally used to refer to Sicilian-based organized crime. *La Cosa Nostra* relates to American-based organized crime, and *'Ndrangheta* refers to the Calabrian Mafia.

12. Home invasions are reported more frequently in British Columbia than elsewhere in Canada. Criminals force their way into a person's home, tie up the family members (often using violence), and steal all of the valuables. Asian homes were initially the main targets, but criminals are now targeting other victims. In addition to the Asian organized crime gangs, gypsy criminals are also involved in home invasions.

13. I am using the familiar term "cartel" even though some critics maintain it is an inappropriate term. A "cartel" is usually defined as a coalition of producers who act together to restrict supply and drive up the price of their commodity. Colombian cartels aim to *increase* production, *decrease* prices, *increase* sales. See *The Economist,* December 24, 1994, p. 22.

Money Laundering in Canada[1]

A Bulgarian diplomat, two lawyers, a policeman, a stockbro-
ker, a firefighter and two rabbis were among those accused of
laundering more than $100 million in drug proceeds [per
year]. ... The range of professionals involved in this was
surprising and somewhat depressing ... the lawyer who was
arrested practiced often at the federal courthouse in Manhat-
tan" (*Narcotics Control Digest* 1994, 6).

In addition to its magnitude and international range, the case
referred to in the above quotation was deemed significant because
of the number of seemingly respectable professionals who were
involved in the criminal laundering of drug proceeds. As New York
Police Chief William Bratton noted, "The only thing missing is the
candlestick maker" (*San Francisco Examiner* 1994). This case
illustrates how narrow our thinking may be in terms of who is or
is not an organized criminal. Business and finance have become
international in scope, and the advantages previously enjoyed by
closed ethnicity-based organized crime groups are now available
to those other criminal groups who have the ability to operate
globally. The case also illustrates the enormous profits to be made
by a criminal group that includes bankers (both in the United
States and Zurich); rabbis and stockbrokers, who serve as cash
couriers; and lawyers, who negotiate the "legalities" of the transactions.

This chapter will define the concept of money laundering; review
those international groups that are currently attempting to work
with countries to ensure that legislation and enforcement policies
are in place to curb money laundering; identify those business and
financial institutions that are particularly vulnerable to money laundering; and follow one particular case through all its stages. Other
case examples will be presented to illustrate how organized criminals operate in Canada and internationally.

Ironically, a major problem for many large-scale organized
crime groups is the cash their crimes generate. Through a process
called money laundering, they must continually turn their illicit

proceeds into some nonsuspicious, spendable form that has the appearance of legitimate earnings. Failure to do so can result in detection, conviction, and the potential seizure and forfeiture of the illicit profits derived from criminal activity. While we often dismiss the eventual arrest and conviction of Al Capone as having been merely for income-tax evasion, in fact his failure was a failure to launder his illicit proceeds adequately and then put into place the evasive strategies that legitimate operations use to lawfully reduce the amounts owing to internal revenue.[2] Today, financial advisers are hired full-time to perform these tasks for "serious" organized crime groups.

Any discussion of money laundering requires acknowledgement of the limitations of cross-jurisdictional or international law enforcement and policing. While there is an increasing emphasis on sharing intelligence and other forms of cooperation in mutual multi-jurisdictional cases, formal mechanisms to facilitate these joint efforts are relatively new and somewhat primitive in comparison to the sophisticated criminal-operated cross-border networks. In addition to law enforcement operational problems, new sovereignty issues are arising as countries attempt to bring other nations into line with their own internal laws, policies, and procedures. More aggressive moves may be perceived to be in violation of the sovereignty and territorial integrity of nations. The international community is being asked to decide what loss of independence it is prepared to accept in order to control cross-jurisdictional crimes.

HISTORICAL BACKGROUND: A FOCUS ON CONTROL

Gold and Levi (1994, 7) call the term money laundering "one of the buzz phrases of crime in the 1990's." Recognition of the importance of the criminal proceeds—in addition to the criminal—has resulted from a long history of small and large shifts in the thinking of governments, law enforcement, and the public. (See Part 3 for a discussion of some of these shifts.)

The 1984 President's Commission on Organized Crime (United States, *Cash Connection*) called money laundering "the lifeblood of organized crime" (7). This report was a significant formal recognition of the need for governments and law enforcement to focus on the money laundering of criminal proceeds. The report recognized three aspects of this criminal practice:

1. "[It] plays a vital role in furthering the activities of organized crime" (*Cash Connection* 1984, 4).

2. The ability of criminals to employ complex laundering schemes is usually reliant on the "modern, sophisticated, often international services of financial institutions" (*Cash Connection* 1984, 3).

3. The private sector, including financial and corporate institutions, must be held culpable if they knowingly profit from organized criminal activity. Corrupt officials, naive and/or ignorant employees, and cash-hungry business entrepreneurs who facilitate the laundering schemes must all be seen as part of the organized crime problem.

The U.S. Financial Crimes Enforcement Network (FinCEN, July 1992) describes money laundering as an *integral support function* common to all profit-producing criminal activities—robbery, fraud, extortion, and, of course, drug trafficking. While this is true of all laundering operations, "professional" laundering is demonstrated by those operations that can sustain a continual—as opposed to sporadic—accumulation of illicit proceeds.

In recognition of the importance of legitimizing the criminal profits, international law enforcement efforts against money laundering have increased over the past 10 years. The international focus on money laundering—including the UN Convention (1986), the G-7 Financial Action Task Force, the CICAD initiative, and bilateral efforts—has helped bring about in various countries legislation

- that facilitates taking the profit away from the criminal via processes of seizing/freezing and eventually forfeiting these proceeds. "Targeting upward" involves targeting the criminal proceeds rather than (or in addition to) the criminals;

- that acknowledges that the money laundering process is critical to organized crime and therefore the laundering process must be treated as a criminal offence;

- that facilitates the gathering of cross-jurisdictional evidence and the development of cases between foreign jurisdictions.

Case-based literature is now available on the schemes and techniques involved in "cleansing" criminal proceeds. For example, within the last four years, the United States, Australia, England, Canada, and the G-7 Financial Action Task Force have separately and together studied and written on this compelling subject.[3]

DEFINITION AND CHARACTERISTICS OF MONEY LAUNDERING

The definition of money laundering used in this book is adapted from the 1988 United Nations Convention Against Illicit Traffic in Narcotic Drugs and Psychotropic Substances. This definition emphasizes that money laundering involves a multi-stage process and that a thorough laundering process will result in the *perception* of a legitimate source or legitimate ownership of the illicit proceeds. While depositing the proceeds of white-collar crime might technically qualify as money laundering conduct, the focus here is on laundering processes that facilitate the continuation of criminal conduct. As Beare and Schneider (1990) summarized the UN definition, money laundering usually involves:

- the *conversion* of illicit cash to another asset, possibly involving the placement of the funds into a financial institution;

- the *concealment* of the true source or ownership of the illegally acquired proceeds, possibly through a technique referred to as "layering" whereby a series of otherwise legitimate transactions are carried out which due to the frequency, volume, or complexity of the transactions create a paper trail that is hard or impossible to follow;

- the *creation* of the perception of legitimacy of source and ownership. By this stage, the funds may be integrated into the legitimate economy so thoroughly as to be interchangeable with legitimate earnings.[4]

Recent cases in the United States suggest that money laundering is being more broadly defined in the courts. Money laundering legislation is being applied to situations unrelated to any traditional notion of organized crime. A laundering law was recently used to prosecute a California lawyer allegedly involved in a personal-injury scam. The government argued that paying a "capper" (runner who directs accident victims to corrupt doctors and lawyers for a share of the settlement) with criminal proceeds served to conceal the nature of the funds and to perpetuate the criminal activity (*Money Laundering Alert,* October and November 1994).

The greater the volume of proceeds and the more frequent the laundering transactions, the more sophisticated the scheme that must be developed. Studies of Canadian police cases similar to those undertaken in other countries, indicate that approximately 80 percent of laundering cases have an international dimension. This percentage varies slightly depending on the jurisdiction. One might expect an even higher percentage of international cases in the future given increasing international markets, the elimination of frontiers, and less expensive global transportation and communication. If the illicit commodity is drugs, the source of the supply is likely from outside of Canada (although not necessarily with drugs such as marijuana or "designer drugs" and illegally diverted chemicals). The market or demand is within North America.

On occasion, Canada plays the dual roles of transit country to the United States and market for the domestic sale of drugs. In addition to the flow of drugs, the illicit proceeds also move across borders. Illicit funds generated in one country may be brought into another country for laundering. Adding this international aspect to the laundering scheme serves to camouflage the paper trail by introducing cross-jurisdictional complications.

LAUNDERING AS AN ENTERPRISE ACTIVITY

While it is informative to list the financial and business institutions and functions that are vulnerable to being used in organized crime laundering schemes, to analyze them as separate laundering vehicles is to lose sight of the linkages between them. Money laundering consists of the series of processes through which criminal proceeds pass in order to appear to be legitimate income. In recognition of this fact, criminal investigations have begun to focus not strictly on the profit-making criminal activity or on separate laundering manoeuvres, but rather on these crimes as the intertwined activities of a criminal enterprise. A legitimate and illegitimate support network will exist beyond any individual activity.

The "enterprise," therefore, comprises the continuing criminal and legitimate activities, structures, and agreements that serve to perpetuate the illicit gain. These networks involve links with legitimate businesses, placement of funds overseas, and complex investment structures. The Australian Transaction Reports Analysis Centre (AUSTRAC) acknowledges the enterprise aspect by calling for an expanded vision that encompasses both the tangible targets and the facilitators who ensure the viability of the criminal enterprises (Coad and Richardson 1993, 43). Edelhertz and Overcast (1993) paint a complex picture of businesses owned or controlled by organized crime, interacting with trade associations controlled by organized crime, interacting with businesses that have had to strike deals with organized crime in order to compete or exist alongside their organized crime-controlled competitors.

TYPOLOGY OF LAUNDERING SCHEMES

Laundering schemes range from the very simple to the highly complex. The following categories are offered as a possible typology of the main laundering schemes:[5]

- simple-limited

- simple-unlimited

- serial-domestic

- serial-international.

Simple-Limited

These schemes are restricted to straightforward financial manipulations that can accommodate a relatively small amount of illicit proceeds. There is a ceiling or a limit on the laundering potential. A typical laundering vehicle in this category would be a tavern, laundry, vending-machine company, pizza parlour—any business that deals in cash and has a "stock" that can be manipulated. Criminals can claim that their legitimate businesses generated a greater profit than was actually the case. The difference between the real profit and the claimed profit is the amount of money that is laundered. This difference cannot be vast, since revenue and law enforcement officials may become suspicious. If little or no legitimate business is conducted, the amount that can be laundered becomes greater—but so do the risks of detection. This category meets the definition of money laundering because the end result is the perception of a legitimate source for the illicit proceeds. Although the businessperson must now pay income tax on these "earnings," it is a small price to pay for the laundering service that has taken place.

Simple-Unlimited

In this category, the ceiling is very high, and made even more "unlimited" by the ambiguous, specialized, and big-budgeted businesses that are used in some of these schemes. They are classified as "simple" in the sense that the manipulation itself is straightforward and involves few transactions. Dredging, waste, scrap metal, construction, and development would be attractive industries for large-scale laundering schemes. The Canadian Hamilton Harbour dredging scandal in the mid 1970s is a perfect example of the use of large-budget industries to launder funds on an ongoing basis. This scheme involved a conspiracy among dredging companies to maintain artificially high prices for dredging services by predetermining which company would win a particular contract. Horace

Grant Rindress, vice-president of the J.P. Porter dredging company, revealed that

> price-fixing has been going on in the dredging industry for at least thirty to forty years. ... the companies maintain "score cards" to keep track of whose turn it is to bid high on a given contract and how much the company awarded the contract must pay as compensation for the others bidding high (Freeman and Hewitt 1979, 162).

The invoice to J.P. Porter was from Wm. Seymour, Electrical Contractor, 1223 Gerrard Street East, Toronto. It carried an apparently legitimate work-order number: HAM 224A-70. It was for expected services: overhaul of diesel engine, etc. $3,250; rewinding of generator, $4,780; replace wiring, $2,640; check and clean ... for a total of $13,500. The work was said to have been completed August 25, 1970 ... Stamler (Rod T. Stamler, RCMP) had almost passed the invoice by when he realized something about it bothered him: there was no telephone number. How many businesses didn't display telephone numbers on their invoices? ... Stamler dawdled along behind a Gerrard Street streetcar looking for 1223, expecting to find a business of some sort there. What he found was a typical Toronto semi-detached house ... The bogus invoice was a key to a door that led to a criminal mind or two—but whose? (Palango 1994, 114).

The payoffs were absorbed into the paperwork of company operations. Few people, aside from other dredgers, are aware of what constitutes legitimate costs in these operations. The full investigation of this particular conspiracy revealed a more complicated international laundering and corruption scheme than would fall under this category in our typology. However, the basic formula was one of price-fixing and the hiding of the illicit funds in a simple invoice scam.

Serial-Domestic
This category involves numerous financial transactions, the total of which is intended to create an impossible paper trail. Many of these schemes may be designed more for the purposes of obfuscation than the actual laundering of funds. Money launderers capitalize on any existing loopholes within the regulatory and

enforcement network as they move their illicit proceeds through a network of transactions—using nominee accounts, dealing with several different banks and exchange houses, purchasing properties and contriving imaginative real-estate flips. Professional lawyers or accountants may be used to help orchestrate this movement of proceeds.

Serial-International

Highly sophisticated criminals with a large, ongoing amount of illicit proceeds to launder must resort to international laundering schemes. The focus on money laundering within Canada and other Western countries has progressed beyond the days when a criminal could with little risk take frequent gym bags of cash into the bank of his or her choice. (Although one makes this claim a little hesitantly!) Bank awareness programs and new legislation adds a culpability factor to persuade people against knowingly facilitating money laundering. Offshore laundering havens, shell corporations, legitimate businesses, smuggling, wire transfers, loan scams, invoice manipulations may all be a part of these international laundering schemes.

Andelman (1994) describes a fairly simple scheme (one he refers to as the "equivalent of the eighteenth-century Triangular Trade") involving Colombian drug traffickers. These drug traffickers purchase legitimate products (e.g., coffee and leather) using Colombian bank loans secured with letters of credit from Panamanian banks, which are backed by drug-generated cash. The legitimate product (i.e., tens of millions of dollars of coffee) is sold in the United States and the proceeds are transferred to shell corporations in Europe. The funds in the bank accounts are, at this stage, the legitimate proceeds of a coffee transaction (Andelman 1994, 101). Depending on the scheme, the "loans" need never be repaid or are repaid with illicit proceeds or a combination of illicit drug proceeds and legitimate coffee profits.

UNIQUE LAUNDERING TRANSACTIONS

The following manipulations may appear in any of the above categories of laundering schemes. These transactions may be used singly in the simple schemes or in combination in the serial schemes.

Loans

Illicit funds are invested into a shell or legitimate company under the guise of a loan. The loans and the ownership of the premises may be in the names of nominees. In these cases, the loans are fictitious, but justify paybacks, interest, and the other financial advantages derived from loaning money to a business.

Loan-Back Schemes

Loan-back schemes are more interesting in that they make use of the tax loopholes offered to foreign investors. Criminal enterprises loan funds to different branches of their own corporate network, but earn tax-deductible interest on the funds. Usually in these schemes, money is loaned by an offshore shell company to a company in Canada. The funds (with interest) are later paid back to the shell company.

Sale of Businesses Once Used to Launder Funds

This is a simple and very effective profit-making scheme. On the books, these businesses will show a considerable profit, and therefore the sale price will be much more than what the criminal originally paid for the business. New buyers may wonder what they are doing wrong when they find themselves unable to generate the same level of profit. The launderer will have gained by having bought the business with illicit funds; continuously used the business to launder funds through with the legitimate profit; and sold the business for a profit—again resulting in "cleaned" proceeds.

Invoicing Schemes

Sometimes the term "double invoicing" is used in the general sense of invoice manipulation. These schemes work best if the criminal organization controls all of the process—the domestic corporation as well as the offshore corporation. Falsified paper can flow back and forth indicating shipments of goods, costs incurred, sales made—whatever will give the appearance of a profit-generating business arrangement. While in some cases "goods" are actually sent and received, in other cases it is a mere paper exchange that results in the repatriation of illicit money to Canada. One particular scheme involves arrangements whereby goods are bought at inflated prices, with the difference between the inflated price and the real value being the proceeds of crime, which are then deposited offshore. Two separate sets of books are kept. The Canadian company will have invoices indicating high prices and therefore taxable profits. The foreign books may record the actual amounts and real costs. The existence of these two conflicting sets of books poses few problems for the criminals due to the difficulty that law enforcement still has in policing across foreign jurisdictions.

Laundered Funds as Salaries

In one case, a video store was in the business of laundering funds for clients. Illicit funds would be picked up from the clients and run through the video store as sales over a period of time. On a regular basis, salary cheques would be made out for the "employees." The video store set rules to maintain an appearance of credibility. Each client could launder to a maximum of only $60,000 per year, so that the salary was realistic. The launderers kept 25 percent as a commission.

VULNERABLE BUSINESSES AND FINANCIAL INSTITUTIONS

A study of the case material from Canada, Australia, and the United States indicates that similar vulnerable financial and business institutions are being used by money launderers. In some instances, the activity is facilitated by the nature of the legitimate operation; in others there exists a regulatory or enforcement gap that is exploited by the launderers. The following functions have been identified in the Canadian report *Tracing of Illicit Funds* (Beare and Schneider 1990), the Australian National Crime Authority report *Taken to the Cleaners: Money Laundering in Australia* (Australia 1991), and separate U.S. reports including the *Assessment of Narcotics-Related Money Laundering* (FinCEN):[6]

- lawyers and accountants

- deposit-taking institutions

- securities industry

- currency-exchange houses

- real estate

- incorporation and operation of companies

- casino operations

- Miscellaneous

  ▸ precious items

  ▸ cults and marathons

  ▸ insurance and travel industry

PROFESSIONAL ASSISTANCE

Lawyers

Sophisticated laundering schemes often involve the services of professionals such as lawyers and accountants. In some of the most notorious cases, the lawyer has been involved in both the creation and implementation of the schemes (and, of course, at the stage of defending the suspect if charged). The lawyer can operate either knowingly as an accomplice in the laundering scheme or as an innocent facilitator.

The 1986 U.S. Commission on Organized Crime spoke directly of "renegade" or "mob-connected" lawyers. In 1985, former U.S. Attorney General Edwin Meese equated professional money launderers to "fences" used by burglars: "They provide a service to the thieves to hide or conceal illegal money. It takes a professional—a lawyer, an accountant, a banker, with all the trappings of respectability—to manipulate these sophisticated schemes" (*Organized Crime Digest*, June 1985, 1. Quoted in Beare and Schneider 1990, 308).

According to the 1987 Australian Fitzgerald report, entitled *Possible Illegal Activities and Associated Police Misconduct,*

> ... it is plain that a wide variety of persons and organizations engaged in legitimate activities are prepared to assist those who are known or suspected of involvement in illegal activities. Those who were shown to have assisted included solicitors, accountants, officers of banks and financial institutions, and real estate agents.[7]

One is struck by the willingness of otherwise law-abiding persons to facilitate criminal activity. Beyond the motivation of greed, there is some concern that the work of "lawyering" within a self-regulated profession places lawyers in too close of a relationship with criminals. Over time, a lawyer may increasingly perceive situations from the client's perspective, and by accepting the justifications of the client be blinded to the true source of the client's proceeds. At the more extreme end of lawyer corruption is the unique "specialization" within law whereby individuals voluntarily become criminals by involving themselves intimately in the laundering schemes of their clients, hence becoming the Mob's money launderer.

At what point does a lawyer who assists criminals in carrying out their legal (if not illegal) dealings become a mobster? In 1966, *Time* was sued for libel by Frank Ragano after the magazine printed a photograph showing Ragano at a restaurant having dinner with major Mafia bosses from Miami, New Orleans, and New York. Ragano had by this time been acting as a lawyer for the Mafia for over 10 years, and yet he expressed shock at being characterized in this manner. At the trial, Robert Blakey, testifying on behalf of *Time*, stated that, "When a lawyer showed up at night to post bail for Mafia figures and defended them at grand jury hearings, you can assume he's in bed with them" (quoted in Ragano and Raab 1994, 247). Blakey based his contention that Ragano was a "house counsel" and "functional part" of Cosa Nostra on the lawyer's long association and frequent social meetings with Santo Trafficante. Although the jury acknowledged that there was no evidence Ragano was a mobster, it returned a verdict in favour of *Time* because no malice on the part of the magazine had been proven and because Ragano had suffered no financial loss. In fact, Ragano admits that the notoriety gained from the publicity of his being mob-connected improved his law business.

The Canadian and the Australian money laundering reports cited earlier identify the following as laundering "services" that are offered by lawyers:[8]

- providing a nominee function;

- incorporating companies;

- conducting commercial and financial transactions;

- managing and physically handling illicit cash;

- coordinating international transactions; and

- buying and selling real estate.

While each of these functions is important, the lawyer's ability to act on behalf of, and in the name of the client in a nominee role is extremely useful. This nominee function can be performed in tandem with the lawyer's execution of commercial and financial transactions using illicit funds. A lawyer thus performs multiple functions in assisting the criminal operation.

Gary Hendin is one of Canada's most famous "professional" money launderers. Now a disbarred lawyer, Hendin pleaded guilty to charges involving the laundering of $12 million over a three-year period (Beare and Schneider 1990, 318–19). While this figure no longer holds any record for the size of the transactions, the diversity of the scheme remains instructive. The flowchart that the police developed for this case (see Figure 4.1) illustrates the benefits of a multilayered scheme. Hendin operated under the auspices of a construction company; purchased real estate; made use of a currency-exchange house; opened law-practice trust accounts for the criminal proceeds; registered a mortgage against properties; and used a tax-haven country as the source of the funds (the source company was owned and controlled by the criminal organization).

Lawyers constitute a powerful lobby group that has been granted special privileges argued to be necessary in order to protect the privileged relationship between lawyers and their clients. In October 1989, the U.S. Internal Revenue Service launched a national operation (the "Attorney's Project") that targeted lawyers for their failure to provide details about their cash-paying clients. Certified letters were sent initially to over 2400 lawyers. Failure to file a Form 8300 is a felony offence in the United States. Lawyers have argued that this filing violates their attorney–client privileges (*Money Laundering Alert* 1989, vol. 1, no. 3).

Similar resistance took place in Canada when the Money Laundering Act (Bill C-89) was introduced. In 1991, the Council of the Canadian Bar Association (CBA) passed the following resolution:

> *Whereas* the Minister of State (Finance) has introduced Bill C-89, the Proceeds of Crime (Money Laundering) Act, which would *seriously undermine the independence of the legal profession and the integrity and confidentiality of the lawyer-client relationship* and which would create a grave strict liability offence whose elements will be defined by regulation;
>
> *Be It Resolved That* The Canadian Bar Association urge the federal government to withdraw immediately Bill C-89;
>
> *Be It Further Resolved That* The Canadian Bar Association urge the federal government to consult with the legal profession before reintroducing any similar legislation to ensure that the independence of the profession and the integrity of the lawyer-client relationship are preserved (Canadian Bar Association 1991, 47).

The legislation was passed following negotiations with the CBA. The automatic claim of lawyer–client privilege is interesting given that the legislation in question requires only that records be kept of transactions over $10,000 cash "to be paid or transferred on another's behalf."

Even with appropriate legislation in place, police cases involving lawyers are particularly problematic. The 1985 President's Commission on Organized Crime emphasized the need for "sting" operations, undercover agents, and electronic surveillance in order to break through the attorney–client privilege, "an impenetrable shield protecting lawyers who engage in a wide variety of criminal actions" (quoted in Beare and Schneider, 1990, 331). In Canada, court cases in the early 1990s have served to illustrate the increasing difficulties the police face as they

F I G U R E   4 . I

Flowchart of a Gary Hendin Money Laundering Operation

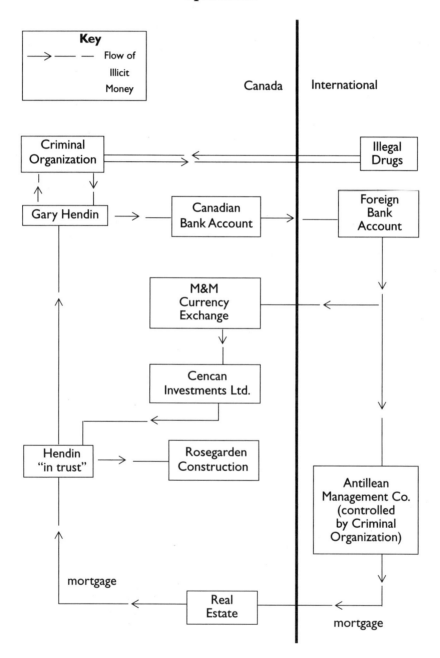

Reprinted by permission of the RCMP.

attempt to build cases against lawyers. As a result of Charter of Rights court decisions, such as *Duarte v. The Queen,* authorizations are now required for the electronic surveillance of private communications. The fear is that judges signing the authorizations, and lawyers helping the police to prepare the authorization requests, may be hesitant to target lawyers.

This fear may be unfounded. While police experiences vary across Canada, there is some evidence that the legal profession has reached a point of wanting to expurge from its ranks criminal, compromised, or incompetent lawyers. Police investigations may be the only means of catching these lawyers given the limitations of the self-regulatory procedures established by provincial law societies that claim they lack the resources needed for spontaneous or random audits. In 1994, the Law Society of Ontario reported that it had to raise $122 million to meet claims against crooked or sloppy lawyers whose actions had cost their clients money (*Globe and Mail,* May 27, 1994, p. A1).

In their study of deviance within the law profession, Reasons and Chappell (1985) conclude that conditions are not likely to change until the profession is viewed in the same way other groups of business entrepreneurs are viewed. Much of the criminal and unethical behaviour within the profession is facilitated by the economic and political power that lawyers enjoy. According to Reasons and Chappell,

> Debate among the legal fraternity about professional deviance has focused on teaching ethics in law school, tougher standards of admission, reducing the number of lawyers, and increasing the policing of lawyers. A greater recognition of [lawyers'] power by the public at large ... could well result in pressures for the state to do more to control the legal profession as another form of business (222).

In addition to serving as either willing or unsuspecting accomplices in the laundering activities, lawyers may undertake the legal defence of their clients in proceeds of crime/money laundering court cases. A sophisticated and expensive defence is generally required for these often long and complicated trials. Debate continues as to whether lawyers' fees should be exempt from the seizure and forfeiture provisions of a country's proceeds of crime/anti-organized crime legislation. The United States does not exempt the fees, but Australia (except Queensland) and Canada do, amid continuing controversy.

Accountants
The role played by lawyers tends to overshadow the involvement of other white-collar professionals in money laundering. However,

they are not alone. Accountants not only advise criminal organizations on their illicit business affairs, but are increasingly important sources of information on legitimate opportunities that can serve some illicit purpose, assist in laundering funds, or actually make additional profit as a legitimate operation.

Corporations, police departments, and governments have increasingly had to turn to private forensic accounting firms to trace the illicit profits of criminals. A high-profile ex-assistant commissioner of the RCMP, the former commissioner of the RCMP, and several other senior officers were recently hired to head the forensic investigative/accounting divisions within the key prestigious forensic accounting firms in Canada. These men, along with numerous retired police officers, are assuming responsibility for an area of police investigations that public police can no longer afford to do—the long, complex, financial cases in which a private business or corporation may be the "victim." Experienced police officers with knowledge in financial investigations are a well paid and courted commodity. Although their cases tend to focus on corporate fraud, money laundering and money-hiding schemes are also a part of this private policing world.

A recently acknowledged difficulty arises when it is discovered (sometimes only after going into court) that members of the same large international accounting firms are involved with both the defence and the prosecution in the same case. As well, forensic accountants are often used in court as "expert witnesses." Care must be taken to avoid the perception of there being a conflict of interest if these "experts" are hired to verify work completed by a member of their own firm—or worse still, to be asked to cast an opinion on the potentially criminal conduct of an affiliated member.

DISPOSING OF THE BULK CASH

The initial stage in the laundering process, known as the *conversion* or *placement* stage, involves disposing of suspicious, often large quantities of small denominations of cash. The greater the laundering needs, the more vulnerable the criminal. It is at this stage that frontline players such as bank tellers, car dealers, brokers, and casino operators become critically important to the process of controlling the money laundering. It is also essential that a record trail (audit or paper trail) begin at this point.

Recent debate has centred on whether transaction records should be reported to some centralized body. U.S. and Australian legislation requires the *reporting* of transactions over $10,000; Canadian legislation requires the *recording* of similar transactions. All three countries have in place a "suspicious transaction" process (either mandatory or voluntary) whereby financial institutions or businesses are encouraged to notify law enforcement of any transactions that seem irregular or unjustified by logical business transactions. As laundering schemes change, so must employees' perceptions of what constitutes a "suspicious" transaction. Britain has introduced new laws that require solicitors, accountants, and other professionals to report suspicious transactions to the National Criminal Intelligence Service. However, the findings from the 1994 Police Foundation of Wales study (Gold and Levi 1994) indicated that the United Kingdom's suspicion-based transactions-reporting system was having only a limited impact on the control or detection of laundering.

Several countries (in some cases encouraged by the work of the Financial Action Task Force) have gradually recognized that banks are not the only places where "banking" occurs. Other financial institutions and businesses must also be brought under greater regulation. The U.S. Money Laundering Suppression Act of 1994 requires that nonbank financial institutions such as American Express and Western Union (and other institutions that handle cheque cashing, money orders, traveller's cheques, and wire transfers) must follow the anti-money laundering regulations.

In August 1994, two bankers for American Express Bank International—a unit of American Express Co.—were sentenced to five- and ten-year prison terms on charges of conspiracy and money laundering (*Wall Street Journal* 1994). In November 1994, American Express Co. settled for US $32 million in exchange for the dropping of criminal charges (the settlement totalled $35.20 million). The total of $40 million in drug profits that the government seized is said to have made this the largest prosecuted money laundering case by any country (*Vancouver Sun* 1994). There is disagreement over the extent to which the banking arm of American Express Co. cooperated during an investigation that involved a large Mexican drug cartel, Colombian cocaine, and the Cayman Islands. Banks may have on paper compliance policies that are not emphasized (or possibly even tolerated) in practice. The following chart indicates the five largest U.S. bank settlements in money laundering cases.

Canada's Money Laundering Act, which requires the keeping of certain records, extends beyond financial institutions to include businesses and lawyers that accept cash on behalf of a third person. This expansion beyond the more narrow confines of traditional financial transactions has been called the "new frontier" of money laundering enforcement (*Economist* June 25, 1994, p. 81).

Legislation may be helping to curtail money laundering, but criminals have proven themselves infinitely capable of adjusting their activities to avoid risks as law enforcement efforts are enhanced. Various mechanisms have not stopped structuring (or "smurfing") whereby money is deposited in numerous transactions that fall under the $10,000 threshold. Organizational corruption and currency smuggling out of the country are other continuing problems. The U.S. Office of the Comptroller of the Currency issued new guidelines in 1993, while the U.S. customs service initiated a project called Operation Buckstop whose aim was to determine the extent and the nature of currency smuggling and to seize unreported outbound currency between 1989 and 1992.[9]

U.S. officials have expressed concern that Canada offers an "easier" border due to the lack of border currency reporting similar to the U.S. CMIR requirements (U.S. Customs Form 4790 Report of International Transportation of Currency and Monetary Instruments). These forms require that over $10K in or out of the United States must result in a record/report. However, the jury is still out on what system works best. A 1994 U.S. General Accounting Office report documents the extent to which the American system fails to prevent the smuggling of currency over the U.S. border. Operation Buckstop seized over $171 million, a minuscule amount compared to how much must be exiting to fuel the Colombian cartel cocaine sales alone. Large quantities of cash are circumventing the formal recording mechanism. The report concluded that the amount of smuggled currency cannot be determined because of the clandestine nature of the criminal activity. Regardless of the amount, the smuggling of cash is undermining the country's efforts to combat money laundering.

The lesson we learn from each new piece of legislation or regulation is that the criminal's reaction to law enforcement can be immediate and dramatic. While law enforcement and government tend to become "comfortable" with certain ways of operating, the criminal remains flexible—prepared to capitalize on whatever gaps remain and to shift away from activities that become too risky. For example, when U.S. police froze $61.8 million in Medellin cartel drug money that was being held in European bank accounts, the cartel responded by reducing the standing balances within the accounts by 90 percent and by increasing the number of accounts—actions all aimed at reducing the risk of doing business (FinCEN 1992, 30).

New routes, partnerships, and smuggling techniques all attest to the criminal's ingenuity. Launderers, fearing to use the U.S. banks due to the Bank Secrecy Act reporting requirements, began to use money orders purchased through such agencies as the postal service, American Express, and Thomas Cook. "Smurfs"[10] bought these money orders in amounts under $10,000 and smuggled them out of the United States. The U.S. Postal Service and the DEA developed software that the Federal Reserve Bank used to identify the Hong Kong Shanghai Bank of Panama as the preferred destination for these money orders. The bank's correspondent account at the Marine Midland Bank in New York was then frozen by government officials—an action that forced the Panama bank to refuse to accept all postal money orders arriving from the United States (Andelman 1994). One door closes, but others are quickly opened as new laundering schemes emerge.

DEPOSIT-TAKING INSTITUTIONS

Research by Beare and Schneider (1990) indicates that Canadian deposit-taking institutions—including chartered banks, trust companies, and credit unions—are the institutions that are used most frequently by money launderers. Although this research was carried out before the bank record-keeping provisions of the Money Laundering Act came into force in 1993, there is no indication that launderers are staying away from banks. The services that have been identified include:

- wire transfers and negotiable instruments
- currency exchange
- denomination exchange
- savings deposit boxes
- government savings bonds, Treasury Bills

Police cases indicate that launderers use more than one account, more than one branch, and often more than one financial institution. The bank-record legislation may encourage launderers to use large numbers of relatively small deposits (and therefore to employ "smurfs" or money couriers) in order to avoid triggering the $10,000 cash deposit record-keeping requirement.

Launderers "work" bank officials by attempting to establish reliable, trustworthy, and wealthy personae. This has become increasingly important following the implementation of "know your customer" policies that encourage bank employees to gain greater knowledge of financial operations and businesses of their regular customers. While some cases have involved the exploitation of unwitting or naive bank officials, others have involved corruption on the part of branch officials. In one instance, over $12 million was laundered through a caisse populaire in Montreal using an account registered in the name of the caisse itself. Police cases also indicate that launderers make use of branches of Canadian banks in tax-haven countries for national or international criminal operations.

The early 1990s witnessed several high-profile cases that introduced the public to the world of international high finance, intrigue, and greed. The Bank of Credit and Commerce (BCCI) scandal and the corruption surrounding the Vatican Bank became front-page news and highlighted the need for greater accountability in a banking system that was being turned into a criminal revenue-generating operation.[11] The transactions of the Banco Ambrosiano involved disguised export-finance deals, fraudulent securities sales, tax-haven bank loans, and shell companies—all of which generated enough cash for payoffs to the Vatican Bank, illegal funding to political parties, payments to Pope John Paul II's favourite charities, secret Swiss bank accounts for the key financial manipulators and friends, and funds for Italian fascist societies (Naylor 1987, 83). In June 1994, the founder and 11 officials were convicted in Abu Dhabi.

"Banks" proper, as stated before, are not the only deposit-taking institutions open to these criminal activities. Beginning in 1987, Canadian banks were allowed to own investment dealers. The "4 Pillars" (banks, securities, trusts, and insurance) of the financial industry are quickly moving toward conglomerate status. Coupled with the internationalization of the securities market and the merging of previously separate and competing firms, the industry is obviously changing rapidly. Although regulations still exist to maintain at least an illusion of separateness, their long-term survival is questionable. One hears of a "wall of secrecy" or "Chinese wall" that supposedly precludes the sharing of client information between banks and their securities operations. However, with common reception rooms, common management, and consent forms through which clients can agree to have their information shared among firms, the walls may have little actual substance.

And what happens to the "know your customer" policies—policies that have been put in place specifically to reduce money laundering—once banks are linked with other services that may have quite different priorities? For example, discount brokerage services operated by the Royal Bank of Canada, the Bank of Montreal, and Toronto-Dominion Bank take orders to buy and sell securities 24 hours per day, seven days per week. Paul Bates, the President of "Green Line Investor Services Inc" (operated by Toronto-Dominion Bank) stated:

> Our clients choose us because they want speed and cheap trades and accuracy ... We had access to brokers around the clock since 1984. The next step was the addition of trading via a client's computer. In the last year, we have enhanced this service. Now you can trade during the night on world exchanges that happen to be open—London for example—in the small hours of the Canadian morning (*Globe and Mail,* July 26, 1994, p. B20).

The frills that these discount brokers have dispensed with include the "know your client" relationships that the banks have attempted to put into place. Discount brokers do not encourage clients to form relationships with their order takers (*Globe and Mail,* July 26, 1994, p. B20). Table 4.1 provides a list of the banks and their affiliated financial institutions.

It may be too early to predict the unanticipated uses to which these convenient services will be put by sophisticated organized criminals and their experienced lawyers. For example, concerns might be raised about the "private banking" services that are being offered to wealthy clients.

As Alan McLaughlin, vice-president of investment services at RBC Dominion Securities and manager of Royal Bank of Canada "Suite 200" in Winnipeg, stated, "Because this is a private banking centre, we're dealing largely with affluent clients, often with sophisticated knowledge and rather complex needs" (*Globe and Mail,* July 26, 1994, p. B20). Some of these confidential and less-visible services may be used to facilitate the laundering of criminal proceeds.

The banks, having bought into the concept that organized crime and money laundering are bad for their businesses, have been educating their frontline staff to detect suspicious transactions. Cash transactions have been made problematic for criminals by the Money Laundering Act. Some of the concerns we might have regarding the combining of separate financial services involve the movement of money *after* it has already undergone initial laundering out of its small denomination cash form. However, the securities companies—even the discount opera-

TABLE 4.1

The Bankers' Research

Bank	Full-service broker	Discount broker	Major trust company	Mutual funds
Bank of Montreal	Nesbitt Burns* (Nesbitt Thomson and Burns Fry)	InvestorLine	Bank of Montreal	First Canadian
Bank of Nova Scotia	Scotia McLeod	Scotia Securities	Montreal Trust	Montreal Trust funds, Scotia funds
CIBC	Wood Gundy	Investors Edge	CIBC Trust	CIBC funds, Hyperion, Talvest
National Bank	Lévesque Beaubien	National Bank Securities	General Trust, NatCan	NatCan funds
Royal Bank	RBC Dominion Securities (took over McNeil Mantha too)	Action Direct	Royal Trust	Royal Trust funds, Royfund
Toronto-Dominion	Evergreen Investment	Green Line (has bought Marathon)	TD Trust (took over Central Guaranty)	Green Line funds
Hong Kong Bank	none	none	none	Hong Kong Bank funds
Laurentian Bank	BLC Rousseau (formerly Select Securities)	none	Laurentian Trust	Laurentian funds

*pending

tions—must still generate a paper trail, and the currency will tend to be cheques or accounts rather than cash. This paper trail may make these services a less attractive tool to launderers. In addition, the one-stop-shopping aspect might be seen as putting too much "paper" traceable in one location.[12]

In addition to formal or semiformal banks, the launderer may also choose to support a parallel banking network of "underground" operations. According to the DEA (United States 1993) the *hawala* or *hundi* underground banking systems originating in Pakistan and India, as well as similar underground systems used by the ethnic Chinese criminal organizations, are assuming an increasingly important role. If any "paper" is kept at all, the hawala broker may maintain a coded ledger. Faxes are sent acknowledging the crediting of an account, but in most cases no actual money moves. The system operates on trust and on the principle of the balancing of accounts around the world. In situations where more currency is being credited than paid, gold, silver, or actual currency may be smuggled in to restore the equilibrium.

Along the same lines as the underground systems, but using a higher level of technology, is the concept of "cyberspace banking" (*Money Laundering Alert*, April 1995, vol. 6, no. 7). In October 1994, First Virtual Holdings opened for business in Cheyenne, Wyoming; the First Bank of Internet opened in March 1995. Enforcement and regulatory agencies are being warned that this "banking" mechanism could be the next popular tool of the money launderer.

THE SECURITIES MARKET

There are two main ways in which the securities market is exploited by launderers: (1) criminals can directly invest illicit proceeds by buying securities through a brokerage firm; or (2) proceeds of crime can be invested in a private company that then goes public and issues shares. While police cases indicate that the former is the more common route, police may become more aware of the second route as they increasingly focus on the legitimate businesses that criminals are linking to their empires. Similarly, in addition to what have typically been included as "organized crimes," the profits from insider trading, market-manipulation offences, and other financial frauds can be laundered through securities investments.

In July 1994, the RCMP seized $1 million worth of stocks held on account at a Vancouver brokerage house. These funds were part of an $8-million tax fraud in Luxembourg. By issuing dummy invoices the individual evaded paying tax, which he then deposited at the main branch of the Bank of Montreal in Vancouver.

These funds were used to buy shares in three VSE-listed companies. Whether or not this qualifies as strict money laundering is debatable. Perhaps even worse than being accused of facilitating money laundering, it has been argued that launderers tend to steer clear of the Vancouver Stock Exchange (VSE) because of its relative instability. The argument being that money launderers may be criminals but they are not stupid! According to Jim Matkin, a lawyer who conducted a provincial government probe into the operation of the VSE:

> The irony is that the VSE's bad reputation ... is one reason [money laundering is] less of a problem here than in New York. The crooks aren't going to risk their money on the VSE stock that might fall out of the sky. They want to buy Microsoft. They don't want to put laundered money into risky, volatile, speculative investments (*Globe and Mail,* July 29, 1994, pp. B1, B6).

Securities brokerage accounts have many of the advantages of a bank account while providing unique securities-related services. Police cases from the United States indicate the complexity of some of these securities-based laundering and profit-generating schemes. One involved the exploitation of a local Teamsters union and the use of an insider in the securities firm. The individuals who controlled the union's resources set up with a securities firm a trading account in the name of the union and separate accounts in the names of their friends and relatives. Securities were purchased and held in the account for a number of days. If the securities rose in value, they were transferred to the accounts of friends and relatives; if the securities lost money, they were transferred to the Teamsters account. The transfers were accomplished by using "trade error correction request" forms (Edelhertz and Overcast 1993, 89). While this activity is more accurately characterized as fraudulent profit generation than as money laundering, the degree of insider assistance points to a considerable laundering potential. International markets now operate 24 hours a day, which opens the legitimate business sphere to 24-hour-a-day international laundering.

A 1992 U.S. Senate report confirms that the globalization of the securities business is making brokerage firms rather than banks the "venue of choice for money laundering" (*Wall Street Journal* 1994). In September 1994, a U.S. joint task force project called El Dorado targeted several Wall Street brokerage firms on suspicion that some of their brokers were laundering illegal drug proceeds. Customer accounts totalling over $10 million were seized at Merrill Lynch, Dean Witter Discoverer, Prudential Securities, and Paine-Webber. Wall Street brokers were accused of accepting suspicious wire transfers, knowingly investing the illicit profits, and creating questionable tax-advantageous trusts and offshore corporations under conditions that should have seemed suspicious. In Canadian cases such as this, the Crown must demonstrate that the firms were "willfully blind" to the source of their clients' funds.

CURRENCY-EXCHANGE HOUSES

Notorious foreign-exchange houses frustrated the efforts of the police across Canada prior to the introduction of the Money Laundering Act. While banks in Canada tend to be highly regulated, the foreign-exchange houses were recognized as a gap within the financial system. These currency-exchange houses may be nothing more sophisticated than a storefront operation, but the existence of legitimate and international exchange houses enables the industry itself to maintain a degree of legitimacy when dealing with deposit-taking institutions. Police cases indicate that currency-exchange houses often served as the intermediary stage between the criminal and the banking institutions, particularly for the purchase of negotiable instruments and wire transfers. While these services would have to be purchased through an official bank, the currency-exchange house would become the "client," thereby enabling the criminal client to maintain a protective distance from the banks.

Converting American currency into Canadian (and vice versa) and converting small drug-dealing denominations into larger, less suspicious denominations are two popular services offered by exchange houses. The American currency serves as an international currency for some drug-trafficking operations and, as such, is required to make drug payments or purchase additional shipments of drugs internationally. As we will see later in Chapter 7, the Neeb/Brook criminal operation used the Friedberg Currency Exchange House in Toronto to convert millions of dollars from Canadian to U.S. currency.

Police cases over the years have indicated both the use and direct participation of exchange houses in drug-laundering schemes. In 1994, RCMP Integrated Anti-Drug Profiteering (IADP) Units in Montreal, Vancouver, and Toronto, in concert with other RCMP ADP units, carried out a nationwide coordinated undercover operation targeted at currency-exchange houses. RCMP officers, often posing as drug traffickers, exchanged large amounts of what should have qualified as "suspicious" cash. Because of the quantities involved, these should have been "recorded" transactions as outlined in the *Proceeds of Crime Money Laundering Act* (1991; regulations to the Act became law

March 26, 1993). Over the course of the undercover operation, the police exchanged a total of $3 million, including individual amounts up to $70,000. On the morning of June 21, 1994, search warrants were executed at 32 locations in Vancouver, Victoria, Calgary, Edmonton, Toronto, Montreal, and Quebec City. According to the RCMP, approximately 190 criminal charges—including money laundering offences—involving 36 corporations and 65 persons were anticipated.[13]

THE REAL-ESTATE INDUSTRY

Laundering schemes involving real estate can involve extremely simple purchases whereby the source of the proceeds are hidden by the sheer volume of transactions. More complex schemes involve the investment in undeveloped industrial and residential properties and the subsequent development of these properties—often with illicit proceeds funnelled through a complex of international lending institutions involving tax-haven countries, crooked lawyers, and shell companies. In addition, since criminals usually like to live in a style that reflects their income, homes and seasonal recreational facilities are purchased for private use.

Real-estate agents, mortgage-broker firms, and development/construction companies all assist (either knowingly or innocently) the criminal in laundering through real estate. Cases from the United States indicate that real-estate agents have worked aggressively with organized criminals to identify businesses that can be used as fronts for other illegal activities. They have also filled out leases in the names of nominal owners of liquor and adult-entertainment businesses in circumstances where the real owners did not have a sufficiently clean record to obtain the licences (Edelhertz and Overcast 1993, 88).

In July 1994, a major DEA/RCMP/Vancouver police drug investigation resulted in the seizure of U.S. properties totalling approximately $57 million, and a possible $300 million in assets worldwide. Properties valued at over $15.8 million were seized in British Columbia. Over 60 police officers from Vancouver Police department and the RCMP were involved in executing the warrants and restraining the property, which consisted of roughly 15 vessels and boats and seven real-estate properties.

This case is considered to be one of the largest asset-seizure case since the Proceeds of Crime legislation came into force in 1989. The seized funds and properties have been handed over to the Seized Property Management Directorate for the mammoth task of managing the properties pending their disposal after conviction. Seized assets, it must be emphasized, are not the equivalent of forfeited assets. This case will have to work its way through the courts before anyone knows the value of the illicit proceeds. It was perhaps with a little too much optimism that the RCMP wrote in its *Press Note* "asset sharing anticipated January '95."

CORPORATIONS

Increasingly, police are having to weave their financial investigations through numerous seemingly legitimate corporations in order to trace the illicit proceeds of criminals. Again, the infamous Neeb/Brook "Spaghetti Jungle" case illustrates the extreme complexity of some of these criminal enterprises. In this case, the drug-trafficking organization incorporated 14 companies in Canada (over 100 corporations in total, with 64 Canadian corporations worldwide) to facilitate the laundering of the drug proceeds. Analysts working their way through the maze of corporations and financial relationships in these cases would marvel at Gottfredson and Hirschi's confident rejection of the structure and sophistication ascribed to major organized crime operations—calling them a mere "illusion of organization" (1990, 213)! (See Chapter 7.)

When we speak of launderers using corporations, we mean both shell companies and legitimate companies. In many of the complex schemes, both types of corporations are combined to facilitate the laundering. Legitimate businesses and corporations can launder proceeds on an ongoing basis within Canada. Businesses that are cash-generating and have a fairly loose inventory are particularly attractive to launderers. Thus, actual laundries are good for "laundering" small amounts of illicit proceeds, since there is flexibility in the amount of legitimate business and therefore flexibility in what can be claimed as legitimate income that would be generated per week, month, or year. A figure can be established for income-tax purposes, and a large percentage of it can be made up of illicit proceeds "cleaned" along with clients' shirts!

Taverns, restaurants, and other entertainment facilities provide the same advantages and also serve as a hangout or office for the organized criminals. Among the transactions that police have identified in money laundering schemes involving corporations are loan-back schemes, phoney business flips, invoice manipulation, and "no job" salaried employees.

LEGALIZED GAMING AND CASINO OPERATIONS

To date, legalized gaming laundering schemes in Canada—at least detected ones—have not been numerous. The relative lack of cases is no cause for complacency. Racetracks, bingos, carnivals, Monte Carlo night events, and casino operations across Canada may be used for minor laundering schemes involving a fairly low ceiling. In one intricate racetrack laundering case, involving collusion with track wicket cashiers, winning tickets were sold for value plus a percentage; the "winnings" were then claimed as a legitimate source of funds. The newly established casinos all have the potential to be vulnerable to larger and more imaginative schemes. Gaming facilities tend to be "cash" businesses. The presence of cash combined with loose credit policies and imprecise record-keeping at the chip cashing and sales areas presents opportunities for launderers to exchange denominations and claim proceeds of crime to be legitimate winnings. It also provides an arena for related criminal activities such as loansharking, drug trafficking, and skimming operations.

The British Columbia Lottery Corp halted a popular game called "Sports Action over/under" in October 1994 because of suspicions that it was being used by money launderers (*Globe and Mail* October 27, 1994). The corporation feared that criminal proceeds were behind the extraordinary amount of wagering (six times the normal). The game pays back 60 to 70 percent of the money bet, an adequate nontaxed rate of return on "dirty" money. The earnings would be "clean" with the required stubs to prove winnings. The Lottery Corp became suspicious the previous summer when the RCMP raided a mansion during a drug investigation and found piles of unclaimed winning lottery tickets that could be turned in for cash any time within a year of purchase. In 1993, the regular "BC49" lottery was temporarily closed down when police feared someone was trying to buy up (possibly with criminal proceeds) all possible winning number combinations.

Concern for organized crime infiltration of gaming is often focussed on casino gambling. In Canada, organized crime casino takeovers are less likely than the prospect of organized criminals availing themselves of casino services. There are ways, however, of minimizing this threat. According to the Parliamentary Joint Committee in Australia,

> Thorough financial, gaming chip, cash handling and cheque issue procedures can virtually eliminate the problem of money laundering" (Grey 1992, 5).

> ... [It is] the discipline imposed upon the industry both by state regulation and by the federal reporting arrangement that makes the environment for systematic ongoing money laundering a pretty difficult process (Pinner 1992, 8).

Although in Canada the same law enforcement priority is given to tracking the proceeds of crime and targeting the money laundering process, we have not put in place at the federal level all of the legislative pieces that are deemed by some critics to be required to protect casinos from use by launderers. Record-keeping and cash-reporting legislation applies to casinos in Australia and the United States, but not to those in Canada—a situation the federal government is currently reviewing.

In Canada, the casinos themselves must take the initiative when it comes to preventing organized crime and money laundering. Even in the absence of federal legislation that covers casino financial transactions, Windsor and Winnipeg take the view that casinos are performing "like a bank" and are therefore subject to the record-keeping provisions outlined in the Money Laundering Act. On the other hand, Montreal takes the position that casinos are not required to maintain records under the current federal legislation and regulations. This is not to say that no paper trail is generated in Montreal, but rather to indicate that there is a lack of uniformity across the country.

While not an ideal method of laundering, the high-stakes slots and tables provide an opportunity to launder cash. For example, the $500 slot machine has a payout of 97.4 percent (with 90 percent confidence over 100 000 tries). With some risk involved, this machine might launder money at a cheaper rate than the going street-laundering price. On the street, it costs the sophisticated money launderer from 6 percent for the small operation to 30 percent for the large multimillion-dollar operation. From a regulatory and enforcement position, the machines themselves are not criminogenic, but there must be a paper trail and surveillance created when the customer buys the tokens so that the final payout cannot be portrayed to be a large win based on a lucky token or two.

Paper trails are essential to the prevention of money laundering. Casino customers must not be allowed to buy $200,000 worth of chips with dirty cash, wander around the casino for a period, cash in the chips, and receive a casino cheque that serves as a legitimate source for the income.

To reduce the opportunities for organized crime, casinos must have the legal recourse to exclude known criminals from their facilities. There is no uniform policy on this matter among Canadian casinos. One casino takes the position that as long as customers do not violate the integrity of the games or break the law during the time they spend in the casino, then there is nothing that the casino management can or should do to interfere with their gambling. Criminal patrons may also be the high-roller customers that casinos strive to attract. These players will be excluded only if the casino has in place a policy that sets the maintenance of a crime-free environment above the economic benefits to be derived from catering to these criminally financed individuals.

> Either through legislation or regulations, the casino must create a paper trail that will assist in the detection and investigation of money laundering.
>
> "Suspicious transaction" reporting to a law enforcement agency should be mandated by casino policy.

Law enforcement and casino security must be well trained in laundering strategies, and open to the fact that launderers come from all classes and do not always match the organized criminal profile. For example, cities that acquire casinos may also enjoy a spinoff in the form of increased revenue for the local restaurants and shops. When businesses claim they have not been positively affected by having a casino in their community, they may in fact be attempting to draw the attention of Revenue Canada away from their newfound incomes. The casino may not only contribute to their revenue in terms of additional customers, but may also serve to launder the relatively small amounts of money on a continual basis for the otherwise legitimate and law-abiding businessperson.

In December 1994, the United States Treasury issued new casino rules that had to be complied with by June 1995.[14] The new rules include the following:

- In reporting cash transactions, casinos must include cash equivalents such as chips, tokens, front money deposits, cash bets, purchase of casino cheques and exchanges of currency, including foreign cash.

- The casino must keep records of customers who have purchased or redeemed slot machine tokens of more than $3,000 in a single gaming day.

- Multiple cash transactions must be treated as a single transaction, if the transactions are "by or on behalf of any person."

- If a customer's cash in or cash out transactions when aggregated exceed $10,000 in a gaming day, the casino must obtain the identification of the customer if it is "reasonably available."

As casinos increase across Canada, Federal legislation must address these same issues.

MISCELLANEOUS LAUNDERING FACILITATORS

Precious Items

The value of precious items for money launderers varies according to their distinct characteristics. For example, some items are particularly easy to smuggle. Cash in one country can be converted into gems, smuggled elsewhere, and converted back into cash or used to purchase drugs. Small, expensive items are less conspicuous and much more easily transported than large quantities of cash. In terms of actual laundering schemes, some expensive items have a value not easily ascertained by the layperson or the customs officer. Laundering schemes can involve using inflated prices for the purchase or sale of these items. Some gems, artworks, and rare coins might be used in various invoice schemes where a false price is used for laundering purposes. Gold has the benefit of a universally stable value, and is usually purchased in certificate form, coins, or wafers. Launderers can purchase gold from nonbank sources including foreign-currency exchanges and private bullion dealers.

Cults and Marathons

The fall of 1994 witnessed two bizarre (alleged) money laundering scenarios. The Solar Temple doomsday cult was accused of being a front for the laundering of funds derived from the illegal international arms trade. As the case developed following the initial deaths of some of the cult members, it soon became apparent that all of the likely orchestrators of this scheme were also dead. Although there appears to be little evidence that money laundering played a significant role in the history of the Solar Temple cult, the case did alert law enforcement to the possibilities of using a cult to facilitate a laundering scheme. When cult members donate their property and wealth to a cult, there is little or no paperwork documenting how much is handed over. This is a perfect environment for commingling the illicit proceeds of criminal activity.

The Los Angeles Marathon corporation was accused of receiving secret contributions from advertisements and then using the proceeds to contribute to the election campaigns of certain candidates. The Marathon corporation would use the secret funds to make payments to city council candidates and others around the time that the council was extending the marathon's contract. In this way, the Marathon company succeeded in giving much larger contributions to the political parties than was legal. While Marathon Corporation was found guilty of money laundering and fined $436,000, the reaction of city officials remains interesting. Several officials still praised the firm's management of the race. City councilman Zeo Yaroslavsky stated

> As a councilman and as a marathoner myself, I can say that [marathon President William Burke] runs a first-class operation. He brings 20,000 people into the city, doesn't cause any problems, cleans up promptly, and does everything he is asked to do (*Los Angeles Times* 1994, pp. B1, B4).

Other Schemes: Travel Agencies and Insurance

We emphasized throughout the *Tracing of Illicit Funds* study that the means of laundering funds seem to be limited only by the amount of professional advice, money, and corruptive power of the organization. Great assistance is provided to the laundering organization by ordinary citizens who choose not to be suspicious of gym bags full of cash for real-estate transactions, the purchase of expensive automobiles, or other commodities. The front-line salesperson is critical to reporting suspicious transactions. Service industries such as travel agencies have a legitimate need to transfer money around the world. These services can be applied to criminal operations.

In the United States, a travel agency and licensed money transmitter is considered a "financial institution" under their Bank Security Act. In late 1992, U.S. Customs Service, with help from FBI, DEA, IRS, and state and local agencies set up a sting operation targeted at World Travel Services Inc. Between February and December 1993, undercover operators supplied World Travel with large amounts of "drug" cash with instruction to wire the money to a bank account in London. Records from World Travel showed transfers of amounts under $5,000 using numerous fictitious names. An indictment seeks forfeiture of $192,000 and charges of money laundering. The owners allegedly only charged 7 percent commission for transferring drug money out of the country—including structuring the transaction and falsifying the documentation (*Money Laundering Alert* 1995, 2).

In different ways, but equally valuable to criminals, is the insurance industry. This industry involves large amounts of cash and somewhat invisible investment opportunities. Again, these legitimate functions can be used to facilitate money laundering.

THE POLICING OF MONEY LAUNDERING

There are no easy answers when it comes to combatting money laundering. There are hundreds of alternative methods for launderers to use when one method is made difficult, expensive, or impossible. There are however, some "points of convergence" through which money prefers to pass—and which cause difficulties when they are not available. If popular laundering routes are made particularly risky, criminals are adept at using alternative transactions. Here again we must appreciate an international component. Easier routes through foreign jurisdictions may be chosen if the regulations elsewhere are perceived to be more rigid.

For law enforcement, the lessons may be graver than merely demanding diligence and more of the same kinds of traditional policing abilities. Developing a worthy money laundering case involves skills, knowledge, and information sharing that we may be only on the verge of recognizing or demanding. A major handicap for the police remains an organizational structure that attaches rank to positions rather than to individuals. Police officers who develop great expertise in one area of responsibility are generally rewarded with a promotion into another area. It makes little sense for an experienced criminal intelligence officer to be transferred into traffic, or for a drug officer to be promoted into personnel work, yet this happens routinely in police departments. International enforcement tools may facilitate the sharing of intelligence between police departments, but there must be intelligence to share in the first place. How the police identify and develop their cases is still critical. If rank were assigned to individual officers, they could earn promotions and remain in the areas of policing where they have gained an expertise.

Large laundering operations must be targeted as if they were multinational corporations. Increasingly, customs agencies from diverse nations, cross-jurisdictional police forces, overseas liaison officers (customs, police, and security agencies) are having to work collaboratively on cases. Each enforcement agency brings to the collaboration its own perspective on criminal activity. When the collaboration works well, the result can be greater than the separate parts. When jealousies and turf battles occur the result may be wasted resources.

Early inquiries into organized crime in Canada emphasized what was seen to be a lack of cooperation, collaboration, and sharing among various police departments. In 1966, Claude Wagner, Quebec's former Minister of Justice, accused his federal colleagues—and specifically the RCMP—of being soft on organized crime. Normand Girard observed in *Le Soleil* that

> ... Wagner did not mince his words ... maintaining that the QPF accomplished more in a year of fighting organized crime than the RCMP had done since 1951. ... The RCMP, he said, made a great display of the grandeur, height, width, beauty,

and efficiency of its force in order to declare that it is the one which should centralize police intelligence. ... "Intelligence was discovered in Ottawa in 1951," he said mockingly (January 12, 1966).

A communiqué signed by the Federal Minister of Justice, Chairman of the Privy Council, and the Federal Attorney General defending the RCMP responded that "[t]he fight against organized crime in Canada can only be carried out with success through the cooperation of all enforcement agencies—federal, provincial and municipal—and not by creating competition amongst them (*Canadian Press,* January 14, 1966 quoted in Quebec 1970b, 127).

Competitiveness between the RCMP and municipal/provincial forces and between the police and customs is of continuing concern. However, joint-force operations are giving officers, departments, and agencies opportunities to work more collaboratively. The fiscal restraint that has characterized recent years has forced the police to pool their resources on certain cases, a practice some police officers say can only add to their effectiveness.

While recognizing the importance of sophisticated international policing strategies, we must not lose sight of traditional police work. The lessons we have learned from community-based policing in general *do* apply to money laundering. The policing strategies—which must be as diverse as the laundering schemes themselves—include:

- specially trained undercover operators and handlers of informants;

- community-based policing or a policing strategy that will ensure that police officers know their neighbourhoods and know the amount of business that a particular establishment is likely to generate over the course of a month, year, etc.;

- specially trained and special-resources "proceeds of crime investigators" (i.e., forensic accountants or police trained in doing money laundering investigations);

- in-house or access to forensic accounting skills, computer intelligence systems, and strategic analysts.

- international components—knowledge of what international regimes exist, international contacts, and specialized training in international investigations.

Large-scale investigations are almost by definition international ones involving the law enforcement efforts of numerous countries, each working its own segment of the same criminal operation. Failure on the part of one undercover operator can jeopardize an investigation not only nationally but internationally as well. Those countries that participate in collaborative cross-jurisdictional police work may not share a common legislative framework, and may not agree on what ethical standards and procedures to follow when building a case. Canadian police must determine whether the different policing practices followed by our most frequent partners should be imitated or whether there are valid reasons for following Canadian policies and procedures. At present, practices vary across Canada. One province works with, say, the DEA according to DEA rules, while another province does not. With legislation in place, the next step might be to study the policies and procedures being followed in the different jurisdictions.

OPERATION GREEN ICE

Operation Green Ice reflects some of the complexities of contemporary money laundering cases. This international case illustrates the global reach of criminal operations and the increasing globalization of some policing efforts. At the termination of a three-year undercover operation, DEA Administrator Robert Bonner stated,

> Money is the lifeblood of the cartels. It enables them to finance the manufacture, the transportation and smuggling, the distribution, the murder and intimidation that are essential to their illegal trade. Through Operation Green Ice, our nations have succeeded in choking off this vital flow of money (Press Statement 1992).

While one might be sceptical of the hype with which the DEA announced the arrests and seizures, this case yielded interesting results in terms of international cooperation. From a Canadian perspective, Green Ice represents the first tangible result generated by the newly created Integrated Anti-Drug Profiteering Units funded under Canada's Drug Strategy.

The case, headed by the DEA, combined the efforts of law enforcement officers working in the United States, Italy, Spain, Costa Rica, Colombia, United Kingdom, the Cayman Islands, and Canada—the first operational international task force formed to combat money laundering. At the end of the project's initial phase, approximately 192 arrests had been made and $54 million[15] in cash and property was seized worldwide. Bonner spoke optimistically of the "global disruption to the Cali and Medellin cartels."

The objective of the project was to infiltrate money laundering enterprises of targeted kingpin organizations run by leaders of the major Colombian cocaine cartels—particularly the Cali cartel.

FIGURE 4.2

Operation Green Ice
Money and Cocaine Routes

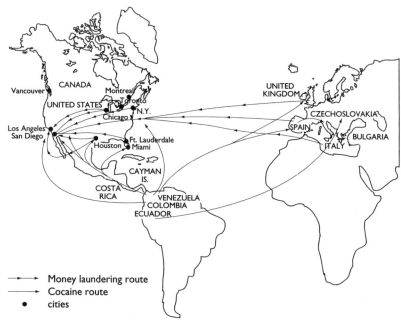

Adapted from data from the U.S. Department of Justice, Drug Enforcement Administration.

Undercover agents posed as money laundering facilitators and used informants to identify several major drug-money brokers in Colombia. These Colombian brokers acted as intermediaries between Cali cartel kingpins in Colombia and money laundering organizations in the United States.[16]

The investigations took undercover agents to Houston, Fort Lauderdale, Miami, Chicago, and New York, where they picked up money and established fronts in the form of leather shops. Drug-money profits were then laundered through the importation of merchandise that legitimized the currency held in banks in Colombia. Leather shops were chosen because Colombia is a cattle-producing country and the export and import of leather seemed a perfect cover. As the case developed, undercover agents were asked to provide money laundering services in Europe,

Canada, and the Caribbean. In the United Kingdom, Her Majesty's Customs and Excise Service was involved; in Italy, the Servico Centrale Operativo; in Spain, the National Police; in the United States, the DEA; and, in Canada, the RCMP. (See Figure 4.2.) To assist the DEA investigation, the RCMP carried out a parallel operation in Canada to accommodate the transfer of money from a Montreal-based cocaine trafficker. Three deliveries of cash totalling approximately $3 million were made to RCMP undercover operators. On September 24, 1992, $1,075,000 was subject to seizure.

As in many large-scale cases, political corruption lurked on the periphery of the action. Carlos Polania was a money laundering expert for Colombia's bank regulatory agency who taught the Colombian police how to recognize clandestine transfers. In his official capacity as a high-ranking government official, he acted as the liaison between Colombia and the DEA, U.S. Customs, and Interpol, and gained valuable information about regulatory changes that might affect laundering activity. On the side, he worked for the cartel.[17]

Perhaps most important about Operation Green Ice was the fact that it established the links between Colombian cocaine cartels and the Mafia organizations operating in Italy (Sicily, Naples, and Calabria) and the United States. In terms of kingpin arrests, officials claim to have arrested seven of the top money managers in the Colombian Cali drug cartel.

TABLE 4.2

Locations	Arrests	Assets	Drugs	
			Cocaine	Heroin
U.S.	121	$40M	745 kg	.45 kg (1 lb)
Canada	1	1.6M	0	0
Cayman Is.	0	.400	0	0
Colombia	0	—	240 kg	0
Costa Rica	4	—	0	0
Italy	50	1.M	0	0
Spain	12	.400	8	0
UK	4	6.M	43	0
TOTAL	192	$54.M	1 036 kg	.45 kg (1 lb)

NOTES

1. Much of the material in this chapter is derived from Beare and Schneider (1990).

2. According to Calder (n.d.), what we know of the Al Capone conviction may be what he terms a "government-crafted history." In 1989, Calder tried through the U.S. Court of Appeals to gain access to the IRS records relating to Capone. He was turned down even though access to these records had been granted to other authors. Those, however, had not been focusing on the conduct of the IRS investigation itself. See *Calder v. I.R.S.* No. 89-5508, U.S. Court of Appeals, Fifth Circuit, December 21, 1989.

3. See, for example, Australia (1991); Beare and Schneidert (1990); Commonwealth Secretariat (1991–92, 1992); Zagaris (1993); *An Assessment of Narcotics Related Money Laundering* (Financial Crimes Enforcement Network, July 1992) and Financial Action Task Force reports, (February 1990, May 1991, June 1992, June 1993 and 1994).

4. Article 3, paragraph 1(b) of the United Nations Convention Against Illicit Traffic in Narcotic Drugs and Psychotropic Substances, Vienna, E/CONF.82/15 of December 19, 1988.

5. A slightly different model appeared in Beare and Schneider (1990, 428). I am not totally convinced that either is accurate. However thinking about specific laundering endeavours with some categories in mind may assist our understanding of the range of activity and allow us to compare across schemes.

6. See each of the reports cited above for detailed discussions of each of the vulnerable institutions, organizations, or facilitating individuals.

7. Report of a Commission of Inquiry Pursuant to Orders in Council (Queensland), op. cit., p. 73.

8. For a detailed discussion, see Beare and Schneider (1990) and Australia (1991, vols. 1 and 2).

9. U.S. Mail was excluded from this initiative because Customs cannot conduct warrantless searches on outgoing mail, although it can inspect outgoing parcels sent via a commercial carrier (United States, GAO 1994).

10. The term "smurfs" originated with the innocuous-looking, mostly blue-haired cartoon characters. Popular laundering "smurfs" have traditionally been thought to be elderly "blue haired" women hired to take the under-$10,000 deposits into banks throughout North America. In fact, youth and every other category of individual are used by launderers.

11. On July 5, 1991, regulators shut down BCCI branches in Britain, the United States, Canada, the Cayman Islands, Spain, France, and Switzerland—1.4-million depositors had placed an estimated $20 billion with the bank, but on that date there were less than $2 billion of real assets. BCCI had been incorporated in Luxembourg, where bank regulations had been flexible and secrecy intense. The power base for the bank, however, was the United Arab Emirates. BCCI had been created in order to absorb and manipulate oil riches. On June 15, 1994, *The Globe and Mail* reported that the founder and 11 former top execu-

tives of BCCI had been convicted of fraud and mismanagement. Their sanctions included prison terms of up to 14 years, and they were ordered to pay a total of US$9.13 billion in restitution to the Abu Dhabi government. See Beaty and Gwynne (1993). For a discussion of the Vatican Bank scandal, see Lernoux (1986) and Naylor (1987).

12. Conversation with Michael Ballard, Vice-President, Security, Canadian Bankers' Association, July 26, 1994.

13. RCMP News Release, *Nation-Wide Money Laundering Undercover Operation Terminated,* June 21, 1994. A similar undercover operation took place in the United States, but instead of currency-exchange houses, another "near-bank" was targeted. A year-long undercover investigation by Customs, the IRS, the DEA, and the NY State Police operating in New York, Washington, and Fort Lauderdale was directed against the subagents of Vigo Remittance Corp. Posing as drug dealers, undercover agents had gone into subagents' offices and asked to have more than $500,000 in "drug" money transferred by wire. The subagents did not resist. The funds were wired and the transaction forms were falsified. While Vigo itself was not charged, the government alleged that it had provided a lax atmosphere that allowed money laundering (*Money Laundering Alert,* July 1994, vol. 5, no. 10).

14. Interestingly, the rules only apply to Atlantic City and Puerto Rico casinos. Nevada casinos are exempted from Bank Secrecy Act regulations (*Money Laundering Alert* 6, no. 3 [December 1994]: 4).

15. This figure runs anywhere between $48 and $54 million depending on which country was reporting.

16. U.S. Department of Justice, DEA News Release, September 28, 1992.

17. See Shannon (1994) and Andelman (1994).

Official Responses to Organized Crime: Policy, Legislation, and Policing

INTRODUCTION

How a society defines organized crime determines whether and/ or how that criminal activity is targeted by law enforcement. This part of the book identifies the sources of the rhetoric that has reflected and promoted a concern with organized crime among law enforcement and the public; discusses the policies, legislation, and operational policing requirements for the implementation of a relatively new approach to organized crime control; describes the processes involved in progressing from an "idea" to acceptance of policy change and the creation of legislation; and concludes by focusing on the operational consequences for the police and other law enforcement agencies, and includes a case study of one international organized crime/money laundering case.

An understanding of the societal and political processes involved in social change is important to our discussion. As Etzioni (1968), argues, societal decision-making is not merely a thought process that carefully balances goals and means. It also involves a political process that balances various power and interest groups. Although a shift to a new policing strategy may seem minor compared to the catastrophic societal changes that have occurred, the process of getting to the point where the anticipated change is accepted is sociologically interesting.

Decisions on policing strategies usually fall strictly under the domain of police management, which as a group is seen to be reactionary rather than change-oriented. Therefore, identifying the motivating forces behind the organizational change becomes important. In our analysis, one sees the role played by external elites such as the UN and the U.S. models; the potential fiscal gains to governments; the growth of prestigious units within policing; and an articulation of claims that the new policing paradigm could solve the seemingly invincible enforcement problems associated with global organized crime. The following diagram illustrates the key aspects of this shift in law enforcement.

Policy, Legislative, and Operational Changes

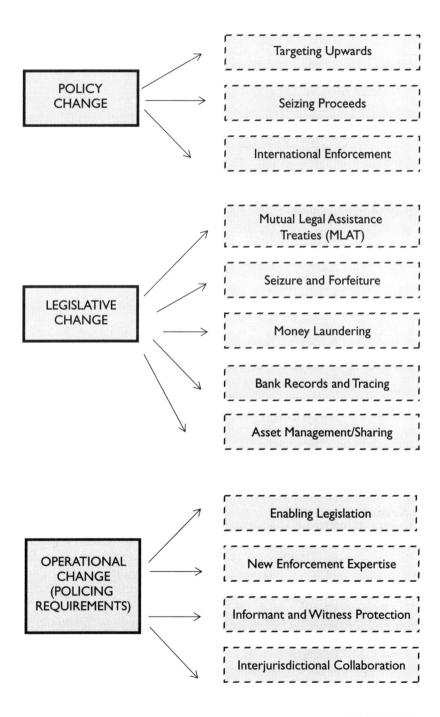

Organized Crime Enforcement: New Policies and New Targets

THE GROWTH OF ORGANIZED CRIME RHETORIC IN CANADA

It may be useful to return briefly to the Canadian use of the term "organized crime" in early inquiries and police reports. While not refuting the existence of independent organized crime activity in Canada and cross-border organized crime operations, the growth of the rhetoric that served as a catalyst for new law enforcement powers and unique proceeds of crime legislation in Canada stemmed largely from the U.S. experience.

When we study the early Canadian discussions on organized crime, it becomes evident that the U.S. commissions had a direct impact on the way not only the United States but also Canada saw and dealt with organized crime. For example, the U.S. McClellan Commission (1963) and the 1967 report to the U.S. Congress directly influenced the statements made by law enforcement officials in Canada, as well as the recommendations put forward by various Canadian inquiries. In the United States, the result was the creation of the Racketeer Influenced and Corrupt Organizations (RICO) Statute; in Canada, it was a series of symposia studying the U.S. experience with RICO, a major federal/provincial study into organized crime, and the eventual drafting of our own legislation.

The interplay between Canadian and U.S. organized crime rhetoric is a recurring theme in the Canadian reports. In November 1961, RCMP Commissioner Harvison gave a speech to the Canadian Club in which he stated,

The American syndicates are showing an increased interest in Canada and they are moving to take over direct control of some existing criminal organizations and to expand their criminal activities. They are already active in the field of gambling, narcotics trafficking, counterfeiting, and in the protection rackets. There are some indications and there is some evidence that the syndicates have already started to treat Canada as an area for expansion of their activities (Ontario Police Commission 1964, 2).[1]

The domestically controlled syndicates were seen to be less harmful and less powerful than their American counterparts. The picture Harvison drew of American organized crime seeping into Canada was compounded by the contrast he enunciated between the "stepped-up activities against the gangsters in the United States" and the relative absence of powers for Canadian law enforcement.[2] This debate coincided with the discovery of police corruption in the anti-gambling squad of the OPP. The result was twofold: the creation of the Ontario Police Commission (OPC) to oversee law enforcement in Ontario; and the appointment of Justice Roach, on December 11, 1961, as Royal Commissioner to examine the extent of crime—including organized crime—in Ontario.

The Roach Report drew the same distinction that Commissioner Harvison had made between domestic "organized crime" and what was seen to be the more insidious U.S.-style "syndicate" crime. The report, which was released on March 15, 1963, concluded that while there was organized crime in Ontario, it did not exist "to any alarming extent except in the field of organized gambling" (Ontario 1964, 6). On August 16, 1963, RCMP Commissioner Harvison gave a press conference at the Canadian National Exhibition in which he made the following remarks about the relationship between U.S. Mafia and the criminal organizations in Canada:

Now whether it is actual Mafia or whether it is developed along the Mafia lines is a subject of debate among policemen. Certainly the form of organization is Mafia-like, their disciplines are Mafia disciplines, so that it follows if the American syndicates are moving into Canada or attempting to move into Canada then this syndicate's being organized along Mafia lines. It's a Mafia-type organization that's coming in, but to say that it is definitely the Mafia, I just don't know ... (Ontario Police Commission 1964, 140).

This less-than-definitive statement encouraged the newly created Ontario Police Commission to request permission from the attorney general to begin its own inquiry into the precise nature of the organized crime threat in Canada. The resulting

1964 *Report of the Ontario Police Commission on Organized Crime* quotes at length from the 1963 U.S. Senate Committee hearings, and specifically from the testimony of Attorney General Robert Kennedy.[3] Kennedy, who was personally directing a concerted attack on organized crime during these years, mentions the 1957 Apalachin (N.Y.) meeting of organized crime families and paints an "ugly picture" of hoodlums moving into legitimate businesses via violence and intimidation. The RCMP Commissioner, in a brief to the Commission on Organized Crime, had confirmed that a number of the men identified as being present at the Apalachin meeting were currently residing in Canada or had financial interests there. He also confirmed that American racketeers had joined with Canadian residents (who were well known to the police) for a hunting party at the James Bay Goose Club. This Goose Club meeting never attained the notoriety of the Apalachin meeting!

The Ontario Police Commission representatives had attended some of the sessions of the Permanent Subcommittee on Investigations of the Committee on Government Operations of the U.S. Senate—presided over by Senator John L. McClellan. As part of the Ontario Police Commission Inquiry on Organized Crime, a team from Toronto, including the Chief of Police for Metropolitan Toronto, travelled to Washington to question the mob informant Joe Valachi regarding comments he had made linking Buffalo mobsters to Toronto. Although Valachi then denied having made these comments, his testimony indicated otherwise.

At the end of 1963, Metropolitan Toronto Police (1964) testified that organized crime had "decreased greatly in the last three years and is described as 50-100% better." However, by 1967, the media, relying heavily on the credibility of U.S. "experts," had adopted organized crime as a priority issue. One *Toronto Star* headline—"Crime Said Moving in on Business"—followed a visit to Toronto by Professor Charles A. Rogovin, adviser to President Johnson on organized crime. Another *Toronto Star* headline informed readers "Mafia Did Feasibility Study on Yorkville."

During this same period, Ralph Salerno, another U.S. organized crime "expert," spoke to the Quebec Royal Commission and was quoted by the *Toronto Star* as predicting that Expo 67 in Montreal would provide a good opportunity for organized crime (April 21, 1967, p. 39). Ten years later, a Quebec Police Commission report confirmed through intercepted telephone calls that a number of U.S. mobsters were operating between Canada and the United States. The Montreal-based Cotroni-Violi gang was shown to have acted as a subsidiary branch of a New York family (Quebec 1977b, 100).

Organized crime activities were beginning to be likened to legitimate business activities in terms of their rules and motivations (which is not to say the methods of conducting business or the reactions to competition were the same). The 1967 U.S. Task Force on Organized Crime served to alert Canadians as well as Americans to the threats posed by criminal investment in legitimate businesses. This marked the beginning of a recognition by law enforcement that organized crime was very much a phenomenon woven into the fabric of legitimate society. In addition, the takeover of legitimate businesses by organized crime was gradually recognized by law enforcement as an essential means of meeting the money laundering requirement of organized criminals. Law enforcement and legislation would eventually link the centrality of this laundering requirement to control efforts.

Following from the U.S. focus on organized crime in the 1960s were a series of federal–provincial conferences held in 1965 and 1966. On August 8, 1967, the report of the January 1966 Federal–Provincial Conference on Organized Crime was released. The conclusions were quite dramatic. Organized crime was said to be involved in nearly all fields of business and commerce. Moreover, it was alleged that "those engaged in organized crime in Canada maintain a close working relationship and personal ties with many of the U.S. crime syndicate ... 'the mafia.'"[4]

The 1966 conference resulted in the creation of the Criminal Intelligence Service Canada (CISC), with a mandate to monitor and control the spread of organized crime; recognition of the need for a centralized police information network (CPIC); and an upgraded training facility for the police community that eventually became the Canadian Police College. The "threat" of organized crime was thereby established, and a consensus among the police departments confirmed the seriousness of the enemy. Law enforcement and the media now proceeded to link this insidious threat to other societal problems. Eventually, new legislation would address organized crime and money laundering, the facilitation of international law enforcement, record-keeping, and proceeds of crime asset-sharing. The targets of the police would shift upward to the illicit proceeds. New forms of police training, different measurements of effectiveness, and new working partnerships would begin to be implemented as Canada moved into the era of international organized crime enforcement.

POLICY CHANGE

However we define organized crime, in essence it involves a process consisting of criminal activity that is carried out by an ongoing organization, that often operates across jurisdictions within an international environment, and that has as a prime objective the making of large amounts of illicit profits. Traditional street-level police strategies eventually came to be regarded as too limited in power and scope. The individual targets of these traditional policing strategies were not critical to the existence of the criminal operations. [Arresting one or even many members of a criminal organization would not necessarily stop the organization from operating.] Even if this were an effective strategy, upper-echelon arrests within criminal syndicates were rare.

Levels of Enforcement

Highest Level

Targeting Criminal Proceeds

International Enforcement

Importers/Bulk Distributors

Street-level Enforcement

Target on Customers

Lowest Level

[The acceptance of this shift in thinking on organized crime developed though a series of royal commissions, inquiries, and organized crime task forces established during the 1950s and 1960s.] More recent national and international working groups, conventions, and conferences expanded on earlier policy recommendations and came to embrace the notion of "targeting upwards" to capture upper-echelon criminals; to shift the focus from the individual criminals to the proceeds of crime; and to recognize that organized crime is an international enforcement problem that can be tackled only from a base of international collaboration and intelligence-sharing. Figure 5.1 illustrates these components.

TARGETING UPWARDS

Law enforcement has gradually turned its attention to the financial gains of criminal operations. "Targeting upwards"—a buzz phrase from the late 1970s and early 1980s—in the beginning involved efforts by law enforcement to take out kingpins responsible for running the organized crime operations. This strategy seemed to be an appropriate and enlightened response to the

FIGURE 5.1

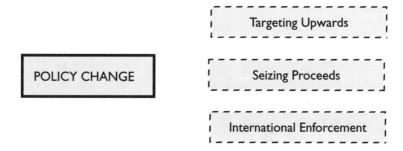

question "Why continue to focus on street-level distributors and pushers if you can hurt the organization farther up in the hierarchical chain"? However, critics soon realized that removing one person from an organization, even a key figure, did not necessarily have a significant impact on the criminal enterprise. Numerous examples existed of organized crime figures running their operations from inside of penitentiaries. In addition, many countries at that time did not have in place the type of legislation that would facilitate the removal of powerful individuals who avoided physical contact with the criminal commodity.

More practical, and possibly more attractive in periods of fiscal restraint, was a philosophy that recognized that these criminals were involved in a specific type of crime in order to generate large amounts of proceeds. Locking up low-level operators would do little to disable the criminal operations, and while it was still occasionally essential to target key criminal figures, seldom was law enforcement able to get high enough to remove the top level. What did seem possible was to focus law enforcement's attention on the money that was illegitimately gained. Focusing on the money was also seen as a way to identify the higher-echelon criminal members. FinCEN (Financial Crimes Enforcement Network) calls the laundering stage the "choke point"[5] of narcotics trafficking. Top-echelon criminals who isolate themselves from the daily operations of trafficking actively take part at the stage where the illicit proceeds return cleansed.

This concern for the criminal proceeds brought an awareness of the necessity to trace illicit proceeds through the complex laundering schemes devised by criminals—hence the increasing focus on international money laundering. While in some cases responses were limited to rhetoric, in others legislation was drafted, agreements were signed, and new responsibilities were assigned and evaluated based on the curtailment of money laundering activity. The international focus on money laundering and criminal proceeds that developed fairly quickly during the 1980s and into the 1990s was made possible by the earlier policy shift.

SEIZING PROCEEDS

The notion of taking the property and proceeds of crime away from criminals is not new. In common law, conviction on a felony offence resulted in the forfeiture of the offender's lands and chattels.[6] No distinction was made between legally gained possessions and those acquired through criminal means. Significant numbers of offenders were rendered destitute by these provisions, and because the creation of a destitute class was felt to inevitably lead to greater criminality, forfeiture of property fell out of favour. The Forfeiture Act of 1880, which was incorporated into the 1892 Criminal Code, abolished the forfeiture of a convicted felon's property.

Over the next 100 years, the focus tended to be on imprisonment or fines rather than the offender's property. The renewed focus on proceeds in Canada stemmed largely from the perceived "threat" from organized crime, which, as we have argued, was largely an American interpretation. In Canada, the thinking of officials had to evolve before the legislation changed. Increasingly, attention was given to evidence that even in the rare instances where courts successfully put key organized crime figures in jail, the criminal organizations continued to operate with very little disruption. In contrast to the draconian measures contained in the earlier forfeiture provisions, criminal proceeds, rather than the total property of the criminal, became the focus of debate.[7]

In the international context, responses to organized crime have generally involved legislation that facilitates taking the profit away from the criminal via processes of seizing/freezing and eventually forfeiting the proceeds. "Targeting upwards" has come to mean targeting the criminal proceeds rather than (or in addition to) the criminals.

INTERNATIONAL ENFORCEMENT

As countries began to talk more about organized crime, there developed a perception of substantive differences between the threat from individual criminals and the threat from organized criminals. The main threat from the latter group was seen to come from the financial power that the organization exerted—power that enabled its members to corrupt officials, create monopolies, and take over legitimate businesses using both legal and criminal means.

Increasingly, countries became aware that they shared not only the same enforcement concerns—they shared the same criminals and a portion of the same criminal proceeds. The crimes that were of the greatest concern to organized crime experts were international in scope and as such required international approaches involving collaboration and mechanisms by which intelligence could be shared and investigations facilitated operationally. The United Nations (Drug Commission and Commission on Crime Prevention and Criminal Justice) has done much to encourage countries to take a global view of criminal proceeds and money laundering. The 1988 UN Convention Against Illicit Traffic in Narcotic Drugs and Psychotropic Substances was adopted by 106 nation-states in December of that year.

Canada was not a passive participant in this process. Rodney Stamler, then Assistant Commissioner and head of the drug directorate for the RCMP, played a major role in the discussions that led to the creation of the 1988 convention, and continued to be involved through the drafting stage. Canada was among the initial signatories to the convention and was among the 20 countries that ratified the convention, allowing it to come into force on November 11, 1990.[8]

The convention urged governments to develop legislation that would allow for the identification, tracing, freezing, and seizing of illicit proceeds. The convention recommended that participating countries have in place:

- legislation to make money laundering an offence;

- legislation that allows for the confiscation of proceeds derived from drug offences;

- procedural tools and cooperation in the investigations necessary to identify, trace, and secure proceeds of crime (Beare and Schneider 1990, 295).

The Convention also outlined a model Mutual Legal Assistance Treaty that is consistent with Canada's preferred bilateral treaty model and compatible with the definition of "treaty" found in the Mutual Legal Assistance in Criminal Matters Act (Bill C-58).[9]

Smoothing the way for this new approach to law enforcement were three factors: the growth of organized crime rhetoric; increased awareness of the movement of money across borders and into legitimate businesses; and dramatic court cases that law enforcement lost due to a narrow interpretation (or the narrow intent) of the existing forfeiture powers. In Britain, the House of Lords decision in *R. v. Cuthbertson and Others* (1980) prompted the Howard League for Penal Reform to set up the Forfeiture

Committee chaired by Mr. Justice Hodgson. This case, known as "Operation Julie," determined that the courts did not have the power under the Misuse of Drugs Act (1971) to deprive defendants of their profits from the illegal manufacture and sale of prohibited drugs.[10]

In Canada, a well-publicized case helped to propel the drafting of the Proceeds of Crime legislation. The case centred on Luis Pinto,[11] a U.S. drug trafficker who admitted to and was convicted of laundering approximately $40 million in U.S. funds. Pinto maintained an account at a Royal Bank branch, in Montreal, in the name of one of his relatives. The RCMP, working with the FBI, discovered that $400,000 in the account were proceeds from drug trafficking. Using Section 312 (now s. 354) of the *Criminal Code,* the RCMP obtained a warrant to seize the funds, but the bank argued that because the money had already been deposited into an account, it was an intangible asset and therefore not recoverable under the available sections of the Criminal Code.

The Pinto case went to the Supreme Court of Canada, where again it was decided that bank credits were not tangible assets and therefore could not be seized (Beare and Schneider 1990, 14). Attempts to seize and forfeit these illicit proceeds were therefore unsuccessful. Under the original Section 312 provisions,

> in order to be seized the asset must be tangible and portable; this precludes, for instance, the seizure of criminal proceeds where they have been converted into real estate, an interest in a business ... The most obvious difficulty lies in relation to moneys deposited in a bank account (MacFarlane 1984–85 425).

The seizure problems were compounded by the fact that once the proceeds of crime had been laundered, they could not generally be frozen. "Proceeds" of crime were not forfeitable unless they were the actual goods or money obtained directly by the commission of an offence.

International meetings, the ongoing work of UN groups, and an exchange of experiences among various countries all served to create an atmosphere that encouraged the search for solutions to the proceeds of crime problem. Australia serves as an example of the global exchange of ideas and conclusions. While it is no surprise that the United States and Canada influence each other, the reaction of Australia illustrates how global policy-making has become. The collected papers from the 53rd ANZAAS Congress, held in Perth, Australia (May 16-20, 1983), show the impact of both U.S. and Canadian experience on Australia. Mr. Douglas Meagher, Q.C., stated that "[Canadians] have researched the American experience, have analyzed it and examined the Canadian scene to determine the extent to which the American practices may be adopted in their own country."[12]

The ANZAAS papers devote considerable space to an analysis of the RICO statute (and its potentially draconian aspects). While various countries seemed determined to create their own made-at-home versions, the model itself remained RICO. Whatever the adaptations, Canada, Australia, and the United Kingdom had by this point made the decision that their legislation needed to be changed to help law enforcement in their respective countries deprive criminals of their illicit profits. As the Commissioner of the 1980 Australian Royal Commission into Drug Trafficking stated,

> It is becoming increasingly recognized that drug trafficking is a business rather than some isolated activity, and, more importantly, one which generates huge profits. ... law enforcement bodies have expressed the view that if detection, arrest, conviction and sentencing of major drug traffickers is to achieve significant and lasting effects in disrupting drug traffic at high levels and immobilising persons or organizations engaged in that activity, *they must be accompanied by measures which attack the working capital of those drug traffickers and strip them of their ill-gotten wealth..*" (italics added; quoted from Australia 1991, vol. 1, p. 13).

Before examining the Canadian legislation, we will look briefly at the American model and some of the key issues it raises.

ORGANIZED CRIME LEGISLATION IN THE UNITED STATES: ROBERT BLAKEY AND RICO

One individual played a key role in the development of the U.S. (and, it could be argued, the Canadian) approach to organized crime. It is fairly unusual for a highly respected academic to hold an influential position as adviser to the U.S. president and then be in a position to draft into legislation the results of his own advice. Such was the case with G. Robert Blakey.

In 1960, Professor Blakey served under Robert Kennedy at the Department of Justice in the Organized Crime Racketeering Section. He also served as Chief Counsel to the McClellan Commission. In 1967, as a law professor from Notre Dame University, Blakey prepared a treatise for the U.S. Congress on a number of laws that he felt would contain the growth of organized crime.[13] The Racketeer Influenced and Corrupt Organizations Statute (RICO) statute, drafted by Blakey, came into force on October 15, 1970, when Congress passed the Organized Crime

Control Act.[14] Other legislative recommendations related to witness protection and electronic surveillance.[15]

During the early 1980s, Professor Blakey was invited at least twice to Ottawa to advise on the possible creation of Canadian proceeds of crime legislation. The RICO statute has had enormous influence on other countries' legislative attempts to seize the proceeds of crime, and is credited with allowing the police to successfully prosecute individuals who previously seemed immune. RICO did not, however, create a money laundering offence in the United States—16 years passed before this occurred with the introduction of the Money Laundering Control Act.

The narrowness of the justifications that were used to "sell" RICO is in sharp contrast to the breadth of the statute's eventual use. Clearly, keeping organized criminals out of legitimate businesses was only one of the statute's targets. Increasingly, white-collar, corporate, and governmental crime and corruption cases have been prosecuted. Critics saw RICO as a "standardless criminal catch-all"[16] and were not reassured when Justice official John Dowd stated, "It's just common sense ... and good judgement ... we will only hit substantial conduct" (Atkinson 1978, 16). The breadth of the "intent" behind the Statute is still being debated by almost everyone except Blakey, who maintains that the current wide interpretations were intended by the drafters. As Blakey himself stated, "I stand in awe at their inability to read the Statute that I wrote."[17] Instructions from the U.S. Department of Justice on the use of RICO state that sections of the statute would give impetus to imaginative prosecutions.

Legislation that allowed the courts to take away illicit proceeds represented at the time a new approach to law enforcement. Police, prosecutors, and courts had yet to educate themselves on this approach. One of the consequences in the United States was that, from 1970 to the early 1980s, RICO prosecutions were rare. Blakey attributes much of the confusion to prosecutors' failure to read the statute and to defence counsel attempts to perpetrate a mythical organized crime stereotypical offender in order to better protect the interests of their business clients. As he stated in 1982,

> There is nothing in RICO that says that if you act like a racketeer you will not be treated like a racketeer, whatever the colour of your shirt or your collar. ... Murderers ought to be called murderers, rapists ought to be called rapists, ... people who run groups by extortion or violence or fraud ought to be called racketeers. And what they engage in is racketeering.[18]

When successful RICO cases showed that racketeering did not have to be "organized" and that enterprises did not have to be legal ones, it became clear that the focus of RICO had wandered far from the early rhetoric used to gain acceptance of the initiative.

Year in which Racketeering State Statutes Were Enacted

1970 Federal Statute

1970 Pennsylvania	1982 Illinois
1972 Hawaii	1983 California
1977 Florida	1983 Louisiana
1978 Arizona	1983 Nevada
1979 Rhode Island	1983 North Dakota
1980 Georgia	1984 Mississippi
1980 Indiana	1985 Washington
1980 New Mexico	1986 Delaware
1981 Colorado	1986 New York
1981 Idaho	1986 North Carolina
1981 New Jersey	1986 Ohio
1981 Oregon	1986 Tennessee
1981 Utah	1988 Oklahome
1981 Wisconsin	1989 Minnesota
1982 Connecticut	

RICO contains both a criminal and civil component. Section 1963 sets out the criminal remedies that are available to the government, while Section 1964 sets out the civil remedies that are available to injured parties.[19] Remedies and sanctions available under RICO include imprisonment, criminal forfeiture, injunctions, and triple damage relief for persons who are injured by violations of the statute.[20] In recognition of the ongoing nature of organized crime activity, RICO allows prosecutors to prosecute "patterns of criminal acts," whether committed by direct or indirect participants in criminal enterprises.

The intent of the "pattern" aspect is to dismantle organized crime groups. Separate offences often appear to be petty until they are seen in the context of a pattern of offending. Take, for example, white-collar crimes. One or two violations would have minor penalties, but together under a RICO prosecution the pattern of criminal activity is considered as the offence. A distinct and controversial benefit stemming from RICO is the power of "threat" it holds against suspects. In some states, a RICO violation is a class 2 felony violation, which tends to encourage suspects to plead guilty to lesser charges (U.S. Department of Justice 1993, 11).

Recent RICO cases include a wide range of "racketeers"—businesspersons, protest/lobby groups, politicians. Among this group are some traditional and not so traditional organized criminals. Since the federal RICO statute was passed, at least 29 states have passed similar legislation. In 1970, Pennsylvania became the first State to pass a "State RICO" statute. In August 1989, Minnesota became the 29th state to enact a RICO statute (U.S. Department of Justice 1993). RICO was the first of many legislative tools to be used against organized crime and money laundering.

U.S. Federal Legislative Tools Against Organized Crime and Money Laundering

- Racketeer Influenced and Corrupt Organizations Statute [RICO] (Title 18, USC s. 1961)
- Continuing Criminal Enterprise Statutes (CCE)
- Money Laundering Control Act (Title 18, USC s. 1956)
- Transactions in Criminally-derived Property (Title 18, USC s. 1957)
- Illegal Money Transmitting Businesses (Title 18, USC s. 1960)
- Bank Secrecy Act (Title 31, USC 5311–5330)
- Cash Reporting by Trades and Businesses (Title 26, USC s. 60501)
- Right to Financial Privacy Act (Title 12, USC s. 3401)
- Willful Violation of Banking Regulations (Title 12, USC s. 1956)

Canadian Legislative Tools Against Organized Crime and Money Laundering

- Mutual Legal Assistance in Criminal Matters Act (1988)
- Proceeds of Crime legislation (1989)
- Act to Facilitate Combatting the Laundering of Proceeds of Crime (1991), Regulations (1993)
- Seized Property Management Act (Bill C-123) (1993)

(Beare 1995, 177)

NOTES

1. In response to this speech, Ontario Attorney General F.M. Cass made the following comment: "The unfortunate division of police responsibilities in this province ... means that the RCMP is the police force which should first become aware of the appearance of syndicated crime, and unless that information is passed on to the Provincial and Municipal police, and a joint plan of action is developed, there is little likelihood of real success in the battle against organized, and united criminal forces" (Ontario Police Commission 1964, 138).

2. This provided an early example of what has continued as a pattern — a criminal situation recognized to be *greater* in the United States results in calls for (or by) Canadian officials to replicate U.S. law enforcement measures. Few question the wisdom of mimicking something that does not seem to be working, and replacing a system that may be adequate or even superior.

3. Even the names of the key individuals in Canada and the United States become interchangeable. Senator John L. McClellan in the United States headed the 1957 Special Committee on Improper Activities in the Labor and Management Field, and became chair of the Permanent Subcommittee on Government Operations, holding the 1963 televised hearings, with the assistance of Attorney General Robert Kennedy, into the Valachi affair. This subcommittee was frequently called a commission, hence the title "Commissioner" McClellan. In Canada, RCMP Commissioner Harvison retired October 31, 1963, and was replaced by George B. McClellan. At that time, the Ontario Police Commission was carrying out its interviews and was usually just referred to as "the Commission" in that era's articles on organized crime.

4. "Big U.S. crime spreading here, police brass warn," *The Toronto Star,* August 10, 1967, p. A1.

5. Organized crime literature also speaks of choke points from the criminal's point of view. If criminal organizations gain control of one critical activity within a larger industry, they are often able to control other aspects of that industry. For example, in New York, criminal control of the concrete operations means that all of those construction activities that rely on the timely delivery of concrete are in the control of the criminal groups. See Edelhertz and Overcast (1993, 65).

6. See Donald (1989). For a full discussion of the early forfeiture provisions, see Finkelstein (1973, 169).

7. Taking proceeds away from criminals may, however, prove too attractive and too addictive for law enforcement. The proliferation of forfeiture statutes in the United States has raised questions about fairness and proportionality. Individuals who have been charged with no criminal offence are finding themselves the subject of civil *in rem* forfeitures, with title of the "offending property" falling to the government as of the time of the alleged illegal act.

8. The 1989 Canadian Proceeds of Crime legislation provided a companion enforcement power to the October 1988 Mutual legal Assistance in Criminal Matters Act. Together they enabled Canada to meet its international commitments under the United Nations Convention Against Illicit Traffic in Narcotic Drugs and Psychotropic Substances.

9. S.C. 1988, c. 37.

10. *Hodgson Committee Consultative Paper*, p.1. In 1986, the Drug Trafficking Offences Act received royal assent in the United Kingdom. The Act provides for the confiscation of drug proceeds in cases where an offender is convicted of trafficking offences.

11. *Royal Bank of Canada v. Bourque et al.*, [1984] 38 c.r. (3d) 363. Otherwise known as the Pinto case.

12. Douglas Meagher, Q.C. *Organized Crime: Papers Presented to the 53rd ANZAAS Congress,* Perth, W.A., May 16–20, 1983, p. 180.

13. See Martens (1991, 99).

14. Blakey has confessed to a fondness for vintage American gangster movies. In 1930, Edward G. Robinson played a character called Caesar Enrico Bandello ("Rico") in the classic "first" American gangster movie titled *Little Caesar.* One suspects that the name for this slightly awkward sounding "Racketeer Influenced and Corrupt Organizations" (RICO) statute is thus explained.

15. In the late 1960s, two Bills designed to fight criminal investment in the legitimate market were introduced into the U.S. Senate—both died in committee. A replacement Bill, introduced by Senators Hrusha and Stevens, was amended and eventually became the Organized Crime Control Act of 1970. RICO was part of this Act. Through much of the debate, the stated purpose of RICO was the "elimination of the infiltration of organized crime and racketeering into legitimate organizations operating in interstate commerce." See Bradley (1980, 844).

16. See Schmidt (1980).

17. Symposium on Enterprise Crime, Ottawa, June 24–25, 1982. More recently, Blakey said, "Read the language [of RICO]. The language says 'any person.' There's nothing about any person who happens to be a member of the mob, or any persona whose name ends in a vowel. It says any person." (quoted in Crovitz 1990, from the original *Nightline* television broadcast, April 12, 1989).

18. Taken from a transcript of proceedings that includes a presentation made by Robert Blakey at a Solicitor General-hosted Symposium on Enterprise Crime held in Ottawa, June 24–25, 1982.

19. In certain circumstances, and in certain states, the state can act as the complainant in a civil suit. For example, under the Arizona Code, the state can sue for triple damages on behalf of the private plaintiffs, resulting in a kind of *parents patriae* situation.

20. To illustrate the sanctions available under RICO, Blakey used the example of an individual who worked for the Gambino family and ran a local Teamsters union. The individual was convicted of extortion, murder, and RICO, and went to jail, but left his relatives in charge of the union's operations. The Department of Justice moved by means of a civil suit in an equity court to take control of the union. People victimized by this individual's crimes could proceed civilly for triple damages. As a result, the gangster would lose control of his enterprise (the union) and be responsible for large triple-damage payments to the victims.

C H A P T E R 6

Organized Crime Legislation in Canada: Background

During the 1970s, as the United States attempted unsuccessfully to encourage the police and prosecutors to use the RICO statute, Canada was conducting more commissions on organized crime. In 1973, Ontario established the Royal Commission on Certain Sectors of the Building Industry which was chaired by Judge Harry Waisberg. The report, published in 1974, established a clear picture of bombings, violence, and organized corruption (Ontario 1974). The 1976 report of the Commission of Inquiry on Organized Crime accomplished the same for Quebec (Quebec 1977b). The findings of both commissions were broadcast on French and English television. Two CBC programs—*Connections I* (June 1977) and *Connections II*—captured the imaginations of Canadians.[1]

Concern was raised at both the provincial and federal levels. In the Ontario legislature, James Renwick introduced a private member's bill, which led the Attorney General of Ontario to refer the matter to the Federal Minister of Justice. In 1975, fears that Canada was becoming a haven for criminals resulted in an amendment to Section 312 (now R.S.C. 1985, c. C-46, s. 354) of the Criminal Code. As Mosley (1989) notes, "concerns about the potential trans-border effects of the American legislation lead to the enactment ... The express object of the amendment was to shut the door to organized crime profits from the U.S." (9). The Criminal Code amendment was designed to prohibit the possession of "any property or thing or any proceeds of any property or thing ... (knowingly) ... obtained by or derived directly or indirectly ... from the commission of an indictable offence in Canada or of a similar offence abroad." Although this amendment was used mainly for possession of stolen property (and was, in fact, not extensively used), it paved the way for later amendments that focused on the seizing and forfeiture of criminal assets.

In 1977, in a first-time ever address to the Canadian Police Association by a federal minister, Solicitor General Francis Fox spoke on the topic of organized crime.[2] In a reference to *Connections I,* he stated,

> That exposé, as none before it, informed Canadians of the insidious presence of syndicated crime in our society. The response to these programmes was immediate. There was a major debate on the subject in the House of Commons. The public, in letters to their members of Parliament, to the Press and, to their Local Officials demanded that firm measures be taken at every level of government to eradicate organized crime in Canada (2).

The CBC program then became research fodder for a 1980 report by the Province of British Columbia. Entitled *The Business of Crime: An Evaluation of the American RICO Statute from a Canadian Perspective,* the report portrayed Canada as a "branch-plant to the U.S. mafia" and argued strongly for the unprecedented provisions in RICO to be introduced, with some adjustments, into Canada.[3] The report argued that because Canadian criminal law was not directly concerned with the profits of crime, attempts to remove criminal proceeds had proven sporadic and ineffective. It also argued that because the existing law applied exclusively to single transactions committed by individual offenders, it therefore failed to address the highly lucrative crime committed by criminal organizations (British Columbia 1980, 2). The *Business Of Crime* report was tabled at the Uniform Law Conference of Canada, Criminal Law Section, in August 1981.

The B.C. report supplemented the continuing pressure from Ontario for the federal government to create legislation that would allow a suspect's assets to be frozen during the period prior to conviction. In response to this two-pronged provincial pressure, the Federal and Provincial Ministers Responsible for Criminal Justice decided, in December 1981, to establish a working group to examine four key issues: the effectiveness and shortcomings of existing legislation for the containment and prosecution of enterprise crime activities; the extent of enterprise crime; comparative foreign law enforcement models; and initiatives directed at freezing, seizing, and forfeiting the proceeds and assets of enterprise crime in Canada. The Federal–Provincial Enterprise Crime Working Group began its study in January 1982.

As part of the work of this group, the Department of the Solicitor General hosted two symposia in Ottawa. The Symposium on Enterprise Crime brought from the United States key experts to discuss their experiences with RICO. The presenters at the June 1982 symposium were Professor Robert Blakey, drafter of the statute; Steven Zimmerman, Office of Chief Counsel, DEA; Brian Murtagh, Acting Attorney-in-Charge of Strike Force 18; and Stephen Horn, a member of the American Bar Association Committee on the Prosecution and Defense of RICO cases. Six months later, the Reparative Sanctions International Consultative Workshop brought together U.S. experts, U.K. members of the Hodgson Forfeiture Committee, and Canadian federal and provincial government officials, academics, lawyers, and law enforcement personnel. When one looks at who attended the two meetings, it becomes evident just how small a circle of expertise was involved. Robert Blakey was a common denominator in both of these meetings, and his extensive writings and broad discussions on the RICO experience were very influential to both the Canadian and U.K. participants.

The Enterprise Crime Study Report[4] found that enterprise crime in Canada generated an estimated $10 billion; that Canadian legislation focused on single transactions committed by single individuals rather than on networks of criminals operating over time; that forfeiture was too limited in that it did not extend to the intangible proceeds of criminal activity such as money deposited in a bank account; and that the existing legislation also failed to provide for the seizure of assets prior to conviction, which would prevent the criminal from disposing of the items. The report rejected aspects of the U.S. RICO statute as being either too potentially abusive or inappropriate because of the differences in the two country's systems of criminal and civil justice. It did articulated the need to develop legislation appropriate to Canada, that would focus on criminal proceeds; to further study issues related to the tracing of illicit funds; and to offer assistance to law enforcement in the form of training, resources, and the provision of forensic accountants/auditors to work with the police in the earlier stages of their investigations.

The two initial results of the Enterprise Crime Working Group recommendations were the Proceeds of Crime legislation (Bill C-61) and an intensive study on money laundering in Canada. The legislation came into force in January 1989, while the research on money laundering was completed in 1990. Both of these initiatives received funding and were packaged as an integral part of Canada's 1987 Drug Strategy.

LEGISLATIVE CHANGE

When demand for legislative change comes, it often appears to come quickly and simultaneously from different directions. The development of the idea behind the change, however, is usually slower and shifting—first an agreement that there is a problem; then an articulation of the issues and eventual consensus as to the answer; and finally, the working out of the details of the solution. When we read about laws being passed, we may experience a sense of a speedy, perhaps even conspiratorial, process by which one group (or "the State") is able to rush through a piece of legislation to the detriment of other less powerful groups. The process may, in fact, on occasion be conspiratorial, but it is usually anything but speedy. There are fixed, rigid, even ceremonial aspects to the process, at the end of which a drafted document reflecting a particular policy takes on the power of the law. Depending on the nature of the legislation being passed, there will be active, aggressive debate, or no debate at all. Of course, the formally prescribed process is on occasion smoothed by "negotiated" compromises between interested "sides" fought out either in advance or during some later stage. For example, when the House is sitting there is normally an all-party House Leaders meeting to determine what priority will be given to the particular Bills that are coming before the House for debate.

Several factors can determine the passage of a Bill into law. The potential visibility of the legislation can be important to its passage. If the issue at stake has a high social or political visibility, the ministers will want to be assured that their constituency is in support of the new legislation. Voters and the promise of their votes have powerful voices, the strength of which varies according to the distance from an election! The strength and credibility of the Minister introducing the legislation may also affect the likelihood of its success. Seldom does a Bill submitted by a private member get debated let alone passed into law.[5] In addition, interest groups such as lobbyists or corporate industry may be in the position to influence the direction taken by government on a specific piece of legislation. Contributions to a particular party, for example, may be intended to buy the ability to "be heard" above dissenting opinions.

Textbook discussions on the role of the law often focus on the latter stages *after* the law is in place. These debates analyze the conduct of law and legal rules, and the ideological intent, but miss the initial law-creation stage (Gavigan 1988; McBarnett 1981). Political power and capital does obviously play an important role, but it is a role that must be negotiated through the democratic process. Any blatant violation of process can result in adverse media coverage and a mobilization of interest groups against the

Creating Legislation

- Consultation
- Memorandum to Cabinet
- Drafting Legislation
- Debates in House and Senate
- Royal Assent and Passage into Law
- Publication of Legislation

legislation. Any exposed surreptitious intent can result in delayed or abandoned legislation. Timing and subtleness often prove to be the determining factors behind successfully passed laws.

The time required to pass legislation within the Canadian system of government may be weeks or years. In emergency situations, it is possible for the process to be accomplished in a matter of hours with all-party agreement. Generally, the process is slower, and in some cases the same legislation will be resubmitted in numerous forms (e.g., as part of a large "omnibus bill") before eventually gaining royal assent. Such was the case with the original Proceeds of Crime legislation, which had been a part of an omnibus Bill (C-19, the proposed Criminal Law Reform Act, 1984). The forfeiture provisions met with strong criticism from defence lawyers, academics, and the media. This Bill was never formally debated in the House because shortly thereafter the 1984 general election was called and the Bill died on the Order Paper with the dissolution of Parliament (Mosley 1989).

This is not to say that nothing was gained by proposing Bill C-19. It provided a mental framework against which to compare other possibly more "temperate" versions of the same approach. The criticisms that had been levelled at C-19 gave the drafters of C-61 a knowledge of what concerns would have to be addressed or avoided. The seizure and forfeiture aspects of C-19 were thus repackaged as a separate Bill (C-61) and introduced by the Minister of Justice on May 29, 1987—four days after the May 25 launch of Canada's Drug Strategy. The Drug Strategy consisted of 51 separate initiatives of which the Proceeds of Crime legislation was one. The Bill came into force January 1989.

To the extent that there is a science or art to getting legislation passed, it has to do with the "packaging" of the product. There are also advantageous "windows of opportunity" for presenting what might be considered controversial legislation. The Proceeds of Crime Legislation is an excellent example of the importance of timing and presentation. In 1986, the prime minister had spoken of the "epidemic" in drug abuse in Canada, and had announced, with much media coverage, the creation of a National Drug Strategy (later known as Canada's Drug Strategy). The public accepted the view that the drug situation was a social problem out of control. Virtually any control mechanism targeted at drug abuse would have received wide public support, with only limited opposition from civil-libertarian groups and specific interest groups such as the defence bar.

The aim was, therefore, to capitalize on this momentum. For government officials, the debate involved balancing the focus on drugs (since the majority of illicit proceeds would most likely be drug-related proceeds) with an equally compelling reality that if the legislation consisted only of seizing the proceeds from drug traffickers, the forfeited illicit proceeds would most likely go exclusively to the federal government, which was responsible for most of the drug law enforcement and prosecutions. The result would be opposition from the provincial governments.

The decision was made to include a fairly wide category of "enterprise crimes" in addition to drugs, but to publicize the potential impact on drug trafficking. The Bill was debated extensively by a legislative committee of the House of Commons and by a Standing Committee of the Senate prior to being passed. The scope and timing of this new Bill worked to the benefit of those who felt that additional enforcement powers should be available under the forfeiture approach. A publication entitled *Action on Drug Abuse: Making a Difference* (released one year after the Drug Strategy launch) informed the public that

> [p]rofits from criminal activities such as drug trafficking are often disguised by complex financial transfers or by filtering the profits through legitimate businesses. Funds "laundered" in this way are used to finance other illegal enterprises. Separating criminals from their profits eliminates the chief motive for these activities, and breaks the cycle of crime. ... Bill C-61 ... will give courts the power to deprive offenders including drug traffickers, of the proceeds of their crimes (Canada 1988, 18).

Legislation addressing these enforcement tools (listed in Figure 6.1) form the bookends between which there has occurred much heated debate, resistance or submission to foreign pressure, and careful negotiations among Canadian business, financial, and professional institutions. Targeting illicit proceeds and enforcing laws within an international environment are relatively new concepts, and the police are not the only players who have had to learn (and believe in) a new rhetoric, acquire new skills, and adopt a new way of doing business.

FIGURE 6.1

THE MUTUAL LEGAL ASSISTANCE IN CRIMINAL MATTERS INITIATIVE

In 1983, Canada began to put into place the mechanisms that would eventually strengthen the country's ability to handle transnational crime. The Mutual Legal Assistance in Criminal Matters Act (Bill C-58) came into force October 1988. This first piece of legislation facilitates international law enforcement collaboration and sharing in cases such as those involving international organized crimes.

The concept of mutual legal assistance is double-barrelled in that a country must (1) first have in place legislation that provides its own courts and officials with the jurisdiction and authority to execute requests from foreign countries, and (2) negotiate specific mutual legal assistance treaties with foreign jurisdictions. There is sometimes a considerable delay between the signing of the treaty and the putting into place of the facilitating legislation. For example, although the first Canadian treaty was signed with the United States on March 17, 1985 (an event that included the singing of "When Irish Eyes are Smiling"), it did not come into force until August 4, 1990, because of the lack of U.S. legislation.

As of July 1995, Canada has 12 treaties in force:

Hong Kong (1990)[6]   Netherlands (1992)
Australia (1990)   United Kingdom (1993)
Bahamas (1990)   Thailand (1994)

United States (1990)   Spain (1995)
Mexico (1990)   Korea (1995)
France (1991)   China (1995)

Canada has signed treaties with Italy, India, Poland, and Switzerland that are not yet in force.

The type of assistance specified in these treaties typically includes:

- executing searches and seizures;

- taking evidence from witnesses;

- gathering and transferring information and evidence; and

- making people available to participate in investigations and proceedings.

The treaties vary significantly across countries. While some refer only to drug-enforcement assistance, others are much wider in scope. The formal signed treaties often merely support the informal routine cooperation systems that have been worked out between officials in separate countries, but they do make the "exchange" expectation clear. Mutual legal assistance treaties encourage sharing of information between countries with varying levels of experience working on common cases, and also serve to protect each country from arbitrary violations of sovereignty by overzealous law enforcement officials.

Other sharing mechanisms include Memoranda Of Understanding (MOU), extradition treaties, and the (among commonwealth countries) Fugitive Offenders Act.[7] Canada has signed Memoranda of Understanding on Drugs Cooperation with Russia and Mexico, and has in place seven extradition treaties.[8] The RCMP has in place numerous MOU with foreign police forces in such countries as the United States, Thailand, Peru, the United Kingdom, Australia, Russia, France, and Turkey.

PROCEEDS OF CRIME LEGISLATION

The Act provides the basis in law for a concerted enforcement effort to strip the profits and hence the incentive from those who engage in the illicit trade in drugs and other crimes in this country. Moreover, it serves notice to the world that Canada is prepared to live up to its international commitments and will not serve as a haven for the profits of crime (Mosley 1989, 15).

GENERAL DESCRIPTION

In January 1989, the Proceeds of Crime legislation (Bill C-61) was brought into force in Canada. This legislation became a new section within the Criminal Code; formed amendments to the Narcotic Control Act (NCA), the Food and Drugs Act (FDA), and the Income Tax Act; and created a new offence of "laundering" the proceeds of enterprise crimes and designated drug crimes.

The term "enterprise crime" is used in the Criminal Code to refer to any one of approximately 24 offences (see Chapter 1 for a list). Although this list is less comprehensive than some critics would wish, the emphasis was on money-generating, serious criminal activities associated with organized crime groups.[9] Besides the enterprise crime offence, the legislation introduces the designated drug offence, which is defined as trafficking in controlled, restricted and narcotic drug offences, the importation and cultivation of narcotic drug offences, and the crimes of possession and laundering of proceeds of these drug offences found in the NCA and the FDA. "Proceeds of Crime" is defined in Section 462.3 of the Criminal Code as: any property, benefit or advantage, within or outside Canada, obtained or derived directly or indirectly as a result of—

(a) the commission in Canada of an enterprise crime offence or a designated drug offence, or

(b) an act or omission anywhere that, if it had occurred in Canada, would have constituted an enterprise crime offence or a designated drug offence.

The new offence of "laundering" the proceeds of enterprise and designated drug crimes relates to dealing in any way with criminal proceeds (uses, transfers the possession of, sends or delivers, transports, transmits, alters, disposes of) with the intent to conceal or convert them. The offence for possession of the proceeds of any indictable offence (the original Criminal Code offence under s. 354) still applies and does not require the additional intent to conceal or convert. The FDA and the NCA have been amended to include the offence of knowingly possessing the proceeds derived directly or indirectly from trafficking in controlled or restricted drugs and trafficking, importing, or cultivating narcotic drugs (Mosley 1989, 16).

Although targeting the proceeds of crime does not necessarily involve tracing these funds through complex money laundering schemes, over 80 percent of Canadian police cases involve an international component and hence some degree of money laundering (Beare and Schneider 1990). The laundering process is not considered complete until the illegitimate funds have been "cleansed" and thus rendered safe for use by the criminal.

BREADTH OF OFFENCES

Which offences should be covered by the Proceeds of Crime legislation is a subject of continuing debate. As mentioned in Chapter 1, the Canadian Association of Chiefs of Police (CACP) Organized Crime Committee recommended that the list of enterprise crime offences be expanded to include all profit-motivated crimes.

Efforts to broaden the legislation to include all profit-motivated crimes would render meaningless the concept of enterprise crime in the legislation, and may negate the original premise upon which the legislation gained approval: the need to fight organized crime, specifically drug trafficking. As law enforcement budgets increasingly reflect the same restraint that other resource-dependent organizations are suffering, and as Canadian police look south to the lucrative forfeiture experiences of their American counterparts, the objectives may become blurred. Quick cash seizures with no organized crime connections prove tempting, even if the police in Canada do not as yet receive the benefits of these illicit proceeds directly.[10]

A second aspect of "breadth" relates to the application of the legislation in foreign jurisdictions. As the law is currently written, "proceeds of crime" includes any property, benefit, or advantage from "an act or omission anywhere that, if it had occurred in Canada, would have constituted an enterprise crime offence or a designated drug offence."[11] Although there is no requirement that the "act or omission" also be illegal in the foreign jurisdiction, there is a requirement that the person subsequently be charged and convicted of the offence in Canada (Gold 1989, 22).

A problem remains for Canadian law enforcement if the person is in jail in the foreign jurisdiction. The legislation allows for forfeiture if the offender has either "died or absconded." However, being in jail outside of Canada is not included as a condition for forfeiture under this section. The CACP Organized Crime Committee has recommended that the definition of "abscond" be broadened to allow *in rem* forfeiture of property located in Canada when a foreign court has found the individual guilty of specified offences and imprisoned.

In situations where the court is unable to order forfeiture because the proceeds have dissipated, left the country, or become irreversibly entwined with other property, the court has the power under s. 462.37(3)(4) to impose a fine equal to the value of the proceeds. The punishment for default on payment of the fine is imprisonment. If the offender is already serving a jail term, the new sentence will run consecutively.

BURDEN OF PROOF

A difficulty experienced by law enforcement in most forfeiture cases is the perceived necessity to link the accused to the commission of an antecedent or predicate (to use American terminology) offence, and also to the proceeds of that criminal activity. The Canadian legislation provides two different standards of proof. Both sections depend on there having been a conviction for an enterprise crime or a designated drug offence.

If the court is satisfied *on a balance of probabilities* that any property is proceeds of crime and that the offence was committed in relation to that property, it shall order the property forfeited. If the person is found guilty of a proceeds of crime offence, but the evidence does not establish the link between that specific offence and the property, forfeiture can still occur if the court is satisfied *beyond a reasonable doubt* that the property is proceeds of crime. Similarly, upon the death or absconding of an accused, property can be forfeited if the court is satisfied beyond a reasonable doubt that the property is the proceeds of crime.[12] Figure 6.2 illustrates the linkages that are required. "A" represents a regular Criminal Code prosecution with no targeting of illicit proceeds. "B" indicates that illicit proceeds can be seized even without an accused if he or she has died or absconded. "C" illustrates two different scenarios: the accused could have been convicted of an unrelated offence, but the court was satisfied beyond a reasonable doubt that his or her proceeds were, in fact, proceeds of crime; or the accused is convicted of laundering illicit proceeds, which is, in fact, an enterprise crime. Finally, "D" represents an actual proceeds of crime case with linkages between the accused, a separate profit-making criminal act, and the illicit proceeds.

The police argue that while the legislation is written to allow for forfeiture in situations where the connection has not been made between the offence and the property but the court is satisfied that the property is the proceeds of crime, in practice Crown counsel have wanted to see the three elements firmly connected before they have been prepared to support the special search warrant or restraint order requests. As the CACP Organized Crime recommendation explains, if the police were able to convince the court that the property was "beyond a reasonable doubt" the proceeds of crime, then the accused would have been charged with another substantive offence. They would like the legislation to be amended so that in cases where the convicted individual is a "career criminal" and a net worth indicates that "on

FIGURE 6.2

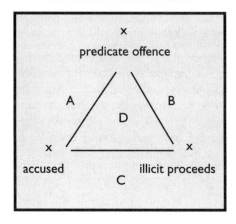

a balance of probabilities" the property is the proceeds of crime, then the property should be forfeitable.

Before the introduction of the Proceeds of Crime legislation, police had become increasingly aware of the large amounts of money that were being professionally laundered by people who specialized in laundering funds. At that time, these people could not be arrested because in many cases they had nothing to do with the crimes that had produced the profits that were now being laundered. From a law enforcement perspective, this was a serious matter. However, the Proceeds of Crime legislation, by making money laundering an offence, has made it theoretically possible for the police, in a particularly strong case, to act against the illicit proceeds.

SPECIAL SEARCH WARRANTS AND RESTRAINT ORDERS

Prior to the passing of the Proceeds of Crime legislation, the main search warrant available to Canadian law enforcement was the s. 487 search warrant, which allowed police to search the premises of subjects of criminal investigations. Proceeds cases require the police to gain information from third-party locations such as banks and other cooperative organizations. The new s. 462.32 search warrant is designed to allow the police to search for and then seize or restrain property that may eventually be forfeited under the Proceeds of Crime legislation.

The police have expressed a number of frustrations with the new search-warrant provisions, and in some cases have preferred to proceed under the original warrant and request the "special" search warrant only *after* the seizure had taken place. The perceived weaknesses of special warrants are outlined below:

- They require that the Attorney General sign an undertaking and accept liability for any costs or damages that may occur. Some provincial attorneys general are reluctant to take this responsibility unless the case is without any risk. Clearly, a body of cases and judgments will not be built unless some risks are taken.

- They can be exercised only by senior judges.

- The paperwork process is so extensive that in some cases the proceeds dissipate before the documentation is received. On a case by case basis, the police have to determine if they have the resources required for the process of obtaining the authorizations. Particularly onerous are multi-property cases, since a separate warrant must be executed for each property targeted for seizure. Police estimate that in some cases preparing, serving, and maintaining the search warrant or restraint order consumed 80 percent of the investigative time.

- Section 462.35 of the Criminal Code requires that special warrants be renewed every six months. This is seen as an unnecessary hardship given that lengthy investigations may require a valid warrant over an extended period of time.

- Unlike s. 487 search warrants, special warrants are not recognized interprovincially. Thus, a judge in one province may issue the warrant, while another, presented with the same facts, may not. Second, third, or fourth hearings, depending on the number of provinces involved, are costly and undermine a sense of fairness when there is not full agreement.

The final criticism is somewhat controversial. Section 462.34 of the Proceeds of Crime legislation stipulates that a judge in Canada may release property under the seizure or restraint order for the purpose of meeting the reasonable business and legal expenses of the accused. According to the *Department of Justice Guidelines and Policy on Attorney Fee Forfeitures*,[13] lawyers must ensure that any transactions between themselves and their defendant clients are not seen to be "sham transactions" intended to shield assets. Also, they must not have known that the assets would be subject to forfeiture at the time of the transfer. To determine the reasonableness of legal expenses, the judge holds an *in camera* hearing.

The CACP Organized Crime Committee report calls this provision "offensive and illogical." It maintains that social services exist to meet an accused person's living needs and that legal aid will cover his or her legal costs. Making an exception for legal costs, the report argues, is akin to "legislative laundering."

The situation is different in the United States. Under the U.S. Comprehensive Forfeiture Act of 1984, Congress incorporated into the forfeiture provisions of RICO and CCE the "relation back" doctrine, which causes the title of all assets derived from crime to vest in the government as of the time that the crime occurred. These assets cannot therefore be put into the hands of a defence lawyer. A defendant in this case has a right to counsel, but not a right to counsel of choice—especially one hired with tainted assets (Wuslich 1988).[14] Much of this debate revolves around the principle of "innocent until proven guilty." As Costanzo (1992) observes, "the rights of a defendant must be weighed against the view that it is iniquitous for a person to be allowed to spend as he chooses property which he derived or realized from the commission of the offence with which he is charged, i.e., tainted property to which he has no moral entitlement" (4).

DISCLOSURE OF INCOME TAX INFORMATION

In designated drug cases, Section 462.48 allows the attorney general, or a person designated by the attorney general, to make application to a judge to order the Deputy Minister of National Revenue for Taxation (or his or her designate) to allow a named police officer to examine (and take away if necessary) all specified information and documents. Without this provision, the documentation would be inaccessible to investigators prior to the "laying of an information," which is the first step in launching a prosecution against a suspect (Mosley 1989, 22). The police would like the provision to be extended to all of the enterprise crime cases. Allowing the disclosure for drug offences only, they maintain, does not give them the tax information they need to facilitate net worth analysis in the wider range of organized crime cases.[15]

DISCLOSURE BY INFORMANTS

Section 462.47 allows a person to disclose to a peace officer, or to the attorney general, any reasonable suspicions that a property is proceeds of crime or that a person has committed, or is about to commit, either an enterprise crime offence or a designated drug offence. This provision protects officials who are in positions of confidentiality with customers or clients from liability for any injury that may occur as a result of their disclosure.

THE PROCEEDS OF CRIME MONEY LAUNDERING ACT (OR THE BANK RECORDS AND TRACING LEGISLATION)

On May 27, 1991, Gilles Loiselle, Minister of State (Finance), tabled legislation on record-keeping that would facilitate the investigation and prosecution of money laundering cases. The Proceeds of Crime Money Laundering Act came into force on June 21, 1991. The regulations accompanying the Act were published in the *Canada Gazette* (Part I) on June 13, 1992, and came into force in March 1993. The financial industry is now required to retain certain records for a five-year period so that they are available for police investigations. The Act applies to:

- banks

- credit unions/caisses populaires

- life insurers

- trust companies

- loan companies

- securities dealers

- foreign-exchange houses

- businesses, professions, and activities that in the course of their business receive more than $10,000 in cash which is to be paid or transferred on another's behalf.

The legislation's greatest impact is likely to be on the foreign-exchange houses, which have not previously been subject to adequate regulation and accountability. The Act's record-keeping regulations are compatible with those already in place in many deposit-taking institutions, and therefore will not necessitate much adjustment. The regulations do address discrepancies across jurisdictions in terms of how long records are kept by financial institutions. In the past, there had been no assurances that records would be available for police investigations going back three or four years.

The new regulations do extend beyond the financial institutions, but this net is not widely cast. Not all businesses dealing in cash over $10,000 are subject to the regulations—only those businesses that receive the cash "to be paid or transferred on another's behalf." Thus, lawyers would be accountable for records under the Act, but only when receiving or holding the cash for another person or transmitting the cash to another person. Large cash payments for professional services are not covered by the legislation, and since no third-party transaction is involved lawyers need not generate paper trails of fees paid to themselves. (This may seem contradictory given that lawyers' fees are protected from the seizure and forfeiture provisions of the Proceeds of Crime legislation.) Bail money deposited with a lawyer is exempt and (as noted in the chapter on money laundering) Canadian casino operations are also exempt.

The Canadian response to the challenge of making financial transactions more accountable is a *recording* scheme—supported by suspicious-transaction reporting to police and the "good practices/know your customer" approach to banking—rather than a *reporting* mechanism, which characterizes the U.S. response. Amid pressure on Canada to duplicate the U.S. system, Canadian officials attempted to determine the actual gains from Currency Transaction Reporting (CTR). While the CTR is in many cases responsible for increasing the size of the seizures, we could not find evidence that it had been responsible for identifying or initiating police investigations. Levi (1991) criticizes the CTR system on the following grounds:

> Overall, despite being sincerely believed in by their adherents, it is arguable that in the context of the United States, where there are many banks and where cash transaction reports are made on paper, currency-reporting requirements are an example of an over-trumpeted intelligence methodology, since except in a targeted investigation, the system has neither the capacity to input the data rapidly (within six months of receipt) nor the capacity of putting the information to sound operational use (35).

Another criticism of the U.S. system, that Australia is seemingly avoiding,[16] is the paper glut that accompanies it. In 1990, 7 324 000 CTR 4789 forms were filed in the United States. Numerous, large fines of the banks have greatly increased compliance within that sector. Our conclusion was that facilitating the reporting of suspicious transactions directly to the police and having thorough and timely records in place for the use by the police during their investigations constituted the appropriate response. Information that cannot be used or relied upon is not valuable.

While the CTR system is considered ineffective, Canadian law enforcement would like a Canadian equivalent of the U.S. CMIR cross-border reporting requirements. At present, Canadian customs officers and the police do not have the right to seize even highly suspicious money that crosses the border. Cases have involved large sums of cash: in one instance, $800,000 in U.S. currency hidden in a spare tire wrapped in foil and plastic. This person was denied entry into Canada and because of the U.S. reporting requirements, the U.S. authorities were able to seize the money. These types of legislative differences between Canada and the United States add to the frustration of cross-border enforcement.

ASSET MANAGEMENT AND SHARING

The Proceeds of Crime legislation was passed with the expectation that it would enable the police to take away the illicit proceeds and property of convicted criminals. Unfortunately, no adequate provision was made for the management and maintenance of the goods seized by police. The difficulty arises from the time lag between the freezing and seizure of the goods and the completion of the legal processes that determines the guilt or innocence of the suspect. Upon a suspect's conviction, the goods determined to be the "proceeds of crime" can be forfeited. However, if the person is declared innocent, the property must be returned—and returned in good order. Court cases can take months or years to complete, and most types of property require professional handling to ensure that they retain some value for whomever assumes ultimate ownership.

The old RCMP line "Never seize anything that eats" should have been applied to the infamous "Ski Montjoie" case—the case that pushed the government to create an asset management and sharing regime. In 1990, the RCMP seized the Ski-Montjoie facility in North Hatley, Quebec. Police investigations had shown that this resort had been obtained through the importation of multi-tonne shipments of marijuana from Jamaica to Florida. The drug money was routed through Switzerland and then "loaned" to the traffickers by a Swiss company. The traffickers were said to have put over $7 million into the resort, which upon seizure had a market value of approximately $4.5 million.

In addition to the difficulties associated with keeping the resort in adequate condition pre-forfeiture, the federal government faced unanticipated legalities in the form of legitimate creditors whose claims for payment exceeded $2.5 million. The ski facility's operating companies were insolvent at the time of the seizure. A judge in Quebec appointed a lawyer to administer the facility (another major expense for the federal government). As of 1995, with an asset management group in charge, the ski facility is actually breaking even—but it still cannot be sold because of the significant decrease in land values in the area.

The liability aspect of the Proceeds of Crime legislation (which falls to the attorney general) makes it particularly essential that all seized property be professionally maintained pending the termination of the court process. A 1990 MOU between the RCMP and National Health and Welfare stipulated that the RCMP was to maintain the property pre-forfeiture, that is, until a verdict was given. If conviction and forfeiture was decided by the courts, National Health and Welfare was to maintain, sell, or otherwise dispose of the property, with the revenue going into the General Revenue Fund. The first flaw in this scenario was the naive assumption that a policing organization would be able (or even willing) to take on professional property maintenance responsibilities. The second flaw was the expectation that provincial and municipal governments would enthusiastically encourage their police forces to assist the RCMP in completing these expensive and prolonged Proceeds of Crime investigations—and then stand by and watch as the forfeited proceeds were handed over to the General Revenue Fund. Professional maintenance of the property and a mechanism for sharing the proceeds with different agencies or levels of government were soon recognized to be essential to the successful handling of seized assets.

In addition to the conflicts arising within its own borders, Canada faced relentless pressure to share seized proceeds with foreign jurisdictions. United States seemed particularly eager to share proceeds of crime with Canadian agencies and similarly share in Canadian seizures arising from joint-force operations or other collaborative efforts. U.S. Customs advertise the extent to which their own seizures pay for their law enforcement costs, and law enforcement officers south of the border boast of the vehicles and other property—including cash—that police forces are able to keep for their own use after forfeiture.[17] A "Miami Vice" approach to law enforcement seems attractive to police forces feeling themselves strapped for funds. However, Canadian government officials, some Canadian police forces, and an increasing number of U.S. officials have expressed concerns that the choice of which cases to pursue can be biased by the vested interest of a police department that is in a position to benefit materially from the decisions that are made. Particular controversy centres on the civil *in rem* forfeiture cases where goods are seized without a person having been found guilty of an offence.

While it is hard to convince some police departments that costs incurred during investigations should come out of their regular budgets without any additional recompense from seizures, it is easier to warn them that evidence from the United States indicates that jurisdictions short of resources tend to build the "expectation" of seizures into the budget process. With varying degrees of subtlety, U.S. police-force budgets are reduced in the expectation that some resources from the seizure of illicit proceeds will be accrued during the year. The upshot is that police forces become operationally reliant on making significant seizures, which again increases the likelihood of bias in enforcement practices. The police may target specific cases not for material gain, but merely to maintain existing resources and viability.

The police are by no means the only group to exhibit a proprietary interest in illicit proceeds. With only minor exceptions, each group (police, community, levels of government) consulted by Canadian government officials on the question of who should share in the distribution of these proceeds named itself as the most worthy candidate. Criminal sanctions have never been so utilitarian!

At one stage government officials were equating the seizure of funds to "priming" the pump that would gush drug prevention programs, treatment, and rehabilitation facilities, with a proportion feeding back into the expensive police investigations that would then produce more dollars. One of these pumps plus a couple of government-run casinos should produce all of the revenue Canada requires! It remains too early to know the potential extent of the forfeiture and sharing.

THE SEIZED PROPERTY MANAGEMENT ACT

Bill C-123, The Seized Property Management Act, was passed by the House of Commons in June 1993 and came into force on September 1, 1993. The Act authorizes the federal government, through the Minister of Government Services, to manage property that has been seized and restrained in connection with criminal offences, and to dispose of property when forfeiture is ordered by the courts. A Seized Property Management Directorate (SPMD) was created to carry out the following functions:

- pre-seizure advice

- control and maintenance of seized property

- management of restrained property

- appraisal

- advancement of funds to preserve property

- inspections

- disposal of property

- satisfaction of claims

- record-keeping.

Funds received are to be shared at "year end" after operating costs of the Seized Property Management Directorate, potential liability for the undertakings, and losses have been deducted—with other levels of government (including foreign governments), but not directly with police forces.

The Forfeited Property Sharing Regulations made under the Seized Property Management Act came into force January 31, 1995. The plan is to begin with a fairly rough percentage split of 90 percent, 50 percent, and 10 percent depending on the extent of a jurisdiction's involvement in a case that leads to assets being forfeited via a federal prosecution. Ten percent always goes to the federal government to cover prosecution, drug analysis, and similar involvements, even in cases that are largely the result of provincial or municipal police involvement. On March 22, 1995, the Minister of Justice signed an agreement to allow Canada to share forfeited proceeds of crime with the government of the United States. The U.S. Attorney General Janet Reno signed on behalf of the United States. Minister Rock stated:

> This agreement underscores the importance of international cooperation and coordination of law enforcement efforts in combatting organized crime and drug trafficking (*Canadian Police Chief Newsletter* 1995, 17).

The Act applies only to federal prosecutions. Provinces are slowly putting into place their own legislation that will allow for the management of properly and sharing of the proceeds from enterprise crimes. Before the introduction of the federal legislation, British Columbia was the first province to create legislation that addressed the disposition of provincially prosecuted proceeds. This legislation (Bill 64-1989) specifies that the proceeds are to be used "to facilitate the administration of criminal justice and law enforcement in the Province."

The B.C. protocol specifies that these funds are to be used for "exceptional" expenditures not otherwise funded in the ministries' budgets. The seized proceeds are not intended to reimburse agencies responsible for the investigations. Again, this seems to reflect the fear that direct reimbursement would build the expectation of seized proceeds for future funding allocations and possibly bias enforcement.

NOTES

1. Some 15 years later, a libel suit is pending against the *Connections* series. Given the impact that the series had at the time, it is ironic that tapes of the shows have been removed from archives and libraries,

with the result that the production is no longer available for public viewing.

2. Canadian Police Association Annual Convention, Toronto, September 23, 1977. Paper entitled *Policing a Changing Society: A National Strategy to Combat Organized Crime in Canada.*

3. The B.C. Coordinated Law Enforcement Unit, which had been monitoring organized crime, published in 1974 an analysis of heroin trafficking, gambling, commercial crime, and major theft at sea and air ports. In 1975, the Second Findings Report, titled *Organized Crime in British Columbia,* focused on other enterprise crimes such as contract killing, loan-sharking, and cocaine trafficking.

4. Department of Justice, June 10, 1983, p. vi.

5. An exception is Bill 205 (anti-smoking), which was introduced by Lynn MacDonald in the late 1980s.

6. The signed document with Hong Kong is an agreement rather than treaty. The pre-1997 regulations prevent Hong Kong from signing treaties that would remain valid after the China takeover.

7. The surrender of a fugitive to a Commonwealth country, unlike extradition, does not require double criminality. Nor is the requesting country bound by the rule of specialty, which precludes the prosecution of the fugitive for offences for which he or she was not surrendered.

8. A revised Canadian Extradition Act, which came into force on December 1, 1992, speeds up the process of extraditing those charged with offences in foreign jurisdictions. Previously, an extradition could take five years to complete, mainly due to appeals.

9. Offences like cigarette smuggling were not seen to constitute enterprise crime at the time the legislation was drafted. Developments since that time resulted in successful demands for amendments to the legislation.

10. Canadian police have ready access to U.S. results. *The Assest Forfeiture News, Quick Release, Significant Sharing Report,* and other bulletins produced and widely distributed by the Assest Forfeiture Office document the "equitable sharing" activity on a daily, weekly, and monthly basis.

11. S. 462.3.(b)(ii) and s. 462.38(1).

12. The court may infer in forfeiture hearings that the property was obtained from the proceeds of crime if it is established that the value of all of a person's property after the commission of the offence exceeds the legitimate income of the offender. Net-worth analysis is used to derive a value of all of the legitimate income and assets as distinct from the worth of the individual, including his or her criminal assets.

13. *The Criminal Law Reporter* 38, no. 1 (1985): 3001–3008.

14. The court may, however, award attorney's fees under the Equal Access to Justice Act [28 U.S.C. 2412(d)(1)(A)] on the finding that the government was not "substantially justified" in delaying its investigation into the source of the seized currency and the initiation of forfeiture proceedings (*Quick Release,* April/May 1992, 2).

15. Comments from RCMP Enterprise Crime members interviewed by Schneider, as well as the CACP Organized Crime Committee.

16. The Australian system will be largely a direct on-line computer system with paper forms completed only by those businesses that do not have access to computer systems.

17. While the amount of seized goods is recognized to be substantial, there was always a degree of margin between the figures quoted and the actual worth of the goods. In some cases, goods seized with a specified value were worth much less by the time the case had gone through the courts. These smaller value figures are sometimes avoided in the hype to sell the merits of seizing assets.

CHAPTER 7

Operational Change (Policing Requirements)

Once the merit of new law enforcement strategies is accepted, the next step is to focus on the technicalities of putting into operation the enabling legislation. The fight against money laundering, for example, requires a network of facilitating law enforcement tools and skills at least as sophisticated as the network the criminal uses to sidestep the law. Enabling tools such as legislation, international agreements, witness-protection schemes, financial/ business cooperation, funding for forensic expertise, and asset-management/asset-sharing mechanisms must operate in unison if law enforcement goals are to be properly served.

We usually speak of the criminal justice system as if it were a single integrated entity. What becomes clear is that the justice system comprises many organizations, each one driven by different survival objectives, and each one working within a distinct culture or environment. In 1992, after several Charter of Rights-related, Supreme Court decisions believed by the police to have seriously limited their ability to do police work, it was suggested that a police officer be seconded to the Department of Justice to collaborate with Justice lawyers in creating legislation that *would* work in the field. The Department of Justice officials interpreted this suggestion to mean that the police wanted to learn how their department operated. They therefore suggested that it might be best to have a number of police officers spending a week or two each within their department so that a greater number could be "informed." This interpretation overlooked the importance of the segments in the justice process becoming *mutually* informed of the tasks, frustrations, and limitations of other segments in the interrelated processes. Each component in the criminal justice system must work in tandem if organized crime enforcement is to be effective.

FIGURE 7.1

Enabling Legislation

While police may have some concerns with the extent to which the new pieces of legislation address their policing needs, the lack of enabling legislation is no longer a main complaint. However, the creation of enabling organized crime legislation coincided with significant Charter of Rights decisions related to police powers— decisions that, from the policing perspective, hindered the ability of police to carry out the complex investigations that the legislation was intended to address.

Since 1990, a number of key decisions have ruled that police practices, particularly in the area of electronic surveillance, violated Section 8 of the Canadian Charter of Rights and Freedoms, which specifies, "Everyone has the right to be secure against unreasonable search or seizure."

Similarly, traditional "ownership" and treatment of investigative materials was deemed to violate Section 7 of the Charter, which states, "Everyone has the right to life, liberty and security of the person and the right not to be deprived thereof except in accordance with the principles of fundamental justice."

These two categories of police powers are deemed by the police to be critically important to their organized crime investigations, which traditionally involve undercover work and massive accumulations of documents and evidentiary materials.

ELECTRONIC SURVEILLANCE

The first significant decision affecting electronic surveillance in police work was *R. v. Duarte* [1990, 53 C.C.C. (3d) 1 (S.C.C.)], a case that illustrates the occasional disharmony between operational police work and the criminal law. The case is particularly important in dictating how undercover operations are conducted. Under the Criminal Code, the interception of a conversation without first obtaining judicial authorization was an indictable offence *except* under conditions termed "participant observation," which involved the wiretapping of communications where one of the parties to the conversation consented to be recorded. Before the Duarte case, it was lawful for the police to place a wiretapping device on an undercover officer, agent, or informer as long as that person consented to wear the transmitter.

The majority opinion in the Duarte case was that there was no logical distinction between participant surveillance (consent wiretaps) and surreptitious surveillance, since in both cases an unwitting person was having his or her words recorded. The Supreme Court argued that its decision was

> not to deny that it is of vital importance that law enforcement agencies be able to employ electronic surveillance in their investigation of crime. Electronic surveillance plays an indispensable role in the detection of sophisticated criminal enterprises. Its utility in the investigation of drug related crimes, for example, has been proven time and again. *But ... it is unacceptable in a free society that the agencies of the state be free to use this technology at their sole discretion. The threat this would pose to privacy is wholly unacceptable* [italics added] (12).

As a result of *Duarte,* the police were required to obtain an authorization prior to carrying out these undercover operations. However, the extensive information that must be presented to a judge in order to obtain the authorizations is usually not available early on in an undercover operation. At this stage, the undercover officer is wired for sound by means of a bodypack, but the objective has more to do with personal protection than with the collecting of evidence. The transmittal of voices reveals to outside police officers the progression of the undercover operation, and allows them to take emergency actions if something goes wrong. In these cases the police would not necessarily have sufficient information needed to persuade a judge to provide authorization.

The dramatic impact of the Supreme Court decision on ongoing police investigations led to an "unofficial" judgment by the legal counsel for the Ministry of the Solicitor General that the wearing of bodypacks strictly for security and nonevidentiary reasons would not be in violation of *Duarte*. This unofficial determination was less than satisfactory since the police never knew when an investigation would be compromised by a judge deciding that a violation had in fact occurred.

R. v. Wong [1990, 60 C.C.C. (3d) 460] extended the application of the Duarte decision to video surveillance. Video surveillance was declared to constitute a search and therefore to require an authorization. In this case, there was no legal vehicle by which to obtain the authorization. The concept of video surveillance had not been previously included in the search-warrant provisions of the Criminal Code.[1]

R. v. Wise [1992, 70 C.C.C. (3d) (S.C.C.)] further extended the restrictions on police work by declaring that a tracking device ("beeper") placed inside a car constituted a search by the police. Once again, the Criminal Code included no mechanism by which a warrant authorizing the installation of a tracking device could be obtained.

Even when it was technically possible to get an authorization in the three types of cases cited, some of the targets of the proceeds of crime investigations were highly placed lawyers, government officials, and wealthy businesspersons. Lawyers in particular have been implicated in major money laundering schemes. Some have "specialized" to the degree that their practices consist of providing money laundering services for their clients. Undercover work is particularly essential in these cases, and there is a fear (perhaps unfounded) that the lawyers who assist the police in preparing the warrant requests might discourage the police from taking such action against a legal "colleague."

AN ACT TO AMEND THE CRIMINAL CODE, THE CROWN LIABILITY AND PROCEEDINGS ACT, AND THE RADIOCOMMUNICATION ACT (BILL C-109)

Bill C-109, an Act to Amend the Criminal Code, the Crown Liability and Proceedings Act, and the Radiocommunication Act was passed in order to rectify some of the most blatant contradictions that had arisen from the clash between court decisions and police work. Bill C-109 came into force in August 1993. With respect to the bodypack/Duarte dilemma, the new legislation allows the police to intercept a private communication if:

- either the originator of the private communication or the intended recipient gives consent to the interception;

- there are reasonable grounds to believe that there is a risk of bodily harm to the person who consented to the interception;

- the purpose of the interception is to prevent bodily harm.

The contents of the interception will be inadmissible as evidence except for the purposes of proceedings in which actual, attempted, or threatened bodily harm is alleged. This Act requires that the police destroy any recordings and any transcript of the recording or notes. The legislation also broadens the pool of people who can apply for judicial authorization and of the number of judges who can authorize the interceptions, and allows for an exceptional or emergency interception by the police without consent or prior authorization. Issues related to video and tracking surveillance were addressed through the creation of a General Warrant. The challenge is to create a balance between granting sufficient powers to the police and protecting people's rights. Some critics feel that Bill C-109 goes too far (Schmitz 1993), while others are pleased that some of the restrictions on police operational work have been modified.

DISCLOSURE

A significant issue from the police perspective relates to disclosure of evidence in court. Until 1991, neither the Crown nor defence had clear principles that would determine what information the Crown had to disclose to the defence. Different jurisdictions, different police forces, and different judges had varying interpretations, particularly with respect to information that was deemed "privileged" and therefore exempted from disclosure. Some of this ambiguity ended with the *Stinchcombe* case.

R. v. Stinchcombe [1991 68 C.C.C. (3d)] specified in great detail what information the police were required to share with the defence:

> *The fruits of a police investigation which are in the possession of counsel for the Crown are not the property of the Crown for use in securing a conviction, but the property of the public to be used to ensure that justice is done.* The defence on the other hand has less of an obligation to assist the prosecution and is entitled to assume a purely adversarial role towards the prosecution. There is a general duty on the part of the Crown to disclose all material it proposes to use at trial on a charge of an indictable offense, and especially all evidence which may assist the accused even if the Crown does not propose to adduce it. This obligation is not however absolute. The Crown has a discretion to withhold information which may be subject to privilege and may delay disclosure so as not to impede an investigation. ... The discretion of the Crown is reviewable by the trial judge [italics added] (2).

The issues arising from the Stinchcombe judgment extend beyond strict disclosure matters to challenge the position of the police relative to the state and the accused. The Stinchcombe case emphasizes that, while police have the task of assembling information and in building cases, neither the separate pieces of information that they gather nor the finished product—the created case—is "theirs." Rather, public funds have paid for a job to be done, and the resulting materials are to be made available to the judge, the Crown, and the defence. The media image of the cop on the beat who finds the guilty party and solves the crime is treated in current court cases as the "dangerous" model. In the words of Judge Sopinka "The purpose of a criminal prosecution is not to obtain a conviction; it is to lay before a jury what the Crown considers to be credible evidence to what is alleged to be a crime" [Stinchcombe, 1991, 68 C.C.C. (3d), 7]. And in *R. v. Denbigh* (1990), the judge takes the position that, in this case:

> right thinking people, i.e., those who recognize that the system of criminal justice is more important than *any* case in it, recognize that the failure of the police to discharge the obligation imposed upon them to be more than "bloodhounds" has clearly resulted in a situation where fundamental principles of our criminal justice system have been violated (quoted in Brucker 1992, 67).

There is a discrepancy between the rhetoric of the judges quoted above and the rhetoric that is used to recruit and motivate police officers. How members of an organization gain a sense of self-worth, esprit de corps, and loyalty becomes extremely important when we look at the issue of police corruption and morale problems. Although society requires police who will maintain objectivity in their search for evidence, stripping police work of the goal of solving crimes may inadvertently turn police work into a blend of paper shuffling, work avoidance, and process-oriented activities. Somewhere between the extremes of "bloodhounds" versus "cogs" in the criminal justice process is a policing model that encourages police involvement in cases—including "solving" a case when the checks imposed by legislation are respected— while ensuring that the relationship between the police and the prosecutors stays within certain parameters.

The U.S. criminal justice process conveys a sense that the police and the district attorney operate as a team to "catch the criminal." This image and operational style is strongly resisted in Canada. For example, when the government wanted to set up pilot projects that would have seen prosecutors working closely with the police in three "proceeds of crime units," concerns were expressed about the development of a "prosecutorial team against the prospective suspect" concept of justice. *Stinchcombe* reiterates (and perhaps exaggerates) this concern.

Although some legal experts maintain that *Stinchcombe* does not fundamentally change the way in which the police are supposed to share their information, this case has in practice resulted in very different disclosure practices. One senior legal analyst called it a "crap-shoot," meaning that it is hard to be certain whether some aspect of the development of the case will be deemed in violation of the Charter. Every case becomes different and the police argue that they never know how to predict the outcome.

The principles for disclosure have been formally made a part of the law, however the law allows police to argue that certain information is privileged and must be exempted from disclosure. This argument would be made most commonly in cases where the police were convinced that the lives of informants or other undercover operators would be at risk if their identities were revealed. That the final decision on disclosure rests with a trial judge introduces a sense of unease into every police investigation involving information that can put individual lives, future working relations, or other criminal investigations at risk. The wide-disclosure expectation also makes it increasingly difficult for Canadian law enforcement to work with foreign police forces that are unhampered by such disclosure provisions.

Even without the consideration of risk to lives, the requirement that police duplicate notebooks and all witness materials and documents they have used or referred to is an acutely burdensome and expensive one. Policy-makers seem unaware of the rooms stacked with bankers' boxes full of photocopied documents, and of the human resources that must be devoted to producing and reproducing the reams of material. This disclosure requirement at times seems more a penalty against the police than a benefit to the defence.

The disclosure implications of *Stinchcombe* were examined at a 1990 Supreme Court closed-door hearing at which it was decided that the RCMP would be responsible for any harm done to Jaworski, an RCMP informant who had been compelled to testify against Colombian cartel members. The case was then handed to the Quebec Court of Appeal judge to determine if Jaworski and his parents were in significant danger. Neither RCMP Inspector Wayne Blackburn nor the judge hearing the case could conclude categorically that an informant who testifies against violent criminals will not be the target of criminal revenge. Jaworski's lawyer argued that

> if the state enforced a subpoena calling for Jaworski to testify while knowing it could kill his parents, this would be an infringement on Jaworski's psychological and emotional integrity. That would contravene guarantees in the Charter of

Rights and Freedoms for the right of a person to life, liberty, and security of the person (Edwards 1991, 203).

(This case is discussed later in this chapter under the witness protection section.)

NEW ENFORCEMENT EXPERTISE: TRADITIONAL POLICING WITH SPECIAL SKILLS AND RISKS

The problem confronting law enforcement is that while new legislation and new demands are being presented to the police, little consideration is being given to whether there exist the skills/expertise, training, and resources that are needed to facilitate the shift toward a new policing style. Changes are also being demanded from within the policing communities as well as from outside, but somehow it is assumed that the new requirements can be accommodated by the older existing structures that have worked for more traditional policing styles. When resources are granted to the police, it is further assumed that those officers who have spent their careers doing "police work" will be able to shift easily into a mode that requires strategic planning, accounting expertise, and a close working relationship with "partners" well outside the sphere of traditional police work.

Performance expectations for the street officers are ambiguous and unrealistic, but so too are the demands on upper management. Although a few police chiefs, commissioners, and senior police managers have been exposed to internationally oriented investigations, most upper-management employees are more comfortable with traditional police work. "Resistance and drift" is often the result. Management may publicly voice support for proceeds of crime investigations but at the same time resist allocating to these investigations the resources (e.g., criminal analysts and forensic accountants) and long-term commitment they demand.

EVALUATING ORGANIZED CRIME ENFORCEMENT

In recognition of the fact that police and prosecutors in Canada are not yet making adequate use of the Proceeds of Crime Legislation, as part of the renewal of Canada's Drug Strategy, the Department of the Solicitor General received funds to set up and monitor three integrated anti-drug profiteering pilot units in Toronto, Vancouver, and Montreal. In addition to the lack of funds that police always cite as being responsible for law enforcement's lack of success using the Proceeds of Crime legislation, other factors include a lack of experience in prioritizing cases, insufficient knowledge of forensic analysis, and a resistance to accepting the skills of nontraditional policing partners. Evaluators were to monitor these pilot sites over a five-year period and report frequently on their operations (culminating with the end of the five-year renewal of Canada's drug strategy in 1997).

Evaluating organized crime control strategies is not easy. A review of the U.S. General Accounting Office Reports and other Task Force Evaluation Reports indicate that most efforts are self-evaluations by agencies and that most of the focus is on administrative data rather than analysis of impact. Most evaluations fail to set out clear, agreed-upon objectives against which to evaluate the projects. Even when objectives are clearly established, there is often a failure to create an overseeing committee that can steer the activities of the units toward their objectives. The Canadian project has tried to avoid some of these shortcomings. Some of its early findings are promising:

- While it is hard to innovate within paramilitary organizations such as police forces, it is possible to bring about some significant "shifts" in the way the work is done.

- Historical or traditional obstacles can be overcome with resources and a change to the physical location and structure of the operations. Having different agencies housed together and working on the same projects does much to break down the hostility—or at least the negative competition between the "partners."

- A major change is possible in the new working relationships between Department of Justice lawyers and the police. Prosecutors worked in the units to advise and assist, which resulted in better working relations between the two groups. The prosecutors assigned to work daily with the police in the unit were not the same ones who would then take the case to court—this was to avoid creating the impression that the prosecutors were being co-opted.

- Although there is some evidence that the units are now making bigger cases that involve more assets, there is little indication that criminal organizations are actually being destroyed.

The final point emphasizes the importance of having clear, agreed upon objectives. *Goal-setting* must be a visible and accountable aspect of organized crime control, otherwise no evaluation of the enforcement efforts will be possible. If elimination of the organized crime problem is not feasible, then the objectives for special-enforcement units, joint-force operations, and special organized crime projects must be enunciated in measurable terms.

POLICING STRATEGIES

Policing should not be applied in like manner across all organized crime groups. Ill-selected strategies might negatively result in specific types of groups forming monopolies and moving toward a greater level of corruption. Strategies that may successfully target the predatory, less socially integrated criminals could be futile against symbiotic/legitimate groups. Below are outlined enforcement strategies appropriate to each of the ideal-type groups that were first introduced in Chapter 2, and are illustrated again in Figure 7.2.

FIGURE 7.2

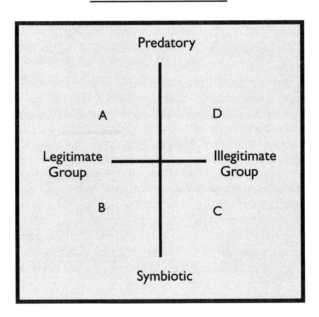

A. The enforcement task will be to distinguish the groups' legitimate activities from their criminal ones. While the organized crime activity will be mainly street-level and nonsophisticated, the legitimate status of the groups may cause political concerns that may have an enforcement impact. Policing strategies designed to limit the criminal activity may be the desired objective. This may involve a "problem-solving" policing approach that works to eliminate the attractiveness of opportunistic organized crime.[2] The longer the criminal activity is allowed to continue, the more sophisticated and entrenched it may become.

B. These organized crime groups represent a great challenge to law enforcement. The schemes often involve violence and may be intertwined with political corruption, networks of legitimate and semilegitimate businesses, and official collusion. The ambiguous status of the group, the ideological commitment of the members, and their willingness to resort to violence adds greatly to the impenetrability of these groups.

C. These organized crime groups have gained the power—political, economic, social—to corrupt the larger society, and may be seen as fulfilling necessary services. These criminals may be the respected members of communities, and their criminal operations are often woven through legitimate businesses. Enforcement efforts must concentrate on building profit-seizing cases that will help to disable the organizations. Enforcement will likely consist of intensive, long-term undercover operations involving specialists trained in forensic accounting and strategic analytical work.

D. In some ways, these groups are the easiest to target with law enforcement efforts because they lack any sense of legitimacy and operates exclusively at the predatory or early parasitic stage. Given the violence associated with these groups, there must be in place a viable witness-protection program to accommodate any would-be informants. Care must be taken to ensure that the enforcement strategies do not simply remove the weakest, most vulnerable groups within this category. Faulty enforcement strategies can lead to the creation of more powerful organized crime monopolies. Policework must address the homicide/violence offences, and gain international police intelligence on the various criminal schemes. Home country/source country links between law enforcement agencies are critical.

THE CRIMINAL INTELLIGENCE PROCESS

The best of intentions in most countries have resulted in only a primitive level of information-sharing between law enforcement jurisdictions, and very little, or sporadic, reliance upon anything approximating true intelligence analysis. The rhetoric may be in place, but the structures and commitment seldom are. Martens

(1990, 1991) identifies some of the reasons behind the ineffectiveness of domestic intelligence. What is missing is the will on the part of police management, government-funding sources, and other policy-makers to insist that police, prosecutors, and other partners in law enforcement set aside "turf" concerns over the ownership of information.

Information is a commodity that has a value within the organization and often beyond its confines as well. For this reason, it is highly protected. Before sharing information, one considers the "exchange" rate, that is, what will be given in return. What is true for all organizations is particularly true for police forces. Information is critical to the accomplishment of policing tasks because evaluation of individual or unit performance is ambiguous, and rewards are still assigned to those who accumulate the largest or biggest statistical numbers of "something," whether it be arrests, seizures, media coverage, or budgets.

Police and law enforcement information must be seen as "corporate" information. Officers must, therefore, be held responsible for making the best use of the corporate property. This points to the depth of the changes that must occur if analytical intelligence work is to become an important part of police work in general and sophisticated money laundering investigations in particular. "Getting on" with efficient police work may require giving credibility to professionals outside of the traditional policing field.

Intelligence work has much in common with research. The best people to hire, whether as civilians or as recruits onto police forces, may have skills different from those typically identified by traditional police recruitment boards. A knowledge of computers, accounting skills to carry out financial audits and net-worth analysis, library research skills, knowledge of law, and an ability to read large amounts of information and capture briefly the essence are all abilities that may be required. Police forces cannot afford to be anti-intellectual or isolationist.

Traditionally, police have worked separately from prosecutors and other professionals who have a role to play in law enforcement. This artificial distance is no longer practical, particularly with respect to complex enterprise crime cases. As Martens observes,

> Enterprise crime is usually committed with the encouragement and/or active participation of attorneys and other professionals. Enterprise criminals are not adverse to using attorneys and other professionals such as bankers, accountants, etc. Why then, should the police not use attorneys and other disciplines to investigate enterprise crime? (1991, 104).

A different philosophy of policing must emerge—one driven by a management that recognizes and rewards clever analytical work. Likewise, and essential to bringing about change, the evaluation of police officers must be based on more than seizure and arrest statistics. The quality of the cases successfully concluded must also be evaluated with recognition given to those cases that involved delicate/negotiative collaboration and sharing with other jurisdictions, forces, or agencies.

Case Prioritization

Long and expensive cases have little merit unless they are worthy of the expenditure of resources. Police management must be able to defend case choices by invoking established criteria such as the "harm" potential of an organized crime network.

We are becoming increasingly aware of the damage that "opportunistic" enforcement can do (Martens (1986). Narcotic enforcement at the street level does not on the surface appear to require an intelligence capability due to the number of opportunities for busts. Cases are easily made and can be "timed" to produce the maximum impact on the department, the media, or the budget. The *unanticipated consequences* of this strategy may, however, undermine law enforcement's wider efforts. For example, we know that law enforcement plays a critical role in the degree of monopolistic control that organized criminals exert over the illicit drug market, and, in some cases, in the amount of violence involved in criminal activity. For this reason, in addition to the limited availability of resources, case prioritization must become more sophisticated.

UNDERCOVER WORK IN ORGANIZED CRIME AND PROCEEDS CASES

Undercover work traditionally involves the use of a combination of informants, paid agents, and undercover officers. Informants are usually "turned" suspects who are exchanging information for some consideration at charging or sentencing. Paid agents either approach or are recruited by the police, and usually receive cash for information. Undercover officers are members of police forces who attempt to penetrate criminal organizations or at least get close enough to gain evidence on the criminal activity of suspects.

Sophisticated proceeds of crime and money laundering cases demand sophisticated undercover work. In addition to the more traditional undercover work involving casual bar contacts, the police are now required to set up elaborate money laundering storefront operations that not only have the appearance of being a viable money-exchange operation, but may in fact be able to carry out transactions. The archetypal scruffy undercover officer has been replaced in these operations by a conservative, suited, banker/accountant type who can "talk" laundering.

It is not merely the appearance and the tasks involved that separate proceeds undercover operations from traditional undercover work. While traditional undercover work may require a significant "flash roll" of cash in major drug investigations, laundering cases may require management to allocate resources months in advance of any action taken against the suspects. Buildings have to be rented and financial arrangements made before drawing in the suspects. Quick arrests and seizures are usually not the objective. Rather than ensnare the first criminal who uses the facility, the goal is to gain the trust of the criminal organization to the point that information on its operations, personnel, and illicit-commodity distribution schemes can be elicited.

The greater the stakes, the greater the risk to the undercover officers, agents, and informants. Evidence from the United States suggests that as penalties increase—particularly with respect to mandatory drug-related sentences—the danger to undercover officers increases. Getting away, even by eliminating the undercover officers, may take precedent over an anticipated life-sentence. Undercover laundering work may overlap with other undercover operations targeted at "lower" levels in the criminal organization. In such an instance, all of the dangers associated with large flash rolls, drug deliveries, and violent criminals come into play. The art or skill of the undercover operator is to be able to control not only the exchanges with the criminals but also their perceptions. If the suspects *think* they are in control and have an opening to take both the money and the drugs—with only the minor inconvenience of inflicting violence or death upon the undercover operator—then the temptation may be acted upon. The information and strategies that the undercover officer can use for self-protection (e.g., having money separated from drugs; having adequate back-up; not being able to obtain the drugs via a phone call) will have the desired effect only if the suspects perceive that they are being controlled (Alvarez 1993).

Management of undercover operators (officers or paid agents) is critical. As Gary Marx (1988) argues, the expanded use of covert tactics may be an organizational response to greater restrictions on noncovert police investigations. In May 1994, the Supreme Court of Canada was asked to consider whether it was a violation of the Charter to not only pay informants, but to make it a condition that full payment be given only if the undercover work leads to charges being laid. Judge Lynn Ratushy of Ontario Court Provincial Division ruled that the rights of accused persons were violated when the RCMP agreed to pay an agent a $10,000 "reward" plus expenses *if* the RCMP was able to "successfully investigate" the subjects (*Toronto Star*, May 24, 1994, p. 11A).

Informants may well be the heart of narcotic enforcement and other consensual crimes, but the risks are great. According to Manning and Redlinger (1978), the informant system by its very nature facilitates extortion, lying, blackmail, and violence. At the root of the problem is the uneasy reality that in many cases criminals are excused because they have information about other criminals that has a higher value to police than their own criminality. The system is turned upside down as informants work off their criminal penalties, and possibly get paid cash in the process, so that the police can build their "targeting upwards" cases (Skolnick 1974; Manning and Redlinger 1978). Evidence from both Canada and the United States suggests that informants are often more capable of "working an officer" than the officer is at "working" them.[3]

The role of informants was explored by the 1991 Judge Marin inquiry into RCMP handling of the investigation against Senator Michel Cogger. In a carefully worded conclusion (that could only have been intended to protect the feelings of the involved parties) the commission found that

> While this inquiry has revealed that RCMP members acted "ethically" in one sense, it has also revealed that they might well have acted differently had there been ethical standards to guide their operational decisions (Board of Inquiry Report, 1991, 119).

In building their money laundering case, the RCMP had used an undercover agent who had a history of unpredictable behaviour. The inquiry acknowledged the difficulties of building such cases against prominent businesspersons and politicians, but their recommendations reflected a sense that the informant had not been adequately controlled by the RCMP, and also that there was a lack of coordination among investigators in other parts of the force. One recommendation called for the establishment of a centralized databank on RCMP informants across Canada. By making informants' previous histories available, this databank allows police to assess their suitability for future projects. Although no databank will remove all of the risks associated with using informants, it may serve to expose the most dangerous or treacherous ones.[4]

OFFICER CORRUPTION AND ORGANIZATIONAL DEVIANCE

The danger of officer corruption, like violence to officers, increases as the stakes increase. Proceeds of Crime investigations by definition involve illicit proceeds, and sometimes those proceeds are in the form of stacks of cash. At every stage, it is relatively easy for officers to justify "borrowing" a portion of the cash. Ordinary investigators working the cases are exposed to the cash at the end of the investigations after the illicit proceeds have been seized by the police; cash is controlled by undercover operators during undercover laundering operations; and cash may be used to bribe individual police officers to tolerate certain lucrative transactions.

Many police forces lack the kinds of accountability procedures that would eliminate this temptation. As in all undercover work, the officer is playing a part—a criminal role. The purpose of rigid policies and procedures is to help officers separate their own ethical standards from the justifications used by the criminals with whom they associate over the course of an undercover operation. Police management must expect corruption—not tolerate it, but "expect" it. In this way police forces work diligently to eliminate the low-risk/high-profit temptations, and to put into place adequate accountability mechanisms.

Of equal concern to individual corruption is the temptation for the organization, intent on gaining a conviction, to act in a deviant or criminal manner. Short of clear criminal conduct are numerous shadings of unethical police organizational behaviour—shadings further blurred by the fact that many of the largest investigations are cross-jurisdictional cases shared with foreign police departments that have very different policies and practices. For example, police in Canada on occasion speak with envy of the freedom with which they see their DEA colleagues operating. In some U.S. drug cases, it is acceptable for undercover operators to use the money from undercover drug sales to fund payments to informants and cover other costs associated with the case. From a Canadian perspective, funnelling money from drug sales directly back into the investigation (rather than tagging and treating it as evidence) is an unacceptable practice. Even short of comparisons with a foreign jurisdiction, different managers and different specialized units in Canada may disagree on what should or should not be done in order to "get the job done."

As concerned as we ought to be for the undercover police officer, there is a "double risk experience" for the paid agent or informant with criminal experience. Although we often hear about the problems police have "handling" informants, we hear little when informants are badly betrayed by the police once their cost to the organization exceeds their value. Documents obtained with the permission of one such agent indicate that while using his services the police were prepared to lie to keep him out of jail. Once the agent's services were no longer considered valuable, the police were equally prepared to tell his co-accused's lawyer about his informant status. Such an action, particularly in high-level organized crime cases, puts an agent's life at risk inside and outside of jail. As difficult as it may be to "quit the mob," the end of an affair with the police can be equally risky.

It is to the advantage of the police that an agent be seen by the criminal world as a very dangerous, high-echelon organized criminal. The funding and other assistance given by the police force helps to substantiate the agent's status and role in the criminal organizations. However, this same role works directly against the agent if he or she is arrested for further criminal activity once work with the police has been terminated. While the public may not feel particularly sympathetic to a criminal who has advanced up into the higher ranks of a criminal operation, a police-funded advancement may indicate an operation out of control. We must also be concerned about a system of justice that has the police negotiating with the National Parole Board and with Correctional Service Canada (CSC) officials in order to gain or maintain access to "use" specific people with criminal experience. The agent is particularly vulnerable if he or she is on parole while working as an informant. By definition, most of the police-directed requirements would normally fall outside of any permissible parole-sanctioned behaviour.

WITNESS PROTECTION AND INFORMANT IMMUNITY

Witness-protection programs and some system of immunity for informants/witnesses were emphasized by Attorney General Robert Kennedy at the McClellan hearings. Speaking of the dangers facing potential informants or witnesses, he stated,

> There is the syndicate gunman who issues threat, and there is the potential witness who receives them, frightened almost inevitably into silence. It is this last aspect which makes the job of fighting racketeering hardest ... A witness who will testify in the face of threats to himself and his family is rare. This is one reason the disclosures by Joseph Valachi are significant: for the first time an insider—a knowledgeable member of the racketeering hierarchy—has broken the underworld's code of silence (Ontario Police Commission 1964, 155).

While we have already discussed the fact that Valachi's testimony became controversial, the testimony would not have been obtained without witness-protection and immunity programs.

In March 1995, the federal government tabled a bill to formally create Canada's first national witness-protection program. Prior to this coming into force, there had been no "national" Witness Protection Program to meet the needs of all police forces across Canada. The 1984 RCMP Source Witness Protection Program (SWPP) was originally designed to meet the requirements of the RCMP exclusively. It has since been expanded to provide service to all Canadian police departments and other enforcement agencies. Services include immediate temporary protection, relocation, change of identity (including new documentation), and subsistence or maintenance funding. Services are provided to non-RCMP forces on a cost-recovery basis, with the RCMP assuming all indirect costs. These programs are very expensive.

The Jaworski case has been mentioned earlier in this chapter. Jaworski and his family won the right to immediate witness protection, court costs for the parents, and compensation for any losses they might suffer as a result of coming under police protection. The witness-protection costs in such cases are staggering. In addition to more normal "domestic" witness-protection costs, the RCMP had to relocate Jaworski's parents and their business interests from the British Virgin Is. where they operated a sail cruise business to a new location.

The RCMP program has evolved into this de facto national program with neither adequate funding nor the infrastructure of training, support services, and policies needed to support the Canada-wide operation. The program costs approximately $3.4 million per year and protects 80 to 100 witnesses at any one time (*Globe and Mail*, March 24, 1995, p. A4). There are several lawsuits pending against the RCMP for its handling of witnesses.

A major weakness of both the U.S. system and the RCMP protection program is the failure to adequately prepare the witness and his or her family for the adjustments they will have to make in their new lives. Of greatest media controversy in Canada have been those few cases where the police have decided that the potential danger to the witness is either very low or nonexistent. The level of protection promised during the process of getting the witness to provide information is on occasion not matched by the level of protection that is actually delivered.[5]

An additional issue is the protection of witnesses who receive a jail term instead of immunity. In the past, many witnesses in the United States were granted immunity in exchange for testimony. However, prosecutors are becoming reluctant in the face of what is seen to be a drug crisis to give drug traffickers total immunity. Deals are still made, but a prison term is often part of the package. (This becomes difficult in those states with mandatory drug sentences.) Over 50 percent of participants in the U.S. Witness Security Program are now in prison. Special facilities must exist in order to protect the informers from the other inmates while still making them accessible to prosecutors or investigative agencies for the provision of ongoing information. The size and number of American prisons allow for segregation of this witness category of inmate. While it is possible in the Canadian male federal prisons, it is more difficult at the provincial level, and extremely difficult in the sole Federal Prison for Women.

Critics of the proposed Bill argue that its primary effect will be to limit the responsibility of the federal government. As mentioned previously, the 1990 Supreme Court decision in the Jaworski case confirmed the responsibility of the police in guaranteeing security to those people compelled to give evidence against criminals on behalf of the state. However, determining when and how much protection is required remains problematic, and has to be determined on a case-by-case basis. The proposed legislation states that *no legal action* can be laid against officials "in respect of anything done or omitted to be done in good faith" (Article 19). Toronto lawyer Barry Swadron, who is representing clients in their civil suits against the RCMP for its handling of their witness-protection cases, argues in response to Article 19 of the new bill that "you can be a bumbler and totally incompetent and be acting in good faith. The victim suffers just as much" (*Globe and Mail*, March 24, 1995, p. A4).

A Marshall's Service administers the U.S. Witness Security Program. No comparable national agency exists in Canada. There is a need for fairly consistent monitoring of these programs. For example, the U.S. system has had to contend with protected witnesses who commit additional crimes while under the program or use their new identities to evade creditors; with separations and divorces of couples in the program and the consequences thereof; and with the continuing need to provide some access to family members who are not in the program. While it is relatively easy to relocate an unemployed or unskilled worker, the task of creating documents, credentials, and a proper work history for a highly skilled individual is considerably more formidable (Tietolman 1984).

The physical protection of the police informant is only one aspect of securing his or her cooperation. The principle behind the concept of immunity is that the goal of obtaining a just and safe society may be better achieved in particular situations by *not* prosecuting every offender in order to secure the conviction of others. If the potential informant is involved in the criminal activity, and is therefore vulnerable to conviction and imprisonment, some "agreement" may be necessary whereby the threat of further prosecution is exchanged for the information. The ability to offer immunity in exchange for information may make it possible to advance a particular case that otherwise would go unprosecuted, to gather information about particular crimes (e.g., the location of bodies), and to gain information that will protect individuals from imminent danger or help to settle labour disputes or quell civil unrest.[6]

At present in Canada, there is no formal system for granting immunity to police informants. This is not to say that there is no *informal* system. Decisions are made by the police and/or prosecutors on a case-by-case basis. While there may be some operating notion of a balance between the value of the immunity and the value of the information to be exchanged, no formal rules or principles exist. Rather than immunity in the sense of absence of charges, the "exchange" more often takes the form of plea bargaining. Serious charges are exchanged for lesser ones (plus the information). However, like plea bargaining itself, immunity in Canada tends to be invisible, unofficial, and lacking in accountability, as suggested by the position taken by the Law Reform Commission of Canada:

> Although police have unofficially entered into agreements to refrain from charging informers, thus conferring on them a kind of informal immunity, the Commission would discourage this practise. It is the Commission's opinion that police lack the political accountability and the independence essential to have the power to grant immunity" (Law Reform Commission of Canada 1992, 3).

Stanley Cohen, the coordinator of the Criminal Procedure Project, at the time of the Commission's research expressed concern that the present situation that allowed decisions to be made informally behind closed doors with no accountability to the public resulted in the potential for justice not to be done—or not to be seen to be done. An openness is required that is not presently there.

INTERJURISDICTIONAL COLLABORATION: INTERNATIONAL POLICING AND INTELLIGENCE WORK

The international character of most organized crime and money laundering cases makes essential the putting into place *and* using of cross-jurisdictional sharing and collaborative mechanisms.

These can take the form of international police organizations, international intelligence systems, and treaties or agreements to assistant foreign law enforcement agencies on a case-by-case basis. An outline of the key international organizations and initiatives that address the globalization of crime follows.

UNILATERAL CONVENTIONS: THE UN AND CICAD

The United Nations

With reference to organized crime and money laundering activity, the main UN programs are the United Nations International Drug Program, the UN Drug Commission, and the UN Commission on Crime Prevention and Criminal Justice. As mentioned earlier in this chapter, the UN Convention Against Illicit Traffic in Narcotic Drugs and Psychotropic Substances was one of the earliest international initiatives against drug trafficking. The 1988 version that came into force in 1990 mandated that signatories create laws to criminalize activities connected with money laundering. As of 1994, approximately 75 nations have ratified this convention.

The Inter-American Drug Abuse Commission (CICAD)

CICAD, a regional organization within the Organization of American States (OAS), comprised 24 member states as of 1993.[7] The main initiatives have included: (1) the creation of Model Regulations for the Control of Precursor Chemicals, Chemical Substances, Machines and Materials; (2) Model Regulations on Offenses Related to the Laundering of Assets from Illicit Drug Trafficking and related Offenses; (3) and the preparation of Model Regulations on the Control of Shipment of Arms and Munitions aimed at preventing smuggling for use in illicit drug trafficking and narco-terrorism (Annual Report of CICAD, March 1994).

BILATERAL AGREEMENTS: MUTUAL LEGAL ASSISTANCE TREATIES/ ASSISTANCE AGREEMENTS AND MEMORANDA OF UNDERSTANDING

Mutual legal assistance treaties have already been discussed earlier in Chapter 6. Canada is now obliged to meet the treaty obligation signed with various countries, and similarly can make requests on behalf of Canadian law enforcement authorities. These treaties are, of course, only useful to the extent that they are used. To date, there is some indication that foreign jurisdictions, particularly the United States, are placing considerable burden on the police with requests under the treaties. Canadian law enforcement, in contrast, is not frequently making requests to other jurisdictions.

From a police and law enforcement perspective, there are some operational difficulties that have yet to be resolved. The procedures for collecting evidence and conducting hearings are so different across jurisdictions that Canadian courts will not always accept the evidence that is obtained elsewhere. Patricia Donald, Crown Prosecutor in British Columbia, has had difficulties obtaining evidence from witnesses unwilling or unable to travel to Canada. In one case, foreign authorities had agreed to honour the Canadian request for assistance, but once the Canadians arrived they insisted that their own procedures be used. The upshot of situations such as these is that the evidence may then not be admissible in Canadian proceedings. Treaties must clearly specify whose procedures will be followed when a requesting state is taking evidence against nationals within their own jurisdiction (Donald 1993, 46). In Donald's view, the MLAT between Canada and the Netherlands addresses many of these problems, and serves as a good example of the type of considerations that countries may want their MLATs to address.

The few countries (12 as of July 1995) with which Canada has formal MLATs in force are not the only ones that will share information and assist Canadian law enforcement. Letters of assistance and MOUs between jurisdictions are also used. However, the picture is still one in which law enforcement works best "locally," despite the fact that crime is very much an international phenomenon.

INTERNATIONAL CRIMINAL POLICE ORGANIZATION (ICPO)—INTERPOL

Interpol is an international agency whose main function is to coordinate and respond to inquiries received from local and foreign law enforcement agencies. As of 1993, 154 countries were members of Interpol. Canada has been a particularly active member both administratively and operationally. Ex-Commissioner Norm Inkster (RCMP Commissioner until July 1994) was elected President of Interpol and served until September 1994. He had previously served three years as Vice-President for the Americas. The RCMP has three permanently seconded officers at the General Secretariat in Lyons, France, and houses at RCMP headquarters in Ottawa the National Central Bureau (NCB), which receives and disperses Interpol inquiries.

Interpol is very active in collecting information on drug movements and traffickers, and has a database set up to store information on money laundering as well as a file on money couriers. However, Interpol is not without its problems. The large number of member states means that interests, priorities, and legislation are not the same in each jurisdiction and numerous small nations can outvote other member states. Some critics argue that Interpol serves mainly as an international mailbox for law enforcement requests from member nations. What appears to be missing is a strong analytical and intelligence component. However, other observers have noted the dangers inherent in having an international police force with a mandate to do operational work as well as intelligence-gathering. Interpol is forbidden by its constitution to intervene in activities of a political, military, religious, or racial character. Unfortunately, some policing issues overlap with these forbidden areas.

Europol

The European Community (EC) has recognized the importance of the intelligence function. Following a meeting of TREVI[8] ministers in 1991, a formal agreement was made to establish Europol. The purpose of this European police organization is to collect and analyze information on cross-border crime with the assistance of a European Drugs Unit (EDU). How this organization will interact with Interpol has yet to be determined. Senior officials at Interpol have criticized the establishment of Europol by arguing that Interpol already has a European Secretariat and a staff of 12 senior officers at Lyon. They fear that EC police may refuse to duplicate their efforts by sharing their police information and intelligence with both Interpol and Europol (*European* 1992).

The European Community is hoping that a "Europol" structure will eliminate some of the problems associated with large numbers of member states. Europe will need a rapid and efficient law enforcement and intelligence network, and a body of police-policy and intelligence managers who will expedite interjurisdictional enforcement among the EC members.[9] As of 1994, the execution of these goals was in the early stages. Europol's first targets are expected to be drug trafficking and money laundering.

World Police Forces: A Future Prospect?

A world police force is a fearful prospect to some people. In reality, we have far to go before such a force, even if created, would be viable. A first step may be to extend the Europol concept of linking together a number of "like nations." While some observers find the Europol concept appealing, others oppose the notion of foreign police officers operating within the borders of distinct nations. In addition, we have only just begun to persuade countries to enter into mutual legal assistance treaties, and there are already many outstanding problems with the small number of treaties in force. Intelligence sharing issues, sovereignty issues, and priorities that vary so vastly across nations would be only some of the difficulties to be overcome.

There is a major difference between criminal operations and the law enforcement activities that are designed to police them. Sense of territory or "turf" may be set aside in organized crime operations if the profit to be derived from collaborating is sufficient. While there is certainly competition for the criminal markets, some of the largest police investigations conducted in the early 1990s have revealed a willingness on the part of Colombian cartels to work cooperatively with the Mafia—all in the interest of operational efficiency. Cases from the 1980s show Mafia members working with Russian Jews to launder money through the jewellery districts of U.S. cities. More recent cases have documented collaborative efforts between the Colombian cartels, the Mafia, and Russian organized crime.

Less comprehensive than the notion of global police is that of global *bank* police whose mandate would be to regulate the operation of banks, and thereby reduce money laundering, by examining sources of deposits in every nation in an attempt to reduce money laundering. As Andelman (1994) notes, however, few countries would agree to cede sovereignty over their national banking system to some foreign body (107). He suggests that a first step might be an international convention on the "beneficial source of money" that might encompass the "due diligence" of attorneys, accountants, and bankers.

While not global in scope, the Basle Committee on Banking Regulations and Supervisory Practices produced a statement of principles titled "Prevention of Criminal Use of the Banking System for the Purpose of Money Laundering."[10] Canada is a signatory to this 1988 document, which encourages banks to:

- verify the identity of the beneficial owners of accounts ("know your customer");

- adopt an explicit policy of refusing significant transactions with customers who fail to provide evidence of their identity;

- avoid transactions they believe are associated with money laundering (i.e., "suspicious transactions");

- cooperate with law enforcement authorities; and

- formally adopt policies to ensure compliance with Basle principles, and arrange an internal audit to test for general compliance.

G-7 FINANCIAL ACTION TASK FORCE: EVALUATING CANADA

The G-7 Financial Action Task Force (FATF) is an excellent example of an international initiative against the utilization of the banking system and financial institutions for the purposes of money laundering. The FATF was established in 1989 by the G-7 Economic Summit in Paris to examine measures that could be taken to combat money laundering.

While expressing concern over the lack of attention some nations have given to money laundering, the FATF discussed but rejected the idea of forming a "blacklist" of noncooperative nations. Instead it has encouraged the adoption of appropriate legislation and enforcement capabilities in the seven original summit participants and eight additional countries. Summit participants were the United States, Japan, Germany, France, the United Kingdom, Italy, Canada, and the Commission of the European Communities. The eight additional countries were Sweden, the Netherlands, Belgium, Luxembourg, Switzerland, Austria, Spain, and Australia. More recently, Finland, Iceland, Norway, Turkey, Hong Kong, New Zealand, and Singapore have become members. As of 1994, FATF membership comprised 28 jurisdictions and regional organizations, representing the world's major financial centres.

The initial FATF report outlined a 40-point legislative, regulatory, and diplomatic approach to money laundering. The 1992 report added "interpretative notes" that built on the original recommendations. Countries are now voluntarily being evaluated against these recommendations, and are participating in the evaluation of other nations. The focus has been on education, the mutual application of international pressure, and cooperation. The 1994 *Annual Report of the Financial Action Task Force on Money Laundering*, emphasized the need for banks to identify customers—particularly in cases where there is no face-to-face contact between the institution and the customer—and to bring nonfinancial institutions into line with the anti-money laundering requirements imposed on financial institutions. The only enforcement power at the disposal of the FATF is the mechanism whereby each of the member countries agrees to be evaluated by its peers.

Canada was officially evaluated in early 1993. The evaluation supported Canada's position that its legislation and practices place it in strong compliance with the 40 recommendations. Some of Canada's initiatives are of an ongoing nature, others are newly implemented:

- Mutual legal assistance treaties have been signed with 12 countries, and many more are under negotiation.

- The new record-keeping legislation ensures identification of customers and the retention of financial records.

- Suspicious transactions are being reported to the police in large numbers (indeed, there have been accusations of over-compliance, with the result that the banks now accuse the police of not following up on potential cases).

- The issue of cross-border transaction records and reporting is currently under review.

The "interpretative notes" included in the June 25, 1992 report of the FATF[11] suggest ways of enhancing the previous recommendations. Canada has debated many of the issues raised in this section:

- The money laundering legislation in Canada does extend beyond drug offences, but not as far as some law enforcement authorities might want. Whether or not there is a natural cut-off point—beyond drugs but short of *all* offences—is an open debate.

- Canada has created an asset management and sharing mechanism. The mechanism and office are beginning to operate.

- Bill C-7, the Controlled Drugs and Substances Act (formerly Bill C-85, Psychoactive Substances Control Act) and its accompanying regulations have met with opposition in the House of Commons subcommittee. This Bill is intended to consolidate the fragmented and outdated 20-year-old Acts that deal with controlled and restricted drugs. In accordance with international obligations, the Bill provides for enforcement regulations to deal with "controlled deliveries" and other enforcement operations of international drug trafficking. Some critics see Bill C-7 as representing an inappropriate "U.S. style war on drugs approach."[12]

FATF officials anticipate that by 1998–99 they will have in place the core of a global regulatory and enforcement mechanism (Andelman 1994, 107). However important the FATF approach, it must not be allowed to shift all of the attention away from the practicalities of doing traditional police work in an international organized crime environment.

ANATOMY OF A CASE: THE OUTRAGE, IOU, AND NEEB/BROOK PROJECTS

Thus far we have examined law enforcement in terms of legislative issues, operational difficulties, globalization of organized crime, corrupt lawyers and government officials, and attempts to obtain evidence for Canadian courts from foreign jurisdictions. One large-scale, multifaceted case included each of these elements. It remains one of Canada's largest drug conspiracies.

Behind this case was the 1985 murder of DEA agent Enrique ("Kiki") Camarena in Guadalajara, Mexico. In 1990, Dr. Alvarez-Machain, a Mexican doctor, was kidnapped by the U.S. government officials, taken to the United States, and charged with using his medical skills to keep Camarena alive while drug dealers tortured and interrogated the DEA agent, who was eventually murdered. In a controversial decision, the U.S. Supreme Court concluded that the kidnapping, while shocking and in violation of "general international law principles," did not violate the U.S.–Mexico extradition treaty.

When we speak of the complexities of large-scale money laundering cases, the reader may be tempted to underestimate the degree of organization that is required to create a viable system of stash houses and a cross-border transportation network involving wholesalers, distributors, importers, couriers, international money launderers, and growers/suppliers. The case under review actually comprises three overlapping projects:

- a Vancouver project (IOU), which focused on Brook as the informant; Cruickshank as a major importer/wholesaler and the controller of the corrupt Canadian Customs officer; a lawyer; and several other importers and distributors.

- a Toronto-based project (Outrage), which focused on Brook and Neeb as equal partners; Donovan Blakeman as principal money launderer for the criminal organization; controllers of stash farms and houses; money collectors and distributors, money couriers and money exchangers; an accountant; and a Canadian citizen who served as a banker in St. Kitts. The Toronto project reached across Canada and internationally.

- a DEA project in San Diego, California, which focused on the major U.S. distributors and the Mexican source suppliers; and the DEA/FBI/Customs project in Grand Rapids, Michigan, which focused on the Klingler transportation network that spread across the United States and Canada.

The criminal organization was headed by Timothy Neeb and Robert Brook, who were equal partners in a North American cannabis distribution network. Neeb had operated in Southern Ontario (London and Kitchener) as a major distributor of narcotics before joining forces with Robert Brook. Brook had access to California suppliers, who bought drugs from Mexico, and limited distribution in British Columbia and Ontario. The partners' strengths reinforced each other—Brook had access to large supplies of drugs and Neeb had an extensive distribution network. Also playing significant roles in this criminal organization were 85 individuals who operated in various locations in North America and Mexico (see Figure 7.3).

FIGURE 7.3

British Columbia 5
Alberta 1
Washington State 1
Manitoba 1
Ontario 34
Michigan 15
New York State 4
Pennsylvania 1
California 8
Tennessee 3
Texas 2
Mexico 10

CASE INITIATION

Cases come to the attention of the Canadian police in a variety of ways: from police leads built up over a number of years; from information provided by foreign (particularly U.S.) police; from other police forces or RCMP units/detachments within Canada; and from "suspicious" information passed to the police by financial institutions.[13] While investigating other cases in Toronto, the police gradually became aware of two recurring names in their files—Robert Brook and Timothy Neeb. Further investigation and police intelligence eventually revealed that the two men were wholesale suppliers and importers of cannabis. Although there was not sufficient evidence to charge them, it had become obvious from the files that Brook and Neeb were behind several of the drug operations of other suspects then under investigation. From approximately 1982 until Project Outrage began late in 1986, information on the case was being accumulated.

The major turning point in the case was the 1987 arrest of Robert Brook in the United States on charges of drug trafficking. The lengthy mandatory sentences under the U.S. Continuing Criminal Enterprise (C.C.E.) statute, a growing fear by Brook that the Mexican criminals might kill him, and a gradual falling out among various segments of the Canadian criminal operation all combined to persuade Brook to turn informant against his own criminal organization.

The same greed that may encourage an individual to join a criminal organization can come back to haunt the organization. Neeb led Brook to believe that their joint profits were significantly less than was in fact the case. When Brook's suspicions led to an agreement between the partners to dissolve their amalgamation, the financial figures Neeb wanted to use were his lower figures. Had the partnership been dissolved using Neeb's figures, Neeb could have bought Brook out in cash! Greed within these organizations can work to the benefit of law enforcement: Much of what is known about this criminal organization, and the roles of the various players within it, are courtesy of Robert Brook.

THE ROLE OF THE INFORMANT

Brook served as an informant and police agent from April to June 1987, until the arrest, in Montreal, of Timothy Neeb and the Mexican supplier, Javier Caro Payan. However difficult it may be to manage informants, the fact remains that they tend to be critically important to major financial investigations. Although police cases are built on the analysis of records and on various forms of surveillance and questioning, information revealing the intricacies of a particular case—the range of players and jurisdictions involved—is often provided by the informant. Ethical concerns are raised by the fact that this information comes at a cost. In exchange for the information he provided, Robert Brook received from the Assistant United States Attorney in California and Michigan, and from the Canadian Federal Department of Justice, immunity from prosecution for his drug-trafficking activities. Upon completion of his testimony, he was relocated somewhere in North America.

The Vancouver Cruickshank et al. investigations began after Brook's arrest and defection. The Vancouver segment may never have materialized had it not been for a reference Brook made about a corrupt Canada Customs official who was facilitating the movement of drugs between the two countries. While not all of the cases went to completion (including the case against the customs officer), Brook provided very specific information to the police. In court, he testified that his first drug dealings with Cruickshank, one of the key accused in British Columbia, was in 1978 or 1979. He outlined for the court a continuous criminal association that extended up to the time of his arrest (1987). He outlined the extent of these dealings and, for at least the Toronto project, listed the transfers and transmittals of funds into various bank accounts and real-estate purchases.

This information played a major role in the success of the Crown's case. Even though it was not possible to connect specific drug transactions to the deposit of specific funds or the purchase of a specific asset, an appropriate inference could be drawn. For this inference, the court relied almost entirely on Brook's evidence. The Justice of the Supreme Court of British Columbia concluded that, in all 16 counts, the property involved was the proceeds of crime. The Justice cited the following reasons for his decision regarding counts 1–7 (having to do with cash deposits into a Zurich bank):

> In analyzing these various matters it becomes perfectly obvi-
> ous that the deposits made by the accused to the Swiss Bank
> account cannot be accounted for by his earnings or any other
> legitimate source. The evidence that he was trafficking in
> narcotics from 1982 onward and the deposits of cash shown
> are consistent with the deposit of the proceeds of crime. ... All
> of this leads me inescapably to the conclusion that the subject
> moneys during that period were the proceeds of the sale of
> drugs (Justice Macdonell, Oral Reasons for Judgement, April
> 16th, 1992, *R. v. Donald Gordon Cruickshank*).

This case is important because of the court's willingness (based largely on the fact that Brook was declared a creditable witness) to analyze the evidence and decide inferentially that in the absence of any other plausible explanation, the presence of the vast proceeds could only have been the proceeds of crime. This made the defendant guilty of a criminal offense with the criminal proceeds forfeitable.

As a result of the information supplied by Brook and the subsequent arrest of 12 major international drug traffickers, criminal proceeds were identified in Ontario, Michigan, Florida, California, Tennessee, Idaho, and New York. Brook thus had been valuable in outlining the scope of the criminal operation, the location of proceeds of crime, the corrupt official involved in the operation, and the money laundering schemes. Although the case against the customs official was unsuccessful (due to a problem of identification), evidence of the existence of a corrupt official was significant in itself. A discussion of Brook's main contributions follows.

- *Participant taping.* Brook made numerous one-party taped pay-phone calls to Neeb and other key members. (After *Duarte*, the police would have required an authorization for this taping.)

- *Arranged meetings.* Brook arranged a meeting with Neeb that was subject to video and electronic surveillance. On June 6, 1987, Neeb, Brook, and the Mexican supplier, Caro Payan, were scheduled to meet in Montreal in the lobby of the Sheraton Hotel to discuss a US $6-million debt and future shipments. It was at this final set-up meeting that Neeb and Caro Payan were arrested.

- *Evidence-building.* RCMP and DEA recorded Brook negotiating with Donald Cruickshank in order to gain evidence against the corrupt Canada Customs officer. Cruickshank was able to cross the Canadian border from the United States with the assistance of a Canada Customs official (Brook had paid Cruickshank as much as $75,000 for border-crossing protection). On June 4, 1987, Brook arranged a "controlled delivery"[14] to Cruickshank of 1 018 pounds of marijuana so that the police could gain evidence on the role of the customs officer. The driver for Cruickshank crossed through Sumas, British Columbia, where a specific customs officer was working. With an authorization, the RCMP/DEA followed the shipment under surveillance. The driver turned the shipment over to an undercover U.S. agent who was posing as a Brook employer.

- *Money laundering scheme.* Brook identified the laundering process for money derived from narcotic sales. He confirmed that over $100 million in Canadian cash was delivered by the couriers to Friedberg Exchange in Toronto for purchase of US dollars. A large percentage of these US dollars were then smuggled by couriers to the United States and Mexico for payment of cannabis received. The profits derived from these drug sales were largely handled by Neeb and Blakeman through offshore financial institutions. Brook never had specific knowledge of where Blakeman and Neeb were stashing the profits other than in real-estate developments in Florida. Brook's evidence on money laundering did, however, indicate the important role played by lawyers in the laundering schemes.

THE ROLE OF FINANCIAL INSTITUTIONS

Given the magnitude of this case, numerous banks and financial institutions obviously played a part in helping to move the money. Of particular note is the extent to which Blakeman and Neeb relied on accounts held in Zurich, Switzerland, and Toronto-based money-exchange houses. The criminal operation transferred money between Bank of Credit and Commerce International (BCCI) in Vancouver and Luxembourg.

Friedberg Money Exchange
Brook estimated that between 1982 and 1987, the Neeb/Brook criminal organization exchanged $100 million through Friedberg Exchange in Toronto. (In the latter period, they were exchanging $1 million per week.) This exchange house played a critical role. The profits from drug sales were converted into US dollars and bearer cheques from Friedberg Currency Exchange. Bearer cheques were used in offshore bank deposits to avoid the suspicions that large cash deposits would arose. (Although less conspicuous than large amounts of cash, these bearer cheques *should* have alerted authorities and bank officials; bearer cheques are very uncommon in legitimate transactions because they can be stolen and cashed by anyone who has them in their possession.[15] Some of the US dollars and bearer bonds were then flown by Blakeman to Brown Shipley Inc. in Jersey Island and England, to First Trust Corporations in St. Kitts, and to Switzerland for deposit into corporate accounts. From these corporate accounts, they were transferred to corporations in the United States, Canada, Switzerland, the Caribbean, and England.

Flight records revealed that on occasion Neeb, Blakeman, and their accountant acted as couriers for these funds, flying them personally to the second stage of what was usually a long route back home. If the Caribbean was to be the destination, the three men would rent a Learjet from Toronto's Pearson International Airport. The remaining US dollars went to the United States, Mexico, and South America for the purchase of more cannabis shipments. Blakeman recognized the benefits of using international tax havens and numerous overseas corporations as vehicles for routing cash back into the criminals' hands that they could not otherwise use (RCMP case files). (See Figure 7.4.)

FIGURE 7.4

Money Laundering Cycle

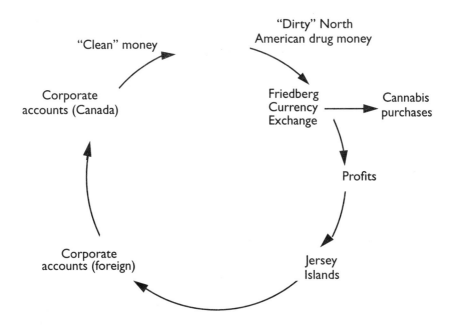

THE ROLE OF LAWYERS

In both the Outrage and IOU projects, lawyers and ex-lawyers played a critical role (see Figure 7.4). Donovan Jackson Blakeman was the main money launderer for the Neeb/Brook organization. Blakeman became involved in the organization in 1979 and retired his law practice in 1981. His role was to "manage" the illicit profits by incorporating domestic and international corporations; maintaining numerous foreign and domestic bank accounts; and concealing, laundering, and investing (in real estate in Ontario, Florida, and elsewhere) millions of dollars of criminal proceeds.

The corporations alone were registered in Liberia, the Cayman Islands, the Isle of Mann, the British Virgin Islands, Ontario, Florida, and North Carolina. A chart, titled by the criminals "What We Got!—Spaghetti Jungle," was seized from Blakeman's residence.[16] The police identified 62 Canadian corporations directly or indirectly related to accused persons in this organized criminal group. Blakeman explained to Neeb his procedure of taking the illicit funds overseas and making deposits in various banks to the credit of numerous corporations. These funds would then be repatriated to North America through offshore accounts and investments in other offshore corporations. As only an indication of their property holdings, Neeb and Brook through Blakeman owned 148 lots in West Palm Beach, Florida. Bank accounts were located in Jersey, the Channel Islands, Switzerland, St. Kitts, Bahamas, the Cayman Islands, Ontario, and the United States.

Major funds were put into the Brown Shipley Inc. accounts in various company names. The companies were set up with little capital and got advances through use of the "spaghetti jungle" maze of corporate entities for financing. The investigation indicated that 62 Canadian corporations, 30 U.S. corporations, and 18 foreign corporations were used (directly or indirectly) to facilitate the movement of drug money. In total, $13,408,845.00 was deposited to Brown Shipley. Figure 7.5 illustrates the vast and complex nature of this laundering operation.

THE ROLE OF FORENSIC ACCOUNTING

Just as the police hired people with accounting expertise to investigate the laundering schemes, the perpetrators of those schemes hired accountants to provide financial advice. The accounting firm of Hogg, Shain and Scheck worked for Neeb and Blakeman; another accounting firm was asked to advise this firm on restructuring the Neeb/Blakeman operation to avoid taxes and to reflect equal partnership between the two principals.

Law enforcement officials have to determine for accountants as well as for lawyers where to draw the line between the provision of professional services and the facilitation of crime. The accountant's advice to Neeb and Blakeman clearly facilitated their money laundering operations.

Price Waterhouse was hired by the police to complete an examination of the financial records and other evidence seized during the investigation. A spokesperson for Price Waterhouse concluded that "the transactions are those normally associated with a laundering scheme, in that the source of funds deposited is confused and funds destination is at times ... camouflaged" (RCMP files). As mentioned in Chapter 4, care must be taken to avoid having the police, prosecutors, or courts hiring an accounting firm affiliated in any way with the accountants used by the charged suspects.

On the matter of income-tax evasion, investigators and revenue officials determined that the following amounts were outstanding between 1983 and 1987: Blakeman ($9,017,623); Neeb ($10,513,282); and other members ($3,482,646).

OBTAINING EVIDENCE FROM FOREIGN JURISDICTIONS

This case provides examples of both failure and success with respect to attempts by law enforcement to obtain assistance and evidence from a foreign jurisdiction *in a form that is required* in Canadian courts.

In the *Good* case (involving a B.C. lawyer named Good), it was necessary to obtain banking and hotel records from Luxembourg, Switzerland, Austria, and England. The evidence was required in the form of business, banking, and government records. Of the four countries, Canada had in force a Mutual Legal Assistance Treaty with England only. Therefore, letters requesting assistance, signed by the designated Department of Justice officials in Ottawa, were forwarded to government officials in each of the other three countries.

In Luxembourg, a challenge to the process by which the evidence was obtained and given to the RCMP was successful. The Luxembourg Court of Appeal declared the seizure of the records to be invalid because the letter from Canada to Luxembourg was not signed by a judge—as required in Luxembourg, but not in Canada. The Luxembourg evidence was critical to the *Good* case. A request by the Crown to the Supreme Court of British Columbia judge to take commission evidence in Luxembourg was denied due to a perceived timeliness issue. The argument seemed to be that the Crown should have anticipated problems relating to the obtaining of evidence, and therefore should have made their request earlier in the process. The Crown entered a stay of proceedings on all charges against *Good*.

In contrast, the challenge to the evidence submitted to the RCMP in Switzerland for the *Cruickshank* case was unsuccessful.

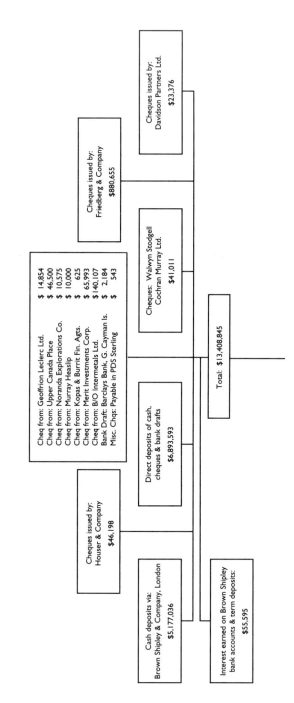

F I G U R E   7 . 5

Summary of Receipts and Disbursements Processed by Brown Shipley (Jersey) Ltd., Channel Isles, British Isles

Cheq from: Geoffrion Leclerc Ltd. $ 14,854
Cheq from: Upper Canada Place $ 46,500
Cheq from: Noranda Explorations Co. $ 10,575
Cheq from: Murray Heaslip $ 10,000
Cheq from: Kopas & Burrit Fin. Agts. $ 625
Cheq from: Merit Investments Corp. $ 65,993
Cheq from: B/O Intermetals Ltd. $ 140,107
Bank Draft: Barclays Bank, G. Cayman Is. $ 2,184
Misc. Chqs: Payable in PDS Sterling $ 543

Cheques issued by:
Friedberg & Company
$880,655

Cheques issued by:
Davidson Partners Ltd.
$23,376

Cheques: Walwyn Stodgell
Cochran Murray Ltd.
$41,011

Direct deposits of cash,
cheques & bank drafts
$6,893,593

Total: $13,408,845

Cheques issued by:
Houser & Company
$46,198

Cash deposits via:
Brown Shipley & Company, London
$5,177,036

Interest earned on Brown Shipley
bank accounts & term deposits:
$55,595

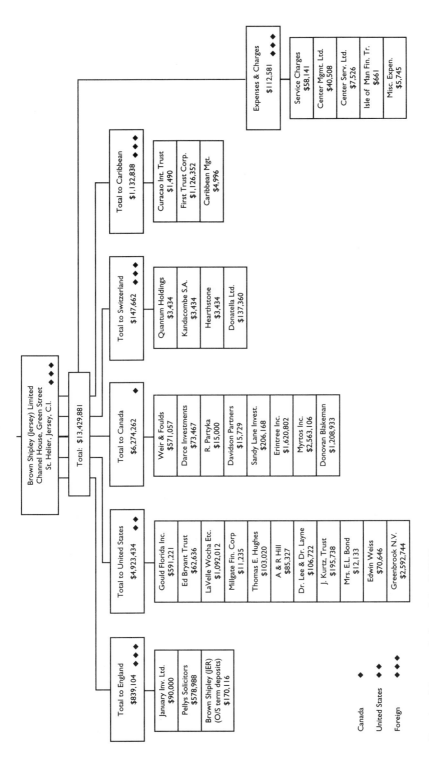

Brown Shipley (Jersey) Limited
Channel House, Green Street
St. Helier, Jersey, C.I. ◆◆◆

Total: $13,429,881

Total to England ◆◆◆
$839,104

January Inv. Ltd. $90,000
Pellys Solicitors $578,988
Brown Shipley (JER) (O/S term deposits) $170,116

Total to United States ◆◆
$4,923,434

Gould Florida Inc. $591,221
Ed Bryant Trust $62,636
LaVelle Wocha Etc. $1,092,012
Millgate Fin. Corp $11,235
Thomas E. Hughes $103,020
A & R Hill $85,327
Dr. Lee & Dr. Layne $106,722
J. Kurtz, Trust $195,738
Mrs. E.L. Bond $12,133
Edwin Weiss $70,646
Greenbrook N.V. $2,592,744

Total to Canada ◆
$6,274,262

Weir & Foulds $571,057
Darce Investments $73,467
R. Partyka $15,000
Davidson Partners $15,729
Sandy Lane Invest. $206,168
Erintree Inc. $1,620,802
Myrtos Inc. $2,563,106
Donovan Blakeman $1,208,933

Total to Switzerland ◆◆◆
$147,662

Quantum Holdings $3,434
Kandacombe S.A. $3,434
Hearthstone $3,434
Donatella Ltd. $137,360

Total to Caribbean ◆◆◆
$1,132,838

Curacao Int. Trust $1,490
First Trust Corp. $1,126,352
Caribbean Mgt. $4,996

Expenses & Charges ◆◆◆
$112,581

Service Charges $58,141
Center Mgmt. Ltd. $40,508
Center Serv. Ltd. $7,526
Isle of Man Fin. Tr. $661
Misc. Expen. $5,745

Canada ◆
United States ◆
Foreign ◆◆◆

Reprinted by permission of the RCMP.

The bank in question agreed that one of its officials could travel to Canada to testify. Cruickshank's business practice was to sell cannabis purchased from Brook. Money from some of these sales was then transported to offshore havens. The conviction of *Cruickshank* on 16 counts of possession of the proceeds of crime is largely due to this Swiss cooperation.

In a detailed paper analyzing the deficiencies in the present system of obtaining assistance from foreign jurisdictions, Donald (1992) makes the following recommendations:

1. When Mutual Legal Assistance Treaties are being negotiated, make sure that little variations in procedures between the countries will not render the evidence received useless for court.

2. Develop some protocol to facilitate communications between the countries while assistance requests are being considered or fulfilled. Designate individuals, possibly lawyers in the International Assistance Unit, to monitor the execution of requests for assistance.

3. Amend the *Canada Evidence Act* to provide for the admissibility of business records which are "verified" by a certificate or other statement. Recognize that when Canada is requesting cooperation Canada cannot always expect that our procedures will be complied with. Some degree of flexibility may be required.

RESULTS: SENTENCES AND COSTS

- Brook received immunity in return for acting as an informant, and entered into the witness-protection program.

- Donovan Blakeman received a two-year jail term for conspiracy to possess the proceeds of crime (relatively short due to medical reasons).

- Neeb received a 13-year jail term for conspiracy to import and traffic in narcotics.

- Roger Heaslip (Neeb's lieutenant) received a nine-year jail term for conspiracy to import and traffic.

- Revenue Canada collected approximately $4,600,000.

- No Proceeds of Crime cases were brought in Toronto. This case was initiated before the Proceeds of Crime legislation was introduced in 1989. It was considered safer to proceed with Revenue Canada and allow viable prosecutions to be undertaken in the United States due to their extensive sentences. The Proceeds of Crime legislation would apply today.

- In British Columbia, the Crown decided that although the offences had taken place before the introduction of the Proceeds of Crime legislation, the corporate possession of the illicit proceeds was ongoing. Thus, the 1989 legislation was used as a tool to facilitate the forfeiture in the case against Cruickshank.

- Cruickshank was found guilty on 16 counts. Ten convictions were registered. He received a five-year jail term (consecutive to the five-and-a-half years he was serving on a previous charge); a fine of $393,000 (three-years imprisonment for default of payment) to equal illicit funds held in a Swiss bank account; and a fine of $209,386.56 (two-years imprisonment for default of payment) to equal the value of the matrimonial home.

- U.S. authorities seized approximately US $22 million in properties, cash, and conveyances/vehicles.

- Caro Payan was extradited from Canada to California, where he received a 25-year jail term.

NOTES

1. Cases involving the absence of this warrant mechanism were still making their way through the courts as of July 1994. In Ontario, Judge D. Latimer ruled that the videotaping in a public washroom of four men who were subsequently charged with indecency was in violation of a "reasonable expectation of privacy." The judge noted that at that time of the police action there was no legislative mechanism in Canada authorizing police to carry out video surveillance; had they waited 15 days, the new legislation would have been in force (*Toronto Star*, July 14, 1994, p. A10)

2. For example, during August 1995, the Director General of the Sûrété du Québec, Serge Barbeau, was widely congratulated for the community-based/negotiative approach he took when assisting the Mohawk peacekeepers to destroy the illicit marijuana plants growing in Kanesatake. This was a highly politicized situation that could have resulted in violence.

3. The term "working" refers to the officer's ability to direct and control an informant, often by building the appearance of a trusting relationship between them.

4. As an aside, perhaps more controversial than the performance of the RCMP was the decision to hold the Marin Commission of Inquiry *prior* to the termination of the criminal investigation. I shall not enter into that debate here, but Rod Stamler's views are "enthusiastically" expressed in *Above the Law* by Paul Palango.

5. A woman who testified against her husband at the 1994 Supreme Court hearing into the David Milgaard case claims she never received the RCMP protection promised to her by Chief Justice Lamer at the time that she testified (*Globe and Mail*, April, 21, 1994, p. A7).

6. See Law Reform Commission of Canada (1992). The Law Reform Commission was disbanded in 1992, and the follow-up to this report is uncertain.

7. Member states are Argentina, the Bahamas, Bolivia, Brazil, Canada, Chile, Colombia, Costa Rica, Dominican Republic, Ecuador, El Salvador, Guatemala, Honduras, Jamaica, Mexico, Nicaragua, Panama, Paraguay, Peru, Saint Lucia, Trinidad and Tobago, the United States, Uruguay, and Venezuela.

8. TREVI was founded in 1975 and is composed of a group of EC ministers. Its original focus was on terrorism and the promotion of international cooperation, but it now focuses on drugs and organized crime. The acronym "TREVI" apparently stands for terrorism, radicalism, extremism, and international violence. The first ministerial conference was held in Rome in 1985 (home of the famous fountain, which must have served to enforce the TREVI name).

9. The eight Schengen countries have set up a Schengen Information Service (SIS) based in Strasbourg. In Great Britain, a new National Criminal Intelligence Service (NCIS) became operational in 1992. Its aim is to "provide a creative and dynamic national criminal intelligence service." A press informational release on the NCIS makes no mention of the system being specifically designed to link to the EC system. In fact, the only reference to the need for international links occurs in the following: "The creation of the NCIS with its constituent HQ units provides a natural focal point for the UK and a conduit through which international intelligence can flow." See Jamieson (1992, 16) for comments about the failure to explore adequately the possibility of a NCIS–EC link-up.

10. The Basle Committee comprised representatives from Belgium, Canada, France, Germany, Italy, Japan, the Netherlands, Sweden, Switzerland, United Kingdom, United States, and Luxembourg.

11. Organization for Economic Co-Operation and Development, Directorate for Financial, Fiscal, and Enterprise Affairs, *Financial Action Task Force on Money Laundering, Annual Report and Annexes 1991–1992*, Par. 68–100.

12. In "U.S.-style drug policy isn't the answer" (*Toronto Star*, July 11, 1994, p. A13), P. Erickson and R. Smart argue that the proposed drug classifications are irrational and inconsistent; that the penalties for cannabis possession should be reduced, not increased; and that what is needed is a thorough review of drug policy following the 1973 Le Dain Commission.

13. The 1993–94 evaluation of the police cases completed since the formation of the three Integrated Anti-Drug Profiteering units revealed that half of the Montreal cases were initiated by a U.S. agency, and the Vancouver site used information from financial institutions in more cases than did either Toronto or Montreal.

14. A "controlled delivery" occurs when the police knowingly allow a shipment of contraband to enter the country with the intention of following the illegal substances and arresting criminals more important than the couriers. This strategy is used in cases involving criminal networks so that arrests can be made of large numbers of suspects.

15. Other peculiar transactions should have caused suspicion. Once the investigation was underway, it became apparent that some of the transactions made no sense in a legitimate business context. For example, money was supposedly being loaned to a Liberian-registered corporation (which made up part of the Spaghetti Jungle network) at the same rate of interest that the money was earning at a St. Kitts trust company—thus the transaction could not have been done in order to generate profit.

16. A copy of this chart appears in Possamai (1992, 118).

CHAPTER 8

Conclusion

This book began by questioning the value of the term "organized crime." As we have seen, the term's usefulness stems from its attempt to encompass a method or process of conducting criminal operations that is distinct from other forms of criminal behaviour. The salient features that define organized crime include the potential for violence, corruption, ongoing criminal activity, and the precedence of the group over any single member.

Our current understanding of organized crime must take into account two significant changes, which together will have a strong impact on law enforcement initiatives against organized crime. First, there has been a broadening of the range of organized crime groups operating. The reasons for this are varied and relate to global political shifts and the entrepreneurial efforts of new criminal participants as market opportunities have become available. In addition, our willingness to "see" beyond the traditional Mafia allows us to recognize other groups who are operating as organized criminals. As we discussed, some of the emerging organized crime groups are relying on violence and intimidation, while the more established groups are able to engage in mutually beneficial relationships with elements of the political and economic status quo. Second, organized crime groups are no longer operating strictly in competition with each other but, have demonstrated a willingness and an ability to work collaboratively. A recent Canadian example discussed in this book was Operation Contrat/ Compote/Creditor, which exposed linkages between the Colombian cartels, the Mafia, and the Hell's Angels.

Continuing to view organized crime as "group specific" leads to wrong policies and wrong policing strategies. We must be aware of the implications of the collaborative, "conglomerate" nature of some organized crime operations. We have already noted the dispensability of individual members of any organized crime group. We now must recognize that one organized crime group working in partnership with another may be substituted if circumstances warrant it. For example, if one group loses some of its members to law enforcement efforts or fails to produce satisfactorily in the view of the other groups, the conglomerate can "redesign" itself. For example, when a particular drug route becomes too risky, a different source country and different importers may be used in a specific conspiracy. Organized crime groups have gone from "owning" a particular illegal commodity to serving as replaceable partners in wider operations. Weaker or less sophisticated groups may function like piece workers, accepting the contracting-out assignments offered by other groups. As in the legitimate economy, efficiency and effectiveness are what determines loyalty within the illicit marketplace.

Focusing on organized crime as a process, rather than on the people engaged in it, allows the investigator/analyst to move away from unconscious stereotyping and to broaden his or her understanding of the range of organized crime operations. The Mollen Commission (New York Police Department Corruption Inquiry) uncovered a group of police officers who recruited new members into their "crews" (hence membership was replaceable/interchangeable); they were prepared to use (and did use) violence and intimidation in order to make huge sums of illicit profits from drug trafficking; and they were organized with the intent to operate on a long-term basis.

In essence, they were operating as an organized crime group. Six officers were described in the Mollen Report as "notorious drug dealers and racketeers in uniform" (*Mollen Commission Report*, Exhibit 8, p. 20). A study on police corruption in New Orleans revealed that police officers were not only committing crimes in an organized crime manner, but had direct links with traditional organized criminals.

The point of this is not to emphasize corrupt police officers, but rather to emphasize the need to redefine organized crime activity based on the process that is used to carry out criminal operations. The process is what adds the additional level of dangerousness and societal threat.

Criminal activities that may in fact constitute organized crime are sometimes assigned less stigmatizing titles such as "fraud" or "corporate" and "white collar" crime. But as Shapiro argues, "It is time to integrate the 'white-collar' offenders into mainstream scholarship by looking beyond the perpetrators' wardrobe and social characteristics and exploring the modus operandi of their misdeeds" (1990, 363).

Calavita and Pontell (1993) attempt to clarify the network of crime categories by proposing a typology based on distinctive "motives and methods" (521). This typology focuses not on those corporate officials who engage in criminal activity strictly for the benefit of their corporations, but rather on those officials who use their corporate positions to facilitate ongoing, conspiratorial criminal activity. Some corporations serve as fronts for criminal networks. Global financial markets and international businesses enable organized crime operations to work out of financial institutions, insurance companies, and most other corporate entities including the health and telecommunications industry.

... The largest settlement ever between the government and a health care provider occurred when National Medical Enterprises agreed to pay the government a $362.7 million settlement ... One of the nation's largest psychiatric hospital chains, the company pleaded guilty to paying kickbacks and bribes for referrals. A former executive, Peter Alexis admitted to arranging $20–40 million of these payments ... more than 50 doctors and others had received payments (*CLEU Line*, November 1994, 10).

While law enforcement focuses on traditional illegal commodities such as narcotics, a parallel international trade in counterfeit watches, clothing, and car parts is being carried out by means of the same criminal processes. Millions of dollars are generated by this trade and are then invested in legitimate and further illegitimate operations. Stan Shillington reports that

> ...the Software Publishers Association estimated worldwide losses for business software of $7.4 billion in 1993 ... The International Intellectual Property Alliance estimates that trade losses due to piracy of movies, books, records and computer programs totalled $827 million in China alone in 1993 (*CLEU Line*, November 1994, 59).

Microsoft claims that 98 percent of the software sold under its name in China is fake. Piracy of this form of intellectual property benefited on at least one occasion from the fact that the offending company was owned by the local government. More generally, it benefits from the sense of ambiguity and public complicity that attaches to it. Nevertheless, it is still organized crime. As the private investigator specializing in copyright and trademark investigations for New York stated, "It's a way for criminal fraternities to support themselves and raise money for other illegal endeavours" (*CLEU Line*, November 1994, 58).

Recognizing these crimes for what they are raises the question of how corporate offenders should be treated (see Pearce and Tombs 1990; Hawkins 1990; and Snider 1993). Officials may determine that the application of "racketeer status" (U.S. terminology) in combination with stiff sanctions involving the loss of criminally derived proceeds might serve most effectively to encourage corporate accountability.

The more we learn about organized crime, the more we appreciate that its penetration into legitimate businesses is *essential* to its existence. Organized crime needs the corporate entity as a front; it needs to launder its cash; and it needs control over "choke points" in certain legitimate industries in order to gain its extortive control over wider industries. International corporations offer a second category of benefits that includes a link to source countries and a legitimizing mechanism for the importation of illicit commodities. International or domestic, it is time to focus on the criminal process and see the racketeer as a racketeer, "whatever the colour of [his] shirt or ... collar" (Blakey 1982).

With respect to police work, there is a critical need to clarify policing objectives and to open debate on what can and cannot be accomplished, particularly in the area of drug enforcement. Where there is a market with a high demand, someone will supply the commodity. In determining which commodities to classify as illegal, society must weigh the consequences in terms of costs, casualties, and corruption. This debate should involve government policy-makers from all of the stakeholder departments, including health and enforcement. The forms of organized crime relate directly to governmental definitions of illicit and licit commodities. The processes involved in carrying out these crimes and levels of violence and corruption used relate directly to social, political, and economic conditions.

The continuance of myth-driven enforcement strategies is futile, expensive, and potentially dangerous. We must identify those major threats that can be most effectively reduced by law enforcement efforts. If certain forms of law enforcement are determined to be deficient, then different strategies must be employed. If in fact new organized corporation-based criminal conspiracies operate globally to steal ideas and other diverse commodities and bilk billions of dollars from the public with an accompanying loss of life, then law enforcement must respond. The shift of the RCMP Anti-Drug Profiteering Units away from the drug directorate in January 1994 served as a recognition of the wider range of illicit economic activity that generates huge profits for criminals. Of course, the enormous resources needed to investigate large-scale financial frauds remain an enforcement problem.

Even with an enforcement structure in place to target organized crime, massive financial frauds are falling somewhere in the gap between public and private policing. The public police seldom have the resources to commit to these lengthy and expensive investigations. Depending on the nature and extensiveness of the loss, corporations that find themselves the victims of fraud are having to hire private forensic investigation firms to carry out the investigation. In addition to other specialized skills and expertise, private forensic accounting firms are now recruiting ex-police undercover officers so that they will be able to offer their paying clients police-trained and court-experienced undercover agents. At present, "policing" tends to be seen either as public (and therefore paid for by the state) or private (for example, forensic accounting firms hired and paid for by the client—often a corporation). Some links and partnerships must connect these two options: new funding arrangements and new joint-force partnerships. Increasingly, the corporate environment is becoming both the victim and the purveyor of organized crimes. Law enforcement must not allow itself to be excluded from this corporate world—not just in terms of the clearly corporate offenses but rather because a wide range of criminal activities may use corporations.

Policing today bears little resemblance to police work of even 10 years ago, and yet much of the academic analysis of police work and to some extent the police forces themselves have not acknowledged the magnitude of the changes. First, there are now both international and financial aspects to police work, and yet police officers are still largely trained, recruited, and promoted on the basis of traditional, jurisdictionally based policing requirements. Even the seemingly traditional and domestic aspects of policing have changed more than is being acknowledged. The structural movement toward community-based policing with the inherent focus on decentralization and levelling of the organization is one example of this change.

A second category of change is occurring simultaneously. The "follow the money" enforcement strategies that drive many organized crime investigations have come to dominate the police work of some units. This trend is equally apparent in the United States, where money laundering prosecutions rose 400 percent from 1991 to 1993 (*Money Laundering Alert*, August 1994). While the arguments in favour of tracking the criminal proceeds are compelling, questions arise as to the ethics of some of the new policing strategies. Money laundering investigations rely heavily on long-term undercover operations involving stings, reverse stings, phoney storefront businesses, currency-exchange houses, and the handling (or mishandling) of informants and paid agents. Of additional concern are the dangers to which undercover officers are exposed.

These dangers must be justified by some clear notion of what society is gaining in return. Policing strategies that incorporate a clearly enunciated set of objectives must be developed, and then guided and controlled by policy and possibly by additional legislation.

This study has identified several areas where legislation may need to be enhanced or replaced and where policies and procedures may need to be changed. However, simplistic rhetoric about the need for a "Canadian RICO" denies what is presently in place and working well in Canada, and also denies the fundamental differences between our justice system, our banking system, and possibly also the magnitude of our crime problem and those in the United States.

Canadian officials must examine, through research and debate, the merits of implementing the following changes:

- *Setting up a system to allow for greater cross-border accountability to monitor and record cash entering and leaving Canada.*

With all of its deficiencies, the U.S. CMIR system (discussed in Chapter 4) provides a model; as well, European systems can provide other types of models. There is also the potential to develop in Canada a mechanism specific to Canadian requirements.

- *Creating a mandatory rather than voluntary suspicious transactions reporting procedure.*

While banks appear to be fully cooperating with the police by training their staff to identify and report suspicious transactions, other financial institutions and "bank-like" operations have been less diligent. The problem for policymakers is that there is no consensus regarding the merits of a mandatory system. The RCMP are currently (Fall 95) studying the mandatory model being proposed in New Zealand. However, U.K. officials have not appreciated an increase in the quality or the significance of reported cases resulting from their suspicious transactions procedures, which include potential criminal liability for those who fail to disclose.

- *Examining the sentences being received by organized crime figures in Canada.*

There is a sense that the current success in the United States of encouraging criminals to become informants is due in part to the fear generated by sentences imposed on those criminals upon conviction. In some U.S. jurisdictions these are mandatory sentences. Great care and consideration must be given to any suggestion regarding the imposition of mandatory sentences. The issues of disproportionality and the unanticipated accommodations to these mandatory requirements in the United States must be avoided.

However, a review of the sentences received by those convicted of organized crime-related offences in Canada should be undertaken. This is particularly true in those cases where white-collar and corporate offences are a part of wider criminal operations. These crimes are often integral to the on-going criminal conspiracies and must be treated as seriously as those offences (like drug trafficking) that are often more associated with "organized crime."

- *Extending the funding for the three (Montreal, Toronto, Vancouver) Integrated Anti-Proceeds Units beyond 1997 and possibly also beyond these three sites.*

The emphasis must not only remain on using these resources to complete high-echelon organized crime investigations, but it should also be placed on learning, training, and experimenting on how best to do the "policing" required to successfully conclude these cases. We still have much to learn about successfully prioritizing and completing long-term organized crime cases. Policies must be developed and expertise hewed to drive these operations in a manner that protects both the safety of the policing personnel and the rights of citizens.

Policing and police strategies are changing, and these changes would be difficult for any organization. The availability of global markets has directly affected the organized crime markets and, indirectly, law enforcement relative to these markets. The concept of organized crime "policing" must be accurately seen to incorporate public, private, and governmental enforcement, regulatory and administrative bodies, plus the front-line workers and members of the public who choose to facilitate or thwart the efforts of these criminals.

By various methods, including funding, governments must encourage the growth of a community of organized crime scholars with links to the policy process. Currently, there is no community of Canadian academic scholarship that researches and writes predominantly on organized crime, global corporate frauds and economic crimes, or cross-jurisdictional enforcement regimes. While there are individuals who have expertise and write in these fields, there is not yet a critical mass of scholarship that will allow for accumulation and replication of data or debate among different approaches. What are perhaps the most lacking are the links between the scholars who do write in these areas and the policy-making and enforcement processes.

New understandings of international organized crime operations, new policing expertise at carrying out complex money laundering investigations, new willingness to let partners enter into and assist with the policing task—coupled with a greater clarity of purpose and objective, and most importantly, the political will and courage to "do the right thing"—will increasingly have a positive impact on the control of organized crime.

REFERENCES

Akers, Ronald L. 1994. *Criminological Theories: Introduction and Evaluation.* Los Angeles, CA: Roxbury Publishing

Albini, Joseph L. 1988. "Donald Cressey's Contributions to the Study of Organized Crime: An Evaluation." *Crime and Delinquency* 34, no. 3 (July).

————, and B.J. Bajon. 1978. "Witches, Mafia, Mental Illness and Social Reality: A Study in the Power of Mythical Belief." *International Journal of Criminology and Penology,* London, 6 (4): 285–294.

————. 1971. *The American Mafia: Genesis of a Legend.* New York: Appleton-Century-Crofts.

————. 1993. "The Mafia and the Devil: What They Have in Common." *Journal of Contemporary Criminal Justice* 9, no. 3, 241.

Alvarez, Tony. 1993. *Undercover Operations Survival in Narcotics Investigations.* Springfield, Ill.: Charles C. Thomas Publishing.

Andelman, David, A. 1994. "The Dirty Money Maze." *Foreign Affairs* (July/August): 94–108.

Atkinson, J. 1978. "Racketeer Influenced and Corrupt Organizations 18 U.S.C. Section 1961–68: Broadest of the Federal Criminal Statutes." *The Journal of Criminal Law and Criminology* 69 (Nov.): 1–19.

Australia, National Crime Authority. 1991. *Taken to the Cleaners: Money Laundering in Australia,* 3 vols. (December).

B.C. Commission of Inquiry. 1994. *Closing the Gap: Policing and the Community.* Hon. Justice Wallace Oppal, Chair. British Columbia.

Beare, M.E. 1995. "Money Laundering: A Preferred Law Enforcement Target for the 1990s," in *Contemporary Issues in Organized Crime,* edited by J. Albanese. New York: Criminal Justice Press.

———— , and S. Schneider. 1990. *Tracing of Illicit Funds: Money Laundering in Canada.* Solicitor General Canada, User Report No. 1990–05.

Beaty, Jonathan, and S.C. Gwynne. 1993. *The Outlaw Bank: A Wild Ride into the Secret Heart of BCCI.* New York: Random House.

Bell, Daniel. 1960. *The End of Ideology.* New York: Free Press.

Bellemare, Jacques. 1988. Quebec Human Right's Commission. "Investigation into Relations between Police Forces, Visible and Other Ethnic Minorities." Jacques Bellemare (Chair). Montreal: Commission les droits de la personne du Quebec.

Blakey, G. Robert. 1983. Comments to the *Reparative Sanctions International Consultative Workshop.* Hosted by the Department of the Solicitor General. Unpublished proceedings (January).

————. 1982. Presentation to the *Symposium on Enterprise Crime Proceedings.* Hosted by the Department of the Solicitor General.

Block, Alan. 1990. "Thoughts on the History of Organized Crime: In Praise of Revisionist Criminology." Paper presented at the American Society of Criminology meetings.

Blumenthal, R., and Miller, J. 1992. *The Gotti Tapes*. New York: Random House.

Bonnano, J. 1983. *A Man of Honor*. New York: Random House.

Book Review of *The Business of Organized Crime* by H. Edelhertz and T. Overcast in *Criminal Organizations* 8, no. 2 (Winter): 27.

Bossard André. 1990. *Transnational Crime and Criminal Law*. Office of International Criminal Justice, University of Illinois Press.

Bradley, C.M. 1980. "Racketeers, Congress, and the Courts: An Analysis of RICO." *Iowa Law Review* 65: 837–97.

British Columbia, Ministry of the Attorney General. 1980. *The Business of Crime: An Evaluation of the American Racketeer Influenced and Corrupt Organizations Statute from a Canadian Perspective* (October).

———. 1994. *CLUE Line*, Policy Analysis Division (May and November).

———. 1994. Policing Inquiry. Chaired by Judge Wallace Oppal.

———. Bill 64–1989, *Attorney General Amendment Act*, 1989; and "Joint Protocol of the Ministries of Attorney General, Solicitor General and Finance and Corporate Relations Regarding the Disposition of Property Forfeited as a Result of Offences," signed July 4, 1989.

Brucker, Theresa. 1992. "Disclosure and the Role of the Police in the Criminal Justice System." *Criminal Law Quarterly* 35: 57–76.

Calavita, Kitty, and Henry Pontell. 1933. "Savings and Loan Fraud as Organized Crime: Towards a Conceptual Typology of Corporate Illegality." *Criminology* 31, no. 4: 519–48.

Calgary Herald. 1995. "Nigerian scam keaves a trail of ruin." *Calgary Herald* (June 15): B10.

Canada. 1988. *Action in Drug Abuse: Making a Difference*. Ministry of Supply and Services.

Canada. Department of Justice. 1995. "Canadian Justice Minister Signs Sharing Agreement with U.S." News Release (March 22).

Canadian Association of Chiefs of Police (CACP), Organized Crime Committee. 1922. *Proceeds of the Crime Legislation: Recommendations and Initiatives*, 1992 Annual Meeting, Victoria, B.C.

Canadian Association of Chiefs of Police. 1993. *Organized Crime Committee Report*. Produced by the Canadian Intelligence Service Canada.

———. 1994. *Organized Crime Committee Report*. "Smuggling" (August 24).

———. 1995. *Canadian Police Chief Newsletter*, 14, no. 1 (Spring).

Canadian Bar Association. 1991. *Resolutions*. 1991 CBA Annual Meeting.

Canadian Police Chief Newsletter. 1995. (Spring): 17.

Cantalupo, J., and Renner, T.C. *Body Mike: The Deadly Double Life of a Mob Informer.* New York: Villard Books.

Chambliss, William. 1978. *On the Take: From Petty Crook to Presidents.* Bloomington, Ind.: Indiana University Press.

CICAD. 1994. *Annual Report of the Inter-American Drug Abuse Control Commission to the General Assembly of the Organization at its Twenty-Fourth Regular Session,* March 8–11, mar del Plata, Argentina.

Clement, Garry, and Brian McAdam. 1993. *Triads and Other Asian Organized Crime Groups.* International Unpublished Paper produced for the RCMP.

Cloward, Richard A., and Lloyd E. Ohlin. 1960. *Delinquency and Opportunity.* New York: Free Press.

Coad, Bill, and David Richardson. 1993. "Reducing Market Opportunities for Organized Crime." Paper delivered at the Australian Academy of Forensic Science, Sydney, Australia (May 20).

Commonwealth Secretariat. 1992. *Basic Documents on International Efforts to Combat Money Laundering.*

———.1993. *Action Against Transnational Criminality.* Papers from the 1991 and 1992 Oxford Conference on International and White Collar Crime.

Costanzo, John. 1992. "Illegally Gotten But Not Gained." Paper delivered at the Commonwealth Director of Public Prosecutions Criminal Asset Branch Annual Conference, Gold Coast, Queensland (October 2).

Cressey, Donald, R. 1969. *Theft of the Nation: The Structure and Operations of Organized Crime in America.* New York: Harper and Row.

———. 1967. "The Functions and Structure of Criminal Syndicates." *Task Force Report: Organized Crime* (annotations and consultant's papers): 25–60.

Crovitz, G. 1990. "How the RICO Monsters Mauled Wall Street." *Notre Dame Law Review* 65, no. 5: 1050–1072.

Dintino, Justine, and Frederick Martens. 1980. "The Process of Ellimination: Understanding Organized Crime Violence." *Federal Probation.* Washington, D.C.: U.S. Government Printing Office.

Dion, Gerard, and Louis O'Neill. 1956. *Political Immorality in the Province of Quebec.* Produced by the Common Front Against Public Immorality (August).

Donald, P. 1989. "A Commentary on the Provisions of C-61, Canada's New Proceeds of Crime Legislation (S.C. 1988, c.51)." *Advocate* 47: 423–31.

———. 1992. "Report on Obtaining Evidence in Foreign Jurisdictions for Investigation and Prosecution of Project IOU."

———. 1993. "Money Laundering—A Legislative Response." Paper presented at the Interregional Money Laundering and Financial Investigations Training Course, Kuala Lumpur, Malaysia (October).

Dubro, James. 1985. *Mob Rule: Inside the Canadian Mafia.* Toronto: Macmillan.

———. 1992. *Dragons of Crime: Inside the Asian Underworld*. Markham, Ont. Octopus Publishing.

Dubois, Alain. 1994. *Code Criminel Annote et Lois Connexes*. Quebec: Les Editions Yvon Blais Inc.

Dutil, Jean L. 1977. "The Fight Against Organized Crime in Quebec." *Quebec Police Commission, Report of the Commission of Inquiry on Organized Crime in Quebec*.

Economist. 1993. "Drug war high in the Andes" (February 13): 45, 46.

———. 1994. "The Mafia: Keep off the grass" (May 28): 49–50.

———. 1994. Money-Launderers on the line" (June 25): 81.

Edelhertz, Herbert. 1987. (ed.). *Major Issues in Organized Crime Control: Symposium Proceedings*. Washington D.C. September 25–26, 1986. Published by U.S. Department of Justice, National Institute of Justice.

———, and Thomas D. Overcast. 1993. *The Business of Organized Crime: An Assessment of Organized Crime Business-Type Activities and Their Implications for Law Enforcement*. California: Palmer Press.

Edwards, Peter. 1991. *The Big Sting: The True Story of the Canadian Who Betrayed Colombia's Drug Barons*. Toronto: Key Porter Books.

———, and A. Nicaso. 1993. *Deadly Silence: Canadian Mafia Murders*. Toronto: Macmillan.

Elliott, Delbert S., David Huizinga, and Suzanne S. Ageton. 1985. *Explaining Delinquency and Drug Use*. Beverly Hills: Sage.

Etzioni, Amitai. 1968. *The Active Society: A Theory of Societal and Political Process*. New York: Free Press.

European. 1992. "Interpol picks up a shadow" (July 30).

———. 1993. "Schengen Express derailed by France" (May 7).

Evening Standard. 1994. "The Russians are coming" (April 15): 8, 10.

Financial Action Task Force on Money Laundering. 1994. *Annual Report 1993–1994*. Prepared by the Organization for Economic Co-operation and Development, Directorate for Financial, Fiscal, and Enterprise Affairs. See also *Annual Reports for 1990, 1991, 1992* and *Annexes 1991–1992*.

Finkelstein, J. 1973. "The Goring Ox: Some Historical Perspectives on Deodands, Forfeitures, etc." *Temple Law Quarterly* 46, no. 2 (Winter).

Firestone, Thomas. 1993. "Mafia Memoirs: What They Tell Us About Organized Crime." *Journal of Contemporary Criminal Justice* 9, no. 3 (August): 197–220.

Fox, Francis, Solicitor General Canada. 1977. Presentation given to the Canadian Police Association Annual Convention. "Policing a Changing Society: A National Strategy to Combat Organized Crime in Canada." Toronto (September 23).

Freeman, Bill, and Marsha Hewitt. 1979. *Their Town: The Mafia, The Media, and The Party Machine*. Toronto: James Lorimer

Friedrichs, David. 1992. "White Collar Crime and the Definitional Quagmire: A Provisional Solution." *Journal of Human Justice,* 3, no. 2 (Spring): 3–21.

Galeotti, Mark. 1993. "Red Mafias and National Security." *Jane's Intelligence Review* (January).

Gambetta, Diego. 1993. *The Sicilian Mafia: The Business of Private Protection.* England: Harvard University Press.

Gavigan, Shelley. 1988. "Law Gender and Iseology." In A.F. Bayefsky (ed.), *Legal Theory Meets Legal Practise.* Toronto: Academic Printing and Publishing.

Gaylord, Mark S. 1990. "The Chinese Laundry: International Drug Trafficking and Hong Kong's Banking Industry." *Contemporary Crises* 14: 23–37.

Geis, Gilbert. 1966. "Violence and Organized Crime." *The American Academy of Political and Social Science* 364 (March): 86–95.

Globe and Mail. 1985. "Court denies Mounties power to seize assets" (May 14): 4.

———. 1994. "Russia's public enemy no. 1: Crime controls everything" (February 25): A1, A12.

———. 1994. "RCMP promises broken, Milgaard witness asserts: Woman says she's frightened, fears for her son's sanity" (April 21): A7.

———. 1994. "Negligence claims against lawyers rise: Law Society needs $122 million to cover costs to errors-and-omissions fund" (May 27): A1.

———. 1994. "RCMP seizes stock in laundering scheme" (July 29): B1, B6.

——— 1994. "BCCI founder, 11 officials convicted in Abu Dhabi" (June 15): B16.

———. 1994. "RCMP break big crime rings: Money-laundering said to involve business people, millions of drugs" (August 31): A1.

———. "Chambly police force taken over: Widespread crime, corruption cited in raid on Montreal suburd" (September 2): A1, A5.

———. 1994. "Five Chambly officers charged" (September 16): A4.

———. 1994. "Laundering fears halt lottery: BC officials suspect sports betting game being used by criminals" (October 27): A1–2.

———. 1994. "Drug boss jailed 10 years: Sentence is half that given to one of his accomplices" (November 2).

———. 1994. "Credit-card scheme backed heroin trade, police charge" (December 15): A5.

———. 1995a. "Star's killing linked to organized crime" (March 3): A12.

———. 1995b. "Former Italian PM charged with Mafia tie" (March 3): A12.

———. 1995c. "Police fear bikers' war threatens public" March 3, A10.

———. 1995d. "Witness-protection legislation shields wrong party, critics say: Police couldn't be sued for failing to carry out duty" (March 24): A4.

———. 1995e. "Rash of biker bombings puzzle police." (August 4): A5.

———. 1995f. "Hell's Angels attend wake for member slain in shooting" (September 20): A6.

Gold, Alan. 1989. *Proceeds of Crime: A Manual with Commentary on Bill C-61*. Toronto: Carswell.

Gold, Michael, and Michael Levi. 1994. *Money Laundering in the U.K.: An Appraisal of Suspicion-based Reporting*. The Police Foundation and the University of Cardiff. London: The Police Foundation.

Gottfredson, Michael R., and Hirschi, Travis. 1990. *A General Theory of Crime*. Stanford, Calif.: Stanford University Press.

Grey, Malcolm. 1992. "Money Laundering Casinos." Paper given at the 2nd Australasian Casinos and Gaming Conference (Oct. 26–27).

Hagan, Frank. 1982. "The Organized Crime Continuum: A New Conceptual Model." Paper presented at the Annual Meeting of the Academy of Criminal Justice Sciences, Louisville, Kentucky (March 27).

Haller Mark. H. 1971–72. "Organized Crime in Urban Society." *Journal of Social History* 5: 210–34.

———. 1987. "Business Partnerships in the Coordination of Illegal Enterprise." Paper presented at the American Society of Criminology meetings, Montreal.

———. 1991. *Life Under Bruno: The Economics of an Organized Crime Family*. Conshohocken, Penn.: Pennsylvania Crime Commission.

Handelman, Stephan. 1993. "Why Capitalism and the Mafia Mean Business." *The New York Times Magazine* (January 24).

Harmon, J.D. 1988. "United States Money Laundering Laws: International Implications." *New York Law School Journal of International and Comparative Law*: 1–45.

Hawkins, G. 1969. "God and the Mafia." *The Public Interest* 14 (Winter): 24–51.

Hawkins, K. 1990. "Compliance Strategy, Prosecution Policy, and Aunt Sally." *British Journal of Criminology* 30, no. 4 (Autumn).

Hirschi, Travis. 1987. Review of *Explaining Delinqency and Drug Use* (by D.S. Elliott et al.). *Criminology* 25, no. 1: 193–201.

Ianni, Francis. 1972. *A Family Business*. New York: Russell Sage Foundation.

———. 1974. *Black Mafia*. New York: Simon and Schuster.

Jamieson, Alison. 1992. "Drug Trafficking after 1992: A Special Report." *Conflict Studies 250*. Research Institute for the Study of Conflict and Terrorism, London.

Johnson, David. 1987. "Economic Behaviour of Professional Criminals: A Case Study of Counterfeiters, 1985–1990." Paper presented before the American Society of Criminology (November 12).

Justice (Department). 1983. *Enterprise Crime Study Report*. Ottawa.

Katz, Jack. 1988. *Seductions of Crime*. New York: Basic Books.

Kelly, Robert. 1986. "The Nature of Organized Crime and Its Operations." In Herbert Edelhertz (ed.), *Major Issues in Organized Crime Control*.

National Institute of Justice Symposium Proceedings (September 25–26): 5–50.

———. 1992. "Trapped in the Folds of Discourse: Theorizing about the Underworld." *Journal of Contemporary Criminal Justice* (February): 11–35.

Kelly, Robert J., Ko-lin Chin, and Jeffrey Fagan. 1993. "The Structure, Activity, and Control of Chinese Gangs: Law Enforcement Perspectives." *Journal of Contemporary Criminal Justice* 9, no. 3 (August): 221–39.

Knapp Commission Report on Police Corruption. 1972 (and 1973 edition). New York: George Braziller.

Lacy, Robert. 1991. *Little Man: Meyer Lansky and the Gangster Life.* New York: Little, Brown.

Law Reform Commission of Canada. 1992. *Communiqué on Working Paper #64 Immunity from Prosecution,* "Giving Police Informants Immunity Necessary and Morally Acceptable But Process Should Be Regulated" (February 12).

Lernoux, Penny. 1986. *In Banks We Trust: Money Making, Lending, and Laundering from Boardrooms to Back Alleys.* New York: Penguin Books.

Levi, Michael. 1991. *Customer Confidentiality, Money Laundering, and Police Bank Relationships: English Law and Practise in a Global Environment.* London: Police Foundation.

Lewis, Clare. 1989. *The Report of the Race Relations and Policing Task Force.* Ontario: Queen's Park.

———. 1994. *Plain Packaging—Its Impact on the Contraband Tobacco Market* (May 10), Toronto.

Los Angeles Times. 1994. "A gaping gateway for drugs." (February 17): A1, 8, 9.

———. 1994. "Reaction mild to Marathon's money laundering." (September 28): B1, B4.

Lupsha, Peter. 1981. "Individual Choice, Material Culture, and Organized Crime." *Criminology* 19, no. 1 (May): 3–24.

———. 1986. "Organized Crime in the United States." In Robert J. Kelly (ed.), *Organized Crime: A Global Perspective.* New Jersey: Rowan and Littlefield.

———. 1988. "Organized Crime: Rational Choice Not Ethnic Group Behaviour: A Macro Perspective." *Law Enforcement Intelligence Analysis Digest.* Published by International Association of Law Enforcement Intelligence Analysts, Washington (Winter): 1–8.

Maas, P. 1968. *The Valachi Papers.* New York: Random House.

MacFarlane, Bruce A. 1984–85. "Confiscating the Proceeds of Crime," *Criminal Law Quarterly* 27: 408–32.

Maltz, Michael. 1990. *Measuring the Effectiveness of Organized Crime Control Efforts*. University of Illinois at Chicago, Office of International Criminal Justice.

Mann, W.E., and L.G. Hanley. 1968. "The Mafia in Canada." In W.E. Mann (ed.), *Deviant Behaviour in Canada*. Toronto: Social Science Publishing.

Manning, Peter. 1980. *The Narcs' Game: Organizational and Informational Limits on Drug Law Enforcement*. Cambridge, MA: MIT Press.

———, and Lawrence J. Redlinger. 1978. "Invitational Edges of Corruption: Some Consequences of Narcotic Law Enforcement." In P. Making and J. Van Maanen (eds.), *Policing: A View from the Street*. Santa Monica, Calif.: Goodyear Publishing.

Marin, Hon René. 1991. "Board of Inquiry on Activities of the RCMP Related to Allegations Made in the Senate of Canada." Ottawa (April).

Martens, Frederick T. 1983. "Market Analysis Applied to the Study of Organized Crime." *Federal Probation* (September), book review on Peter Reuter's *Disorganized Crime: The Economics of the Visible Hand*. Cambridge, Mass.: MIT Press.

———. 1993. Book review on "The Business of Organized Crime" by H. Edelhertz and T. Overcast in *Criminal Organizations*. Cambridge, Mass.: The International Association for the Study of Organized Crime.

———, and Michele Cunningham-Niederer. 1985. "Media Magic, Mafia Mania." In *Federal Probation*. Washington, D.C.: Government Printing Office (June): 60–68.

———. 1986. "An Enforcement Paradox: The Intelligence Dilemma in Narcotic Enforcement." *Journal of Justice Issues 1*, no. 2 (Fall): 1–14.

———. 1990. "The Intelligence Function." In Paul P. Andrews and Marilyn B. Peterson (eds.), *Criminal Intelligence Analysis*. Loomis, Calif.: Palmer Enterprises.

———. 1991. "Transnational Enterprise Crime and the Elimination of Frontiers." *International Journal of Comparative and Applied Criminal Justice* 15, no. 1 (Spring): 99–107.

Martin's Annual Criminal Code. 1975. Agincourt, Ont.: Canada Law Book Limited.

———. 1993. Agincourt, Ont.: Canada Law Book Limited.

Marx, Gary. 1988. *Undercover: Police Surveillance in America*. Berkeley: University of California Press.

Matza, David. 1992. *Delinquency and Drift*. New Brunswick, U.S.A.: Transaction Publishers (originally published 1964).

McBarnet, Doreen. 1981. *Conviction: Law, the State and the Construction of Justice*. London: Macmillan Press.

———. 1992. "Legitimate Rackets: Tax Evasion, Tax Avoidance, and the Boundaries of Legality." *Journal of Human Justice* 3, no. 2 (Spring): 56–74.

Meagher, D., Q.C. *Organized Crime: Papers Presented to the 53rd ANZAAS Congress*. Perth W.A. (May 16–20).

―――. 1967. *On Theoretical Sociology*. New York: Free Press.

―――. 1968. *Social Theory and Social Structure*. New York: Free Press (originally published 1957).

Metropolitan Toronto Police. 1964. *Report to the OPC Inquiry on Organized Crime, OPC Inquiry Report*, Toronto.

Mills, James. 1986. *The Underground Empire: Where Crime and Governments Embrace*. New York: Doubleday.

Moley, Raymond. 1926. "Politics and Crime." *The Annals of the American Academy of Political and Social Science* XXV, no. 214 (May): 78–84.

Mollen Commission Report. 1994. Commission to Investigate Allegations of Police Corruption and the Anti-Corruption Procedures of the Police Department (July 7).

Money Laundering Alert. 1995. (April): 2.

Montreal Gazette. 1995. "Lawyer handed 13 years prison sentence for overseeing money laundering scheme" (June 30): A4.

Moore, Mark. 1987. "Organized Crime as a Business Enterprise." In Herbert Edelhertz (ed.), *Major Issues in Organized Crime Control*, National Institute of Justice Symposium Proceedings (September 25–26).

―――. 1992. "Problem-Solving and Community Policing." In Michael Tonry and Norval Morris (eds.), *Modern Policing*. Chicago: University of Chicago Press.

Moore, William Howard. 1974. *The Kefauver Committee and the Politics of Crime 1950–1952*. Columbia, Miss.: University of Missouri Press.

Morris, N., and G. Hawkins. 1970. *The Honest Politicians Guide to Crime Control*. Chicago: Chicago University Press.

Mosley, R. 1989. "Seizing the Proceeds of Crime: The Origins and the Main Features of Canada's Criminal Forfeiture Legislation." Unpublished paper (March).

Murray, Tonita. 1988. "Organized Crime: A Comparison between the Experiences of Canada and the United States." *Law Enforcement Intelligence Analysis Digest*, published by International Assoc. of Law Enforcement Intelligence Analysts, Washington (Winter): 9–15.

Nadelmann, Ethan A. 1988. "The DEA in Latin America: Dealing with Institutionalized Corruption." *Journal of Interamerican Studies and World Affairs*, University of Miami.

Narcotics Control Digest. 1994. "Professionals Busted in International Laundering Ring." (December 7): 6.

Naylor, R.T. 1887. *Hot Money and the Politics of Debt*. Toronto. McClelland and Stewart.

―――. 1993. "The Insurgent Economy: Black Market Operations of Guerrilla Organizations." *Crime, Law and Social Change* 20:13–51.

New Jersey. 1978. *Organized Crime Control Planning and Evaluation: Implications for Public Policy.* New Jersey State Police Intelligence Bureau (January).

———. 1983. *Commission of Investigation,* Public Hearing on Statutory and Regulatory Controls Over Casino Credit and Casino Industry Credit Practices (March).

Newman, Peter. 1978. *The Bronfman Dynasty.* Toronto: McClelland and Stewart.

New York Times. 1994. "Mob tightens secretive style in retreat from prosecutors" (May 29).

Nonna, J.M., and Corrado, M.P. 1990. "RICO Reform: 'Weeding Out' Garden Variety Disputes under RICO." *St. John's Law Reform* 64, no. 4 (Fall): 825–48.

Office of the Chief Coroner (J. Cain). 1994. Report of the Task Force into Illicit Narcotic Overdose Deaths in British Columbia (September). British Columbia: Ministry of Attorney General.

Ontario. 1974. *Report of the Royal Commission on Certain Sectors of the Building Industry,* Judge Harry Waisberg, Chairman, vols. 1 and 2. Ottawa: Queen's Printer.

———. 1964. *Report of the Ontario Police Commission on Organized Crime,* Judge Bruce Macdonald, Chairman (January 31). Ottawa: Queen's Printer.

———. 1963. *Report of the Royal Commission on Gambling,* Justice Roach Chairman. Ottawa: Queen's Printer.

Oppal, Hon. Wallace T. (Commissioner). 1994. *Closing the Gap: Policing and the Community,* vols. 1 and 2. British Columbia: Commission of Inquiry into Policing in British Columbia.

Palango, Paul. 1994. *Above the Law: The Crooks, the Politicians, the Mounties, and Rod Stamler.* Toronto: McClelland and Stewart.

Pearce, Frank, and Steve Tombs. 1990. "Ideology, Hegemony, and Empiricism." *British Journal of Criminology* 30, no. 3 (Autumn).

———. 1990. "Policing Corporate 'Skid Rows.'" *British Journal of Criminology* 30, no. 4 (Autumn).

Pennsylvania Crime Commission. 1991. *Organized Crime in Pennsylvania: A Decade of Change, 1990 Report.* Commonwealth of Pennsylvania.

Pfohl, Stephen. 1994. *Images of Deviance and Social Control: A Sociological History.* New York: McGraw-Hill.

Phillips, Alan. 1963–64. "The Mafia in Canada." Five-part series in *Maclean's magazine,* August 24, 1963; September 21, 1963; October 5, 1963; December 2, 1963; March 7, 1964.

Pinner, Graham. 1992. "Money Laundering—The Compliance Environment." Paper given at the 2nd Australasian Casinos and Gaming Conference (October 26–27).

Possamai, Mario. 1992. *Money on the Run: Canada and How the World's Dirty Profits Are Laundered.* Toronto: Viking Penguin Group.

Potter, Gary W. 1994. *Criminal Organizations: Vice, Racketeering, and Politics in an American City.* Prospect Heights, Ill.: Waveland Press, Inc.

———, and Cox Terry. 1991. "A Community Paradigm of Organized Crime." Unpublished paper—possibly presented to the ASC.

Poulin, Anne. 1990. "Symposium—RICO: Something For Everyone." *Villanova Law Review* 35, no. 5 (September): 853–64.

Quebec. 1970a. "Crime in Quebec: Organized Crime." *Crime, Justice, and Society.* Commission of Inquiry into the Administration of Justice on Criminal and Penal Matters in Quebec, Yves Prevost, President.

———. 1970b. "Crime in Quebec: Organized Crime." *Crime, Justice, and Society.* Commission of Inquiry into the Administration of Justice on Criminal and Penal Matters in Quebec, Yves Prevost, President.

Quebec Police Commission. 1977. *Inquiry on Organized Crime.* "Organized Crime and the World of Business," editeur officiel du Quebec. Judge Denys Dionne, President.

———. 1977. "The Fight Against Organized Crime in Quebec." Report of the Commission of Inquiry, presented to the Quebec Solicitor General, Jean L. Dutil (September 30, 1976). Québec Official Publisher.

Quebec Judgement. 1993. *The Montreal Report*, translated by Wayne and Maria Field, "Public hearing of the Regie into the Video Lottery Technologies Inc." (December 22).

Queensland (Australia). 1989. *Commission of Inquiry into Possible Illegal Securities and Associated Police Misconduct.* Report of a Commission of Inquiry Pursuant to Orders in Council (Chairman G.E. Fitzgerald).

Ragano, Frank, and Selwyn Raab. 1994. *Mob Lawyer.* New York: Charles Scribner's Sons.

Reasons, Charles E., and Duncan Chappell. 1985. "Crooked Lawyers: Towards a Political Economy of Deviance in the Profession." In T. Fleming, ed., *The New Criminologists in Canada: Crime State and Control.* Toronto: Oxford University Press.

Reed, Gary E., and Peter C. Yeager. 1991. "Organizational Offending and Neoclassical Criminology: A Challenge to Gottfredson and Hirschi's General Theory of Crime." Paper prepared for the 1991 Annual Meetings of the American Society of Criminology, San Francisco.

Resolutions. 1991. Mid-Winter Meeting in Regina, Legal and Government Affairs publication.

Reuter, Peter. 1983. *Disorganized Crime: The Economics of the Visible Hand.* Cambridge, Mass.: MIT Press.

———. 1987. "Methodological and Institutional Problems in Organized Crime Research." In Herbert Edelhertz (ed.), *Major Issues in Organized Crime Control.* National Institute of Justice Symposium Proceedings (September 25–26).

———. 1988. *Can the Borders be Sealed.* Santa Monica, CA: Rand.

Rogovin, Charles, and Frederick Martens. 1992. "The Evil That Men Do." *Journal of Contemporary Criminal Justice* (February): 62–79.

Rollnick, Roman. 1992. "Interpol Picks Up a Shadow." *The European* (July 30).

Rosner, Lydia. 1986. *The Soviet Way of Crime: Beating the System in the Soviet Union and the U.S.A.* South Hadley, Massachusettes: Bergin and Garvey.

Royal Canadian Mounted Police. 1993. *News Release* (May 19). Project TOME.

Royal Canadian Mounted Police Gazette. 1994. *Outlaw Motorcycle Gangs* 56, nos. 3 and 4.

Ryan, Terry (RCMP Assistant Commissioner). 1994. *Development and Trends—Drugs.* Presentation to the Canadian Association of Chiefs of Police, annual meeting. (August).

Sacco, Vincent F., and Leslie W. Kennedy. 1994. *The Criminal Event.* Scarborough, Ont.: Nelson Canada.

San Francisco Examiner. 1994. "Money-laundering scam cracked: Rabbis, bankers implicated in $100 million-a-year drug profit scheme." (December 1): A10.

Schmidt, W.L. 1980. "The Racketeer Influenced and Corrupt Organizations Act. An Analysis of the Confusion in Its Application and a Proposal for Reform." *Vanderbilt Law Review* 33: 441–80.

Schmitz, Christin. 1993. "Electronic Surveillance: Defence Lawyers Believe Proposed Legislation Will Expand Police Powers at the Expense of Civil Liberties." *The Lawyers Weekly* 12, no. 42 (March 12): 1, 12, 13.

Schwartz, Martin D., and David O. Friedrichs. 1994. "Postmodern Thought and Criminological Discontent: New Metaphors for Understanding Violence." *Criminology* 32, no. 2: 221–46.

Scott, Peter Dale, and Jonathan Marshall. 1991. *Cocaine Politics: Drugs, Armies, and the CIA in Central America.* Berkeley: University of California Press.

Shannon, Elaine. 1994. "The Ice Queen." *Working Woman Magazine* (March). 45–47.

Shapiro, Susan P. 1990. "Collaring the Crime, Not the Criminal: Reconsidering the Concept of White-Collar Crime." *American Sociological Review* 55: 346–65.

Sharkey, Jacqueline. 1988. "The Contra-Drug Trade-Off." *Common Cause Magazine* (Sept./Oct.): 33.

Sheehy, Patrick. 1993. *Inquiry into Police Responsibilities and Rewards.* London, England. HMSO.

Shelley, Louise. 1993. The American University, "Post-Soviet Policing: A Historical Perspective" and "Post-Soviet Organized Crime: Implications for the Development of the Soviet Successor States and Foreign Countries." Paper presented at the American Society of Criminology Meeting, Phoenix.

Skolnick, J. 1974. *Justice Without Trial.* New York: Wiley.

Snider, Laureen. 1989. "Models to Control Corporate Crime: Decriminalization, Recriminalization and Deterrence." Department of Sociology, Queen's University mimeograph.

———. 1993. *Bad Business: Corporate Crime in Canada.* Scarborough, Ont.: Nelson Canada.

Solicitor General Canada, unpublished *Proceedings*, from the 1982 *Symposium on Enterprise Crime.*

———. *Proceedings,* from the unpublished *Reparative Sanctions International Consultative Workshop*, 1983.

South China Morning Post. 1995. (May 9): 15.

Southerland, Mittie D., and Gary Potter. 1993. "Applying Organizational Theory to Organized Crime." *Journal of Contemporary Criminal Justice* 9, no. 3 (August): 251–67.

Stamler, R.T. 1992. "Organized Crime." In R. Linden (ed.), *Criminology: A Canadian Perspective.* Toronto: Harcourt Brace Jovanovich.

Sterling, Claire. 1994a. *Thieves' World: The Threat of the New Global Network of Organized Crime.* New York: Simon and Schuster.

———. 1994b. *Crime Without Frontiers.* New York: Little Brown.

Stier, Edwin H., and Peter Richards. 1987. "Strategic Decision Making in Organized Crime Control: The Need for a Broadened Perspective." In *Major Issues in Organized Crime Control*, National Institute of Justice, Washington, D.C., Symposium Proceedings.

Strafer, G.R. 1989. "Money Laundering: The Crime of the 90s." *American Criminal Law Review* 27: 149–207.

Tepperman, L., V. Grabb, and C. Wilton. 1976. "The Modernization of Crime." Research report prepared for the Solicitor General of Canada.

Teresa, V., and Renner, T.C. 1973. *My Life in the Mafia.* New York: Doubleday.

Thornberry, Terence, P., et al. 1994. "Delinquent Peers, Beliefs, and Delinquent Behavior: A Longitudinal Test of Interactional Theory." *Criminology* 32, no. 1: 47–83.

Tietolman, R. 1984. "Enterprise Crime—Witness Security." Discussion paper for the Police and Security Branch, Ministry of the Solicitor General, Canada.

Toronto Star. 1994. "Singapore denies dad's claim caned teen bloodied, in pain" (May 8).

———. 1994. "U.S.-style drug policy isn't the answer" (July 11): A13.

———. 1994. "Judge stays washroom sex charges" (July 12): A10.

———. 1994. "25 arrested in cross-Canada heroin ring raids" (September 15): A3.

———. 1994. "25 arrested in heroin bust" (September 22): A7.

———. 1994. Reputed Mafia boss arrested in Metro" (November 8): A5.

———. 1994. "Crowds line London streets as East End buries hero mobster" (March 30): A3.

United States. 1976. *Gambling in America*. Commission on the Review of the National Policy Toward Gambling. Charles H. Morin Chairman, Washington.

———. 1984. President's Commission on Organized Crime. *The Cash Connection: Organized Crime, Financial Institutions and Money Laundering*, Washington D.C.

United States, Drug Enforcement Administration (DEA), Operations Division. 1993. *Money Laundering in Southwest Asia*. Washington, DC: DEA Publications Unit, Intelligence Division. September.

———. 1992. "Operation Green Ice," *Release* (September 28).

United States, General Accounting Office. 1984. *GAO Report to the Congress: Bank Secrecy Act Reporting Requirements Have Not Met Expectations, Suggesting Need for Amendment*, Washington, D.C.

———. 1994. *GAO Report on Money Laundering: U.S. Efforts to Fight It Are Threatened by Currency Smuggling*, Washington, D.C. (March).

U.S. Department of Justice. 1993. "Local Prosecution of Organized Crime: The Use of State RICO Statutes." Bureau of Justice Statistics Discussion Paper (October).

United States Financial Crime Enforcement Network (FinCEN). 1992 (July). *An Assessment of Narcotics-Related Money Laundering*. U.S. Department of Treasury.

Vancouver Sun. 1993. "Crime chief linked to two city companies" (March 20).

Waisberg, Judge Harry. 1974. (Chairman) *Report of the Royal Commission on Certain Sectors of the Building Industry*, vols. 1 and 2. Ontario: Queen's Printer.

Wall Street Journal. 1994. "Tale of two bankers in laundering case sets stage for brokers" (September 21): A1–A3.

Wolf, Daniel R. 1991. *The Rebels: A Brotherhood of Outlaw Bikers*. Toronto: University of Toronto Press.

Woodiwiss, Michael. 1988. *Crime Crusades and Corruption: Prohibition in the United States 1900–1987*, London: Printer Publ.

Woods, G., Beare, M.E. 1984. *The RICO Statute: An Overview of U.S. Federal and State RICO Legislation*, User Report No. 12. 1984 Department of the Solicitor General, Canada.

Wuslich, Raymond B. 1988. "Procedural Due Process and the Defendant's Right to Choice of Counsel Under the Comprehensive Forfeiture Act." *American Journal of Criminal Law* 15, no. 83: 115–60.

Zagaris, Bruce, and Sheila Castilla. 1993. *Implementation of a World-Wide Anti-Money Laundering System: Constructing an International Financial Regime*. Police Executive Research Forum, Washington (July).

———, and Scott B. MacDonald. 1992. "Money Laundering, Financial Fraud, and Technology: The Perils of an Instantaneous Economy." *The George Washington Journal of International Law and Economics* 26, no. 1.

LIST OF STATUTES AND REGULATIONS

An Act to Amend the Criminal Code, the Food and Drugs Act and the Narcotic Control Act, S.C. 1988, c.51.

Anti-Drug Abuse Act of 1986, Pub. L. No. 99–570, tit. I, § 1352(a) 100, Stat. 3207 (codified as amended at 18 U.S.C. §§ 1956, 1957 [Supp. IV 1986]).

Bank Records and Foreign Transactions Act, Pub. L. No. 91-508, 84 Stat. 1114 (1970) (codified as amended in scattered sections of 12 U.S.C., 15 U.S.C., and 31 U.S.C.).

Bank Secrecy Act, Pub. L. No. 91-508, 84 Stat. 1114 (1970) (codified as amended at 12 U.S.C. §§ 1730d, 1829b, 1951–1959 (1982 & Supp. IV 1986) and 31 U.S.C. §§ 321, 5311–5324 (1982 & Supp. III 1985), *amended by* 31 U.S.C.A. §§ 5312 (a) (2) (T), (u) (5), 5316 (a) (1) – (2), 5316(d), 5317(b)-(c), 5318(a)-(f), 5321(a)(1), (4)-(6), 5321(b)-(d), 5322(a)-(c), 5323 (a)-(d), 5324 ([West Supp. 1987]).

Canadian Charter of Rights and Freedoms, Part I of the *Constitution Act, 1982*, Schedule B of the *Canada Act, 1982* (U.K.), 1982, c.11.

Civil Remedies for Racketeering Activity, Indiana Code § 34-4-30.5-1 et seq. (1988).

Comprehensive Drug Abuse Prevention and Control Act of 1970, Pub. L. No. 91-513, 84 Stat. 1236 (1970) (codified as amended at 21 U.S.C. § 848 (1982) and 21 U.S.C. s.881 (a) (6) (1982)).

Comprehensive Forfeiture Act of 1984, Pub. L. No. 98-473, § 303, 98 Stat. 2044 (1984) (current version at 21 U.S.C.A. § 853(A) (2) ([West Supp. 1986]).

Controlled Substances Act, 21 U.S.C. § 801 (1982).

Criminal Code, R.S.C. 1985, c. C-46.

Food and Drugs Act, R.S.C. 1985, c.F-27.

Internal Revenue Code, I.R.C. § 6050I (1984).

Mutual Legal Assistance in Criminal Matters Act, S.C. 1988, c.37.

Narcotic Control Act, R.S.C. 1985, c. N-1.

Organized Crime Control Act, Pub. L. No. 91-452, 84 Stat. 922 (1970), *codified at* 18 U.S.C. §§ 1961-68 (1988).

Proceeds of Crime (money laundering) *Act,* S.C. 1991, c.26.

Proceeds of Crime (money laundering) *Regulations,* C. Gaz. 1992.I.1744.

31 C.F.R. § 103.22(a) (1) (1987).

31 C.F.R. § 103.23 (a) (1987).

31 U.S.C.A. § 5316 (a) (2) (West Supp. 1987).

LIST OF CASES

R. v. Duarte [1990, 53 C.C.C. (3rd) 1 (S.C.C.)]

R. v. Wong [1990, 60 C.C.C. (3d) 460]

R. v. Wise [1992, 70 C.C.C. (3d) (S.C.C.)]

R. v. Stinchcombe [1991, 68 C.C.C. (3d)]

R. v. Denhigh [1990, 4 C.R.R. (2nd) 141]

Calder v. I., R.S. No. 89-5508, U.S. Court of Appeals, Fifth Circuit, December 21, 1989.

INDEX

Madonia, Guiseppe, 82
Macdonnell, Justice (B.C.), 206
Macfarlane, Bruce A., 148
Machain, Alvarez, 203
Maclean's magazine, 73
Mafia, 75, 107, 141, 219
  in Canada, 70, 142, 143, 156
  and Colombian cartels, 86, 133
  as community choice not deviance, 58
  and consequences of financial exposure, 44
  as criminal conspiracy, 30
  established families, 65
  informants, 28 (*See* also *pentiti; omerta*)
  and limitations of the term, 18
  in Montreal, 70, 71, 93, 95
  mythology, 58, 90
  as parocial obsession, 64
  and prohibition, 59
  skepticism about existence of, 20
  Sicilian, 28, 44, 81
  as source of mob memoirs, 26
  targetting of, by U.S. law enforcement, 27
"Mafias," 68
Mafiosi, *see* Mafia
Maltz, Michael, 14
Mandatory sentencing, 225
Mann and Hanley, 70
Manning and Redlinger, 191
Marin, Judge, 191
Marshall's Service (U.S.), and witness protection, 195
Martens, Frederick T., 35, 187, 188, 189
Martens and Cunningham-Niederer, 60
Marx, Gary, 190
Matkin, Jim, 111
Matza, David, 55, 57
McBarnet, Doreen, 158
McClellan Commission (U.S.), 140, 149
McClellan hearings, 28, 193
McClellan, John L., 142
McLaughlin, Alan, 117
Meagher, Douglas, 148
Medellin, 86, 131
  See also Colombian cartels
Media
  Connection I and II (CBC), 155–56
  effect on criminal self-image, 25, 28
  effect on legislation, 158, 160
  as generators of crisis, 33
  as information source, 34
  investigative journalists, the usefulness of, 24
  and law enforcement, 143
  and legitimization of the Mafia, 59
  press attraction to organized crime, 21
  role in romanticizing criminals, 60
  and witness protection controversy, 194
Meese, Edwin (Attorney General U.S.), 107

Membership, advantages of, in organized crime, 44
Merton and Martens, 40
Merton, Robert, 30, 51, 53, 56
Merton's Theory, Figure 2.2, 53
Methodology
  range of techniques in, 5
  and sources of access to information, 21
Metropolitan Toronto Police, 146
MI5 (U.K.), 69
Minister of Government Services, 173
Minister of Justice (Rock), 173
Ministry of the Solicitor General, 179
Misinformation, as a police strategy, 30
MLAT (Mutual Legal Assistance Treaties/Assistance Agreements), 162, 197, 198, 200, 214, 215
Mobsters, 58
Mohawk communities, 55
Moley, Raymond, 20
The Mollen Commission (U.S.), 220
Money-exchange houses, 208
Money laundering
  and accountants, 104
  awareness of, 104
  and brokers, 120
  in Canada, 36
  and Canadian cases, 100
  by Colombian cartels, 86
  continuity of, 99
  and corporate/financial institutions, 99
  and corruption, 114
  and creation as an offence in Canada, 163
  as enterprise crime, 165
  and exploitation of unions, 120
  internationally, 97, 104, 120, 129,
  and lawyers, 104, 107, 108
  legislation, 112, 113
  and legitimacy, need for, 100
  and links between elements of, 101
  and lotteries, 124
  means of, 104
  and ordinary citizens, 128
  and outlaw motorcycle gangs, 81
  professionals, 166
  and regulatory loopholes, 103
  role in criminal practice, 98, 99
  schemes, types of, 123
  and U.S. legislation, 100
Money Laundering Act (Bill C–89), 109, 113, 115, 117, 125,
  applicibility of, 169
  exemptions under, 170
Money Laundering Control Act, 150
Money Laundering Cycle, Figure 7.4, 209
Money Laundering Suppression Act (U.S. 1994), 113
Monopoly of crime commodities, 23
Montreal, Le Devoir, 71
Montreal, Le Soleil, 129

Moore, Mark, 36
Morra, Rocco, 86
Mosley, R., 155, 162, 168
MOU (Memoranda of Understanding), 162, 197–98
  between RCMP and Health and Welfare, 172
Murtagh, Brian, 157
Mutual Legal Assistance in Criminal Matters Act (Bill C–58), 147

Nadelmann, Ethan A., 69
"Narcoterrorism," 69, 197
Narcotic Control Act (NCA), 163
Narcotic enforcement, and informants, 191
National Criminal Intelligence Service, 113
National Parole Board, 193
National Police (Spain), 133
Naylor, R.T., 116
NCB (National Central Bureau), Interpol, 198
Ndrangheta, 75, 81
  See also Mafia
Neeb/Blakeman operation, 210
Neeb/Brook operation, 121
Neeb/Brook organization, 208, 209
  map, Figure 7.3, 204
Neeb, Timothy, 203, 205, 207, 208, 210, 214, 215
"New mafia," 27
Newman, Peter, 74
"Neutralization processes," 55
Nigerian organized crime, tribal base of, 90
Nigeria, flights from, Figure 3.2, 91
Non-bank institutions, financial, 113, 127
  and FATF, 201
Non-police professionals, use of, as investigators, 188

Obront, William, 74
Offshore banks, 208
Omerta, see Mafia
Ontario Court Provincial Division, 191
Ontario Police Commission, 72, 141, 193
  Report on Organized Crime, 142
Operation Contrat/Compote/Creditor, 219
Operation Buckstop, 114
Operation Green Ice, Figure 4.2, 132, Table 4.2, 133
OPP (Ontario Provincial Police), 80, 86
Opportunistic crime, 77, 187
Opportunistic enforcement, 189
Organizational deviance, 192
Organized crime
  categories of, 75
  characteristics of, 14, 15
  concept of, 1, 12
  consensual nature of, 22
  as corporate structure, 66
  defining, problems of, 1, 12, 138, 219
  as demand driven, 21

and determinants of nature and scope, 4
early reluctance to acknowledge in Canada, 72, 73
early use as term in Canada, 140
estimates of scope of, as misleading, 3
groups (Canadian), 47
and official responses, 138
and legal definitions, 19
legitimate society and relation to, 4
and links to legitimate business, 85, 95, 142, 222
and links to political structure, 43, 44
and links to terrorism, 70
and need to redefine, 220
as perceived threat in Canada, 146
and political exploitation as threat, 28
as a process, 14, 50, 143, 219, 220
the promoting rhetoric of, 142
and Quebec Study (1970b), 23
and rhetoric as catalyst, 140
societal threat, opportunistic use as, 21
theoretical explanations of, 39
theoretical framework, lack of, 12
types of, 75
and U.S. expansion to Canada, 141
Organized Crime Committee Report, see CACP
Organized Crime Control Act (U.S. 1970), 149
"Out-group" explanation of criminal behaviour, 40
Outlaw Motorcycle Gangs
  cultivation of separateness by, 55
  internationally, 78
  Joint Force operations against, 81
  Mafia affiliation with, 78
  Policing, effects of, 80
  in Quebec, 78
The Outlaws, see Outlaw Motorcycle Gangs
"Outrage," "IOU," "Neeb/Brook" Projects, 203–215

Packaging legislation, 159
Packer, H.L., 40
Palango, Paul, 103
Paper trails, 119, 125–26
Paramilitary organizations, 56, 185
  See also Outlaw Motorcycle Gangs
Parasitic groups, 46, 187
Parliamentary Joint Committee (Australia), 124
"Participant observation," 179
Participant taping, 207
Passamai, Mario, 36
Pearce and Tombs, 222
Pennsylvania Crime Commission (1991), 12
People's Republic of China, 67
Pentiti, see Mafia
Perception of injustice, as factor in criminal acts, 55
Pfhol, Stephen, 53

Public policy on organized crime control, 35
Public sources of information, as revealed in
   confidential documents, 24

QPF, 129
Quebec Commission of Inquiry on Orga-
   nized Crime (1971), 22, 155
Quebec Court of Appeals, 183
Quebec Police Commission, 22, 142
Ouebec Provincial Police, 70
Quebec Royal Commission, 142

Racketeers, range of, 152
"Racketeer status," 222
Ragano, Frank, 107
Rand Foundation, 36
Ratushy, Lynn (Judge), 191
RCMP, 29, 32, 36, 71, 80, 82, 86, 93, 95, 112,
   119, 122, 129, 133, 140, 142, 148, 162,
   171, 183, 191, 194, 195, 198, 205, 207,
   209, 214, 222, 224
Reasons and Chappell, 111
Reed and Yeager, 52
"Relation back" doctrine, 168
Reno, Janet (U.S. Attorney General), 174
Renwick, James, 155
Reparative Sanctions International Consul-
   tative Workshop, 157
*Report of the Commission of Inquiry on
   Organized Crime,* 74
*Report of the Royal Commission on Certain
   Sectors of the Building Industry,* 72, 155
Research
   aspects of, in common with intelligence
      work, 188
   bias, potential for, 12
   difficulties of, 21
   extent of, 21
   of groups over time, 50
   information, need to distinguish accu-
      racy of, 30
   sources, extent of, 21
   role of, in commissions, 33
   and traditional social science analysis,
      36
Reuter, Peter, 15, 25, 28, 36, 43
Revenue Canada, 125, 215
Rhetoric, variance of, among police and
   judges, 182
RICO (Racketeer Influenced Corrupt Orga-
   nizations Statute, U.S.), 4, 26, 27, 138,
   149–52, 156, 168
Riina, ("Toto") Salvatore, 28
Rindress, Grant, 103
Rizzuto, Vito, 95
Roach Report, 74, 141
Roach, W.D. (Justice), 72
The Rock Machine, *see* Outlaw Motorcycle
   Gangs
Rogovin, Charles A., 142
Russian organized crime, 61, 66, 68, 88, 200

and gangs in Canada, 90
and threat to Russian national security,
   69

Sacco and Kennedy, 75
Salerno, Ralph, 142
Samper, Ernesto, 60
Satan's Choice, *see* Outlaw Motorcycle
   Gangs
Scarfo, Nicky, 27
Schmitz, Christin, 181
Schwartz and Friedrichs, 50
Search and seizure, 178
Search warrants, 180
Secondary crime activity, organized crime
   as, 45
Secrecy
   and banking, 116
   in biker gangs, 56
   government overclassifying of informa-
      tion, as cause of, 24
   in Nigerian gangs, 91
   in police work, 24
   in organized crime groups, 22, 23, 28
   as research difficulty, 22
Securities-based money laundering, 120
Seizure of assets, 75, 88, 95
Seizure and forfeiture, 156,
   in Britain, 147–48
   in Canada, 148
   and early limits of legislation, 157
   and police budgetting, effect on, 172
   and U.S. influence on Canada, 164
Seized Property Management Act (Bill
   C–123), 173
Seized Property Management Directorate,
   122
Senate Foreign Relations Subcommittee on
   Terrorism, Narcotics, and International
   Operations, 69
Senate Standing Committee, 160
Serebrikou, Valerly (Lt-Col.), 90
Serrano, Diego, 86
Servico Centrale Operativo (Italy), 133
Sevillano, Joachin, 88
Sharkey, Jacqueline, 69
Shillington, Stan, 221
"Ski Montjoi" case, 171
Skolnick, J., 191
Smith, Dwight, 20, 28
Smuggling
   and aborignal groups, 77
   arms, 65, 77, 90, 197
   and Bill C–102 (tobacco), 20
   and couriers, 208
   of currency, 170
   and money laundering, 127
Smuggling routes (tobacco), Figure 2.4, 56
"Smurfing," 114, 115
Snider, Laureen, 222
Social control theories, 51, 52

and economic purposes, 45
as indicating levels of corruption, 42
and inter-gang escalation, 78
and predatory crime, 45, 187
Volpe, Paul, 27, 73
VSE (Vancouver Stock Exchange), 119–20

Wagner, Claude, 129
Waisberg, Harry (Judge), 72, 155
White-collar crime, 16, 23
    See also Organized crime; Corporate
    crime; Legitimate business
Wiretaps, interpretation of, 30
Wise case, 180

Witness protection, 27, 148, 150, 187
    and immunity, 193–96
    and limits of programs, 90
Wolf, Daniel, 56, 57
Wong case, 180
Wuslich, Raymond B., 168

Yakuza, see Boryokudan
Yamaguchigumi group, 85
Yaroslawsky, Zeo, 128
"Yellow Mafia," 65, 66
Yeltsin, Boris, 68

Zimmerman, Steven, 157